Vote Jesus Christ

"The problem with Scott Spencer's book is that it is too perceptive to be listed among the political theology books. There is a pastoral theology in abundance, institutional critique cropping up, and personal discipleship challenges on every page. Plus, it's clever and fun and satirical all at once. I hope churches preach this book in the run-up to elections because it offers a bold Jesus- and cross- and kingdom-shaped vision of Christianity, the church, and Christian leaders. This book shows that we have failed to realize this vision more than we care to admit."

—**Scot McKnight**, visiting professor, Houston Theological Seminary

"F. Scott Spencer has written a fun and fascinating book describing the Jesus of the Gospel of Luke as if he were running for public office. Strange as it sounds, it is in fact a genius way to show how Jesus was campaigning for God, God's kingdom, and God's people to live a new kind of story—not according to the cut-throat politics of the world, but based on the theme of love for God and love for neighbor. The book also puts into sharp relief the difference between Jesus and many other political campaigners of our day. An enlightening volume!"

—**Michael F. Bird**, deputy principal, Ridley College

"F. Scott Spencer masterfully walks his readers through Jesus's life and ministry according to Luke's Gospel. Along the way, Spencer distinguishes Jesus's aims, approaches, and values from those of politicians in antiquity. The real genius of this book, however, lies in Spencer's contrast between Jesus and contemporary politicians, who are commonly characterized by self-aggrandizement and grandiose promises. He exhorts Christians to assess whether their devotion to Jesus guides their participation in the American electoral process."

—**Andrew E. Arterbury**, professor of Christian Scriptures, George W. Truett Theological Seminary, Baylor University

"This book is for people who have committed to basing their ethical decisions (including voting) upon the life and ministry of Jesus of Nazareth as presented in Christian Scripture. Read this book by seasoned New

Testament scholar Scott Spencer alongside the Gospel of Luke. By doing so, you will gain insight (and warning) about the dangers of submitting to authoritarian rulers who idolatrously divinize themselves, demand total allegiance, and crucify their opponents, whether Roman Emperors in the first century or tyranny-driven politicians of the twenty-first century."

—**Jaime Clark-Soles**, professor of New Testament, Perkins School of Theology, Southern Methodist University

"Quite a few scholars have tried to turn the Bible against the wave of right-wing Christian authoritarianism. They don't change anyone's mind. But Scott Spencer has the imagination to do something different: to re-read the Jesus story as a campaign. Jesus's story is kryptonite to Christian authoritarianism if we'll just listen."

—**Greg Carey**, professor of New Testament, Lancaster Theological Seminary

"F. Scott Spencer brings together an analysis of the American political landscape with an astute reading of the third gospel. Given his long history as a renowned biblical scholar and his significant publications, especially his Two Horizons commentary on Luke, Spencer is uniquely positioned to offer hope for today. The Easter story of the gospels finds its basis in hope, and despite frightening possibilities, this excellent book puts forth an insightful story of hope. Every Christ-follower should read it before voting."

—**Matthew Tennant**, senior minister, University Baptist Church, Charlottesville, VA

"This is an amazing, insightful, and prophetic book, at once a commentary on the Gospel of Luke and a political manifesto on the continuing struggle for the freedom of democracy in the face of autocratic control. Through it all, Jesus becomes the Lukan guide, then and now."

—**Bill J. Leonard**, founding dean and professor emeritus of divinity, Wake Forest University

Vote Jesus Christ

A Political Riff on Luke's Gospel and Cautionary Tale for Evangelicals and Other Concerned Citizens

F. SCOTT SPENCER

CASCADE *Books* • Eugene, Oregon

VOTE JESUS CHRIST
A Political Riff on Luke's Gospel and Cautionary Tale for Evangelicals and Other Concerned Citizens

Copyright © 2024 F. Scott Spencer. All rights reserved. Except for brief quotations in critical publications or reviews, no part of this book may be reproduced in any manner without prior written permission from the publisher. Write: Permissions, Wipf and Stock Publishers, 199 W. 8th Ave., Suite 3, Eugene, OR 97401.

Cascade Books
An Imprint of Wipf and Stock Publishers
199 W. 8th Ave., Suite 3
Eugene, OR 97401

www.wipfandstock.com

PAPERBACK ISBN: 979-8-3852-0788-6
HARDCOVER ISBN: 979-8-3852-0789-3
EBOOK ISBN: 979-8-3852-0790-9

Cataloguing-in-Publication data:

Names: Spencer, F. Scott, author.

Title: Vote Jesus Christ : a political riff on Luke's Gospel and cautionary tale for evangelicals and other concerned Christians / F. Scott Spencer.

Description: Eugene, OR: Cascade Books, 2024 | Includes bibliographical references.

Identifiers: ISBN 979-8-3852-0788-6 (paperback) | ISBN 979-8-3852-0789-3 (hardcover) | ISBN 979-8-3852-0790-9 (ebook)

Subjects: LCSH: Jesus Christ—Political and social views. | Bible. Luke—Criticism, interpretation, etc. | Christianity and politics—campaigns.

Classification: BS2415 S667 2024 (paperback) | BS2415 (ebook)

VERSION NUMBER 05/30/24

In Honor of

Jimmy Carter

President of the United States (1977–81)
in his centennial year

Contents

Preface: Confessions of a Confused Citizen | ix
Acknowledgments | xvii

Entering the Race | 1
Testing the Candidate | 17
Launching the Campaign | 34
Recruiting Staff | 52
Raising Funds | 68
Making Speeches | 84
Working the Crowds | 103
Dividing the Electorate | 114
Taking a Poll | 133
Making the Last Push | 153
Facing Defeat | 173
Keeping Hope Alive—and Active | 197

Postscript: Resolutions of a Concerned Citizen | 211
Bibliography | 217

Preface
Confessions of a Confused Citizen

I'VE LONG SINCE GIVEN up burning the midnight oil in favor of a good night's sleep. Age and common sense eventually prevail. Except on November 8, 2016, the night of America's fifty-eighth presidential election. I didn't get to sleep until 4:00 AM the next morning. I stayed awake until the unthinkable (for me) results were confirmed: Donald J. Trump would be the forty-fifth president of the United States. I did not rest well or long.

    I somehow got myself together to teach my three-hour New Testament Greek class, beginning at 8:20 AM. My teaching assistant, who voted for the winning candidate, saw my face and asked, with genuine concern (no gloating), how I was doing. I grunted, "Not well." He let me be. I got through the class, but I was pretty wracked for the rest of the semester and have remained politically unsettled ever since. I make no claim to political correctness. I may be wrong; I've been before. I could understand how reasonable people might be less than thrilled with Trump's opponent. I had supported losing candidates in other elections and moved on. But this one threw me for a triple roller-coaster loop. I was not alone on this scary ride.

    I remain a concerned, confused citizen on the brink of paralyzing cynicism. Shortly after the midterm elections of 2022, when the aggrieved Trump, still refusing to concede the 2020 race, announced his candidacy for 2024, I decided to try something for my mental health in this long (so very long) campaign season, specifically, a little Jesus therapy. Therapists recommend writing, so I decided to imagine a political campaign manual *as if* Jesus were running for president today, or more accurately, *as if Jesus had run for Messiah* in his day as a countermodel for those who aspire to authoritarian leadership in contemporary America and other democracies that care about fair elections.¹

Of course, as a New Testament scholar I know that historically Jesus ran for no office—messianic, prophetic, royal, priestly, or otherwise—in first-century Israel. These "offices" weren't up for popular election; nobody voted on them. Ideally, they were based on *divine election*, confirmed by proper pedigree. Jesus descended from the "house of David" (Luke 1:27, 32, 69), which fit a standard messianic profile, but no one expected the Messiah to come from the hamlet of Nazareth in Galilee (John 1:46; 7:52).² Moreover, campaigning and voting for high offices in the Roman Republic waned under the Roman Empire dominating Jesus's world.³

So admittedly, my Jesus campaign guide is something of a fantasy. But not purely or primarily so. I've added no witches or wardrobes, wizards or quidditch matches. My political musings are rooted in Luke's Gospel or Evangel (*euangelion*, "good news")—a fundamental evangelical account of Jesus's career.⁴ Through the years, I've written a fair bit about Luke, including an extensive commentary published in 2019.⁵ The present volume is rooted in solid Lukan scholarship. It offers no revisionist history. It might be better labeled "envisionist"—envisioning Luke as a cautionary political tale.

I'd like to claim loose precedent for a biblical scholar's imaginative construal of Jesus's story in Gerd Theissen's *The Shadow of the Galilean: The Quest of the Historical Jesus in Narrative Form*. This compelling book, which I regularly assigned as a supplemental text in undergraduate courses early in my teaching career, reports Jesus's career from the perspective of a fictional Jewish character named Andreas, whom Pontius Pilate blackmails into investigating the political threat of Jesus's fledgling movement. Though Pilate tries to pass off the assignment as "research," it

---

1. On authoritarianism in modern history, see Applebaum, *Twilight of Democracy*; Arendt, *Origins of Totalitarianism*; Ben-Ghiat, *Strongmen*; Gessen, *Surviving Autocracy*; Naím, *Revenge of Power*; Snyder, *On Tyranny*.

2. Unless otherwise specified, all Scripture citations are from the NRSVue.

3. See Cicero, *How to Win*; Beard, *Emperor*, 29-37, 49-50; Vishnia, *Roman Elections*.

4. Michael Bird, a leading evangelical biblical scholar *and* Trump critic (see "Someone Needs to Grab America") published an illuminating overview of Luke-Acts (*Bird's-Eye View*) just as I was concluding this project. His study opens with a compelling chapter on the central importance of Luke's work in the New Testament canon and its special relevance for contemporary Christian faith and practice.

5. Spencer, *Luke*; see also *Gospel of Luke* and *Salty Wives*.

feels more like "spying" to Andreas, who though no follower of Jesus, is even less a fan of Pilate.

Theissen's work is a historical-political novella with endnotes referencing various Gospel and other ancient sources,[6] whereas mine offers a narrative-political reading of one Gospel, hewing closely to Luke's text while also recasting it in modern political terms, including sidebars on presidential candidates and campaign strategies. My book also contains touches of satire. It may fairly be called a political riff on Luke's Gospel. I'd be happy to occupy a small corner of Theissen's "shadow."

Still, assuming there is a place for creative projects in biblical scholarship, am I not running the risk of spinning out of control with this interpretive experiment multiple levels beyond the historical Jesus? Luke's story, composed several decades after Jesus's death, constitutes secondary and tertiary interpretations of Jesus's mission from eyewitnesses to written sources to Luke's account (Luke 1:1–4). Throughout Christian history, teachers and preachers have used various analytical tools to interpret Luke's interpretation. Now I add another interpretive layer with satirical sprinkles on top.

All this may be too much for some Christian readers. Isn't it a tad presumptuous, to saying nothing of irreverent, to be riffing on Jesus's story like this for political purposes? Perhaps, but not any more presumptuous, I would argue, than the sizeable bloc of evangelical American Christians who believe that their commitment to Jesus and the Bible demands their vigorous support of authoritarian-strongman, nationalist-supremacist politics, Trumpian and otherwise.

I confess to wondering: What Jesus are they following? What Gospels are they reading? What "good news" are they consuming? To be sure, Luke and the other canonical evangelists have political aims to persuade people to trust, honor, and obey Jesus as the chief agent of God's rule. Various views of God's Anointed One—the Messiah/Christ—in early Judaism shared a political angle focused on a royal figure in the mold of King David.[7] But Jewish scriptural notions of God's kingdom also include sharp critiques of earthly monarchical power (e.g., Deut 17:14–20; 1 Sam 8:1–22). Moreover, American politics has historically declared independence from dictatorial rule and protected the free exercise of

---

6. Further, each chapter is preceded by a brief introductory letter to the (fictional) Dr. Katzinger, an avatar of traditional biblical scholarship.

7. See A. Collins and J. Collins, *King*; Novenson, *Grammar*.

religion—including no religion—separate from state control. The foundational "canonical" text is the US Constitution, not the Bible.

Of course, it's perfectly legitimate, even incumbent, for believers to seek scriptural guidance for their politics (integrating faith and practice). But unfortunately, dogmatic claims of biblical support for Christian authoritarian nationalism too often reflect superficial analysis, selective prooftexts, and minimalist portraits of Jesus. Russell Moore, a leading evangelical thinker, has recently issued an urgent "altar call for evangelical America," based in large measure on a stunning pattern of biblical ignorance and resistance among those who most vigorously profess to uphold biblical values. He reports "having multiple pastors tell me essentially the same story about quoting the Sermon on the Mount parenthetically in their preaching—turn the other cheek [Matt 5:39; cf. Luke 6:29]—to have someone come up after and to say, where did you get those liberal talking points? And what was alarming to me is that in most of these scenarios, when the pastor would say, I'm literally quoting Jesus Christ, the response would not be, I apologize. The response would be, yes, but that doesn't work anymore. That's weak. And when we get to the point where the teachings of Jesus himself are seen as subversive to us, then we're in a crisis."[8]

The crisis becomes most acute among some avid Trump-supporting evangelical leaders who deny there is a crisis. They know Jesus's teachings and claim to accept them but only in their proper spiritual compartment, strictly segregated from secular politics. They almost revel in a sharp conflict of interest between the morality of Jesus we need to practice in our daily lives and the machinations of the authoritarian strongman we need to run our government. For example, Robert Jeffress, pastor of the prominent First Baptist Church of Dallas, Texas, breezily justified his endorsement of Trump in 2016: "I was debating an evangelical professor on NPR, and this professor said, 'Pastor, don't you want a candidate who embodies the teaching of Jesus and would govern this country according to the principles found in the Sermon on the Mount?' I said, 'Heck no.' I would run from that candidate as far as possible, because the Sermon on the Mount was not given as a governing principle for this nation. . . . Government [needs] a strongman to protect its citizens against evildoers. When I'm looking for somebody who's going to deal with ISIS and exterminate ISIS, I don't care about that candidate's tone

---

8. Detrow, "Russell Moore"; Moore, *Losing Our Religion*, 156, 174, 189-90.

or vocabulary. I want the meanest, toughest son of a you-know-what I can find."⁹

To which I would say to Rev. Jeffress in his own language, "What the heck? I don't know what you're talking about, dude." Most of the Texas Baptists I grew up with (I spent the first twenty-five years of my life in this milieu), however staunchly they advocated the legal separation of church and state, still believed that *moral character* mattered in government and that *Jesus Christ* was the quintessential embodiment and teacher of such character. That doesn't require an honorable politician to be a member of any particular church (or even, theoretically, a Christian, though most Baptists would draw the line here) or a candidate for sainthood. But the common good, including the common political good (the commonweal), bears more than a tenuous link to good habits of the heart, mind, and body (including the body politic). And make no mistake, Jeffress and company very much want the government to promote good Christian values (as they perceive them). They just don't care *how* the government, or more accurately, the autocrat who runs the government, does that. The end justifies the means.

At the tangled intersection of biblical interpretation and contemporary politics, this book stands out as an imagined political campaign guide based on a creative deep dive into Luke's vibrant evangelical account of Jesus's messianic mission, challenging any group that blithely claims Jesus's endorsement of their partisan agendas today, but especially those trumpeting authoritarian rule. Close attention to Luke's narrative discloses a distinctive figure who strikingly ill fits standard strongman profiles and indeed all straitjacket labels. To follow Jesus cuts across party lines, ancient or modern, secular or religious. Though affecting the politics of his day—and ours—Jesus proves to be an inept politician and weak candidate by normal measures.¹⁰ His wisdom and power operate through

---

9. Reported in Bean, "Jesus" (an op-ed piece discussing the phenomenon of "Jesus/John Wayne dualism"; cf. Du Mez, *Jesus*); see also Fea, *Believe Me*, 39; Schiess, *Ballot*, 142-49, adding Jerry Falwell Jr. into the mix of Christian strongman acolytes of Trump.

10. Obery Hendricks Jr. takes a different tack, describing Jesus as a "master political strategist" (*Politics of Jesus*, 10) and unpacking seven strategies (mostly based on Matthew and Mark) such as "Treat the People's Needs as Holy" (strategy one) and "Give a Voice to the Voiceless" (strategy two) (99-188). My work resonates with Hendricks's overall Gospel portrait of Jesus. I agree that Jesus knew what he was doing and set out with all due urgency to fulfill his "true revolutionary" mission (subtitle; 1-10). I approach the matter from a more imaginative angle (concentrated on Luke), tracing twelve "strategies" in Jesus's countercultural "campaign" that ill fit modern political playbooks. Hendricks Jr.'s *Politics of Jesus* (2006) also contains trenchant analyses of

foolish and anemic means by worldly standards. He is most glorified as the *crucified* Christ for the sake of the lowly and powerless in society (Luke 10:21; 22:14-27; cf. 1 Cor 1:17-30). Even so, "Take up your cross daily and follow me" (Luke 9:24) has to be the worst campaign slogan of all time.[11] Who wants to mark their ballot with a *cross*, that is, a *Roman cross* that brutally X-es out its victims?

Luke lays his political cards on the table from the start. The angelic announcement of "good news of great joy for all the people: to you is born this day in the city of David as Savior, who is the Messiah, the Lord" peals forth in antiphony to the despotic "decree . . . from Emperor Augustus that all the world should be registered" (2:1, 10–11). And John the Baptizer blazes the trail for the coming Jesus Messiah "in the fifteenth year of the reign of Emperor Tiberius, when Pontius Pilate was governor of Judea, and Herod was ruler of Galilee" (3:1). Jesus's messianic mission inherently challenges the powers that be.

Accordingly, this study calls for rigorous re-engagement with Luke's "evangelical platform" endorsing Jesus Messiah in marked tension with "all the kingdoms of the world" (4:4), including the modern American version. Whether or not Luke's portrait of Jesus changes your vote, it might well shake up your worldview and change your life.

I confess to being a fan of Jesus and Luke—as I understand them.[12] I can't get out of my physical, psychological, or political skin (I'm not a snake), though I can try to improve my skin condition. The interpretation that follows is mine. I'm responsible for its inevitable flaws. But I would at least plead that my position is no mere parroting a party line. As it happens, I am a little snaky. I've shed a fair bit of ideological skin over the course of my life. From the cradle, I was immersed in the skewed faith and politics I'm confronting in this book. The fierce Independent Baptist church I grew up in did not in fact encourage *independent* thinking at all.[13] But as I got older, I took this independent spirit seriously and ap-

---

the Reagan and George W. Bush presidencies (191-255). More recently, he has trained his critical eye on right-wing evangelical distortions of Scripture in *Christians Against Christianity* (2021).

11. Cf. Moore, *Losing Our Religion*, 190: "If the American church thinks 'turn the other cheek' is weakness and surrender, then wait until they hear 'take up your cross and follow me.'"

12. I'm also happy to call myself a "believer," though I make no claim to being a model believer. I prefer the clunky label of "faith journeyman."

13. This and related churches proudly styled themselves with the quasi-denominational label of Independent Baptists over against the Southern Baptist Convention and

plied it to serious biblical study that my family and church led me to do. Little did they know.

So, finally, the truth set me free, or so I hope, at least to some extent. But I'm sure, even in my senior years, I have much more to learn. Yet I find myself less patient these days with facile pretensions of freedom at the expense of truth and, especially, with blatant distortions of the gospel by authoritarian leaders that project a "Christ" and "Christian" way of life that bears little relation to the Jesus of the Gospels.

---

other Baptist groups, all of whom were deemed too liberal (yes, liberal). In my teenage years, I became a member of an SBC church in Texas. I couldn't tell the difference.

Acknowledgments

I'VE NEVER MET JIMMY Carter in person, and he wouldn't know me from Adam. I did hear him speak in 2014 at the joint American Academy of Religion/Society of Biblical Literature meeting in San Diego on women's and environmental issues (related to his book, *A Call to Action*). He had turned ninety the month before. He spoke briefly, extemporaneously—yet powerfully—about critical problems in our world he had devoted his public life to solving. By all accounts a life honorably—and humbly—lived across a century (at this writing, Carter is in hospice care; I hope he makes it to one hundred on October 1, 2024). Though driven, ambitious, and proud of his achievements, as a man of deep Christian faith, he makes no claim to perfection or grandiosity and readily acknowledges his dependence on God's grace and forgiveness. It's no accident that he took the oath of presidential office with his hand on the KJV Bible (given by his mother) open to Micah 6:8, which he also cited in his inaugural address: "He hath showed thee, O man, what is good, and what doth the Lord require of thee; but to do justly, and to love mercy, and to walk humbly with thy God."[1]

In short, Carter is a countermodel to the narcissistic, hyper-authoritarian strongman politician so inexplicably adored by many American evangelicals today and so antithetical to the life and teachings of Jesus Christ. As the historian Randall Balmer comments after listening to tapes of Carter's Sunday school lessons delivered to his home church in Plains, Georgia, "I recognized . . . both in Carter's conversance with the biblical texts and in his asides, the depth of his understanding of evangelicalism. . . . Identifying oneself as evangelical, he declared in one

---

1. Carter, "Inaugural Address"; K. Bird, *Outlier*, 152.

of his lessons, entails more than claiming the label *Christian*. Instead, believers should emulate the life of Jesus, especially his example of 'love and respect and concern' for others. 'Let that be the primary evangelical capability that we exhibit.'"[2]

Amen. Hence, my dedication of this book to Carter, and my humble identification, for what it's worth, amid the convoluted Baptist battles over the last forty years, as a "Jimmy Carter kind of Baptist." (I heard that somewhere and it immediately resonated, though I don't come close to matching Carter's extraordinary Christian service.)

I am most grateful to Michael Thomson, the acquisitions and development editor at Wipf & Stock (Cascade), for accepting this book, expediting its timely publication, and encouraging me in the final stages of writing and editing. Sincerest thanks, too, to Rodney Clapp for editing the completed manuscript and offering gracious support. The entire administrative staff at Wipf & Stock has been top-notch. This is my first publishing venture with the press. I hope it's not the last.

---

[2]. Balmer, *Redeemer*, xxxv–xxvi (emphasis original).

Entering the Race

Strategy 1
Don't put yourself forward for public office or service. Seek only to serve God and answer God's call to serve others. God "elects" the servant-leader(s) of God's people.

CONVINCED OF AMERICA'S STATUS as God's "chosen" nation aligned with God's biblical chosen people of Israel, male political candidates commonly give lip service, and often wholehearted witness, to God's calling them to run for office. With all due humility (ahem), after much prayer and soul-searching, they each proclaim themselves as God's man for the moment. In a pinch, the odd woman like Esther might do, but Father God prefers a man, a strongman, to serve as earthly ruler of his people.

A brazen example of this conviction of divine appointment emerged in the 2022 gubernatorial campaign of Ron DeSantis. DeSantis was running for a second term as Florida's governor and also auditioning to be the Republican nominee for president in 2024. Days before the 2022 election, his adoring wife blasted an audacious audio-video ad on Twitter as if produced by a heavenly studio (not Hollywood) and narrated by God's official spokesman (not Morgan Freeman).[1] Here's the transcript:

> And on the eighth day, God looked down on his planned paradise and said, "I need a protector." *So God made a fighter.*
>
> God said, "I need somebody willing to get up before dawn, kiss his family goodbye, travel thousands of miles for no other reason than to serve the people, to save their jobs, their livelihoods, their liberty, their happiness." *So God made a fighter.*

1. See Jenkins, "'God made a fighter' ad."

God said, "I need someone to be strong, advocate truth in the midst of hysteria. Someone who challenges conventional wisdom and isn't afraid to defend what he knows to be right and just." *So God made a fighter.*

God said, "I need somebody who will take the arrows, stand firm in the wake of unrelenting attacks, look a mother in the eyes and tell her that her child will be in school. She can keep her job, go to church, eat dinner with friends, and hold the hand of an aging parent, taking their breath for the last time." *So God made a fighter.*

God said, "I need a family man. A man who would laugh, and then sigh, and then reply with smiling eyes when his daughter says she wants to spend her life doing what dad does."

So God made a fighter.

That's about as blatant as it gets: God is invoked ten times (a new Decalogue) in a minute-and-a-half. Not just on Friday, November 4, 2022, but from the eighth day of the foundation of the world, the Divine Creator ordained DeSantis's strong rule as a "fighter." In fact, God *needed* this man to protect and defend his "planned paradise" (which apparently God didn't plan very well) from enemies foreign and domestic. God also needed a strong family man, truth-teller, and savior of vulnerable mothers, children, and elderly folks. With God on his side, how could DeSantis lose? He didn't. He won reelection as Florida's governor by a landslide.

This fervent religious rhetoric has a distinct messianic ring, effectively announcing DeSantis as God's "anointed" leader authorized to save God's persecuted people. Not that DeSantis would dare declare himself the Messiah. As a good Christian and churchman, DeSantis serves Jesus Christ, God's one true Messiah. All glory be to Jesus whom the good governor humbly serves and fights for. Still, the ad elevates DeSantis to Messiah-like status, the closest thing to Jesus we're likely to see before the second coming.

Of course, Christlikeness is the worthy goal of all Christ's followers. As the apostle Paul said, "Be imitators of me, as I am of Christ" (1 Cor 11:1). The issue, then, for DeSantis or any would-be Christlike leader concerns how much they fit Jesus's model of service during his time on earth. Times have changed, of course, and there is no need to be silly about microcopying Jesus's example. No sandals are required (flip-flops might work better in Florida) nor rowing across waterways (Lake Okeechobee is over ten times larger than the Sea of Galilee). But a couple of substantive contrasts between Jesus of Nazareth and Ron of Tallahassee (as idolized in the ad) stand out from the start: Jesus was not a typical family man (no wife or kids), and for all the lofty titles the Gospels assign Jesus (Messiah, Savior, Lord, Beloved Son, Son of Humankind, Good Shepherd, Light of the World, etc.), "Fighter" or "Warrior" is not among them, although many of these titles presume protective and liberative roles.

Throughout this book, I engage in an imaginative exercise juxtaposing the evangelical "campaign" of Jesus Messiah in Luke's narrative with current political campaigns, often conducted under the name of Christ. How do these campaigns square up? Let's start by considering Jesus's role as God's chosen ruler on earth. How and when does Luke's Jesus come to know and embrace this God-anointed vocation?

BORN TO RUN

Politics tend to run in families—like the powerful Roosevelt, Rockefeller, Kennedy, and Bush dynasties—along with more modest political clans. DeSantis's five-year-old daughter already says she wants to do what Daddy does. Bred in the bone, born to run for public service: many voters find this pedigree and predestiny for leadership reassuring. Others, however, particularly in America's rugged individualist tradition, prefer mavericks, (so-called) self-made men who buck the establishment and stick up for common folk. So how does Jesus fit these portraits? Was he a regal legacy figure born to be Israel's Messiah or a "marginal" newcomer and reformer?[2] Was he Son of God or Son of Humankind? Luke eschews such dichotomies in favor of a multifaceted depiction of Jesus.

Conception and Birth

We're used to birth announcements on cards and yard signs ("It's a girl/boy!") with pink/blue balloons and, among close family and friends, conception announcements ("We're pregnant!") with projected due dates. But *pre*-conception announcements by a divine messenger, not so much. That's what a young woman named Mary received one day in the Galilean village of Nazareth. The archangel Gabriel suddenly appeared to her and said, "Do not be afraid, Mary, for you have found favor with God. And now you will conceive in your womb and bear a son, and you will name him Jesus. He will be great, and will be called the Son of the Most

---

2. See Meier, *Marginal Jew*.

High, and the Lord God will give to him the throne of his ancestor David. He will reign over the house of Jacob forever, and of his kingdom there will be no end" (Luke 1:30–33).

What good news! What a lucky girl, destined to be the mother of God's Son who will rule over Jacob/Israel's people and David's kingdom forever. So why isn't Mary shouting and jumping for joy? She'll get there, but first she has some serious concerns about this whole arrangement. How will this divine impregnation business operate in her body (1:34), and (by implication) what will people say about her swelling belly as a (supposed) virgin engaged to be married? What will fiancée Joseph say and do (cf. Matt 1:18–25)?

Suffice it to say that Mary had not been praying her whole life for this magical messianic moment, as if this were every devout Jewish girl's dream (it wasn't). Oh, let it be me, Lord! Again, she gets there ("Let it be with me according to your word," Luke 1:38) but not before becoming "much perplexed" and needing to "ponder" this shocking news (1:29). Thankfully, Gabriel supplies Mary some key "conceptual" information: "The Holy Spirit will come upon you, and power of the Most High will overshadow you; therefore the child to be born will be holy; he will be called Son of God. . . . For nothing is impossible with God" (1:35). Good to know, since this supernatural, Spirit-seeded conception seems pretty impossible, in fact totally unique in human history after God breathed life into Adam and Eve and then left reproduction up to them,[3] with a few miraculous interventions here and there to aid "barren" women.[4]

Though actively engaged in responding to God's plan for her body, Mary is not given much choice in the matter: she will be overshadowed with divine creative power to gestate God's Son and Messiah in her womb.[5] And nothing gets easier from that point: the supernatural conception leads to natural pregnancy and delivery. No special reduction of nine-month term, no exemptions from morning sickness, hormonal surges, labor pains, and other maternal rigors. No miraculous birth. The human Mary bears Jesus in the normal way.

---

3. Gen 1:26–30; 2:7. The strange story in Gen 6:1–4 of heroic warriors produced from the sexual union of the "sons of God" and "daughters of humans" (reminiscent of Greco-Roman mythology) perverts God's purpose for creation.

4. E.g., Sarah (Gen 21:1–7), Rachel (30:22–23), the wife of Manoah (Judg 13:2–24), and Hannah (1 Sam 1:1–2:10)—and Mary's relative Elizabeth (Luke 1:5–7, 24–25, 35–36).

5. See Spencer, "Woman's Right to Choose?," in *Salty Wives*, 55–100.

Actually, it becomes a harder-than-normal way, as late in her pregnancy Mary is forced to travel with Joseph seventy miles south to his tribal hometown of Bethlehem in Judea. At least Joseph hasn't abandoned the pregnant Mary (does he accept her wild Spirit-conception claim?); he remains engaged to her (2:5) but has not yet consummated the marriage, ceremonially or sexually. At any rate, the Bethlehem trip is not a social call but rather a political duty decreed by the Roman Emperor Augustus to register for tax rolls in home districts (2:1–4).

The taxing journey, physically and financially, and tight lodging arrangements take their toll on Mary's body, and she winds up delivering baby Jesus in Bethlehem and using a manger (an animal feed trough) as his first crib. The situation is not quite as dire as often portrayed. There is no "inn" (or innkeeper), stable, or barn in the story. The popular translation, "there was no room in the inn" (2:7 KJV) misleads today.[6] "Room" is better rendered "place" (*topos*) and "inn" better rendered "lodging room" within a house; hence, "there was no place in the guest room" (NRSVue; cf. CEB). Most likely the setting was a small family residence now crowded with relatives who had come to Bethlehem for Caesar's tax census. Space was tight throughout the house but more open in the main living room, where it was common for poorer families to allow a work animal (donkey or ox) to rest and feed inside, out of the cold. Hence the indoor *manger*, which in this case doubles as a makeshift crib for baby Jesus. Mary does not deliver Jesus all alone in a cold, dank barn. But a crowded home is still hardly an ideal maternity ward and certainly no birthing suite fit for a king. You can bet no scion of Caesar would be laid in a manger. To a manger born, this Jesus Messiah, not to the manor born.

Luke's nativity story, along with its later embellishments in Christmas creches, easily resonates with American frontier legends. Think Lincoln's log cabin origins, trudges through the snow to a one-room schoolhouse, and rough-and-tumble political career in the Midwest before ascending to the White House. Just like Jesus, sort of. But while Luke clearly distances the "lowly" Jesus Christ (1:48, 52) from Caesar Augustus, Luke also has a loftier aim in the Bethlehem birth story. Jesus's messianic candidacy inevitably raises "birther" issues.[7] No one expected the

---

6. See Bailey, *Jesus*, 25–37; Carlson, "Accommodations."

7. "Birtherism"—attacking opponents' nationality and legitimacy—is a common feature of autocratic politics. Such attacks became the stock in trade of Tea Party and Trumpian calumny against Barack Obama, despite his certified birth on American soil in Hawaii. See Levitsky and Ziblatt, *How Democracies Die*, 159–60.

Messiah to come from the one-mule, no-account village of Nazareth in Galilee. John's Gospel reports heated debate about Jesus's origins: "Some in the crowd said, 'This [Jesus] really is the prophet.' Others said, 'This is the Messiah.' But some asked, 'Surely the Messiah does not come from Galilee, does he? Has not the scripture said that the Messiah is descended from David and comes from Bethlehem, the village where David lived?' So there was a division in the crowd because of him" (John 7:40–43; cf. vv. 45–52). Luke is not so explicit about the "birther" crisis, but his Bethlehem nativity is clearly aimed to "certify" Jesus's messianic heritage.[8]

Bethlehem represents the ideal messianic birthplace, since that's where David was born and first anointed as Israel's king, while still a lowly shepherd (1 Sam 16:1–10). Though not Jesus's biological father, Joseph seems to assume legal responsibility for Jesus during the engagement period with Mary. As one "descended from the house and family of David" (Luke 1:27; 2:4), Joseph brings Jesus into the Davidic-messianic line. Jesus's birth in David's hometown then seals the deal, along with the fact that the Lord's angel issues a special birth announcement to local shepherds (à la David): "I am bringing you [shepherds] good news of great joy for all the people: to you is born this day the city of David a Savior, who is the Messiah, the Lord" (2:8–11).

Thus Luke's Jesus is born to be God's chosen Messiah-King. "Glory to God in the highest heaven!" (2:14). But such good news is not yet widely known. The shepherds disclose to Mary, Joseph, and company what the angel had revealed to them. Naturally, the Bethlehem community is "amazed" by the shepherds' report (2:17–18), but amazement is not the same thing as belief or commitment. Shepherds were far from the most noble, honorable men in this society. Can they be trusted? The present group rejoin their fellow shepherds who stayed behind to watch the flock, "glorifying and praising God for all they had heard and seen" (2:20). But it doesn't appear that they share much beyond their circle.

While Mary remains the most clued in about Jesus's identity, the shepherds' visit only gives her more to mull over "in her heart" (2:19; cf. 1:29; 2:51). We should not underestimate her ongoing cognitive and emotional struggle to understand all that is happening with her and her special son, who at this stage has no clue himself about his destiny.

---

8. I leave aside here the thorny question of the historicity of the Bethlehem nativity stories in Luke 2:1–20 and Matt 2:1–12.

Childhood and Adolescence

Now that Jesus has come into this world, how are Mary and Joseph supposed to raise this special Christ child, this incarnate Son of God and Savior, destined to mend the tattered world? As with his birth, the answer seems to be—as normally as possible. There's no singling out Jesus back in Nazareth as the "chosen one"; no treating him with kid gloves. He's circumcised on his eighth day of life, like every other Jewish boy (2:21; cf. 1:59) and is soon brought to Jerusalem for dedication in the temple, as the law required for the firstborn in every household. At the same time Mary offers a postpartum purification sacrifice of two doves or pigeons, an acceptable option for those who couldn't afford a sheep (2:22–24; cf. Exod 13:2; Lev 12:6–8).

Luke then jumps a dozen years in Jesus's life to another temple incident, this time at the Passover festival in Jerusalem, which the family attended every year (Luke 2:39–52). What happened in Jesus's childhood before age twelve, a common time of transition to young adulthood in this culture? Good question—to which Luke and the other evangelists give no answer. Only Luke offers a glimpse of twelve-year-old Jesus, and from there he zips to Jesus's work around age thirty (3:23). Mark dives right into the mission of the adult Jesus, and Matthew bounces from Jesus's nativity and early childhood directly to his mission. The so-called "hidden" years of Jesus's life are not meant to be spooky, still less filled with Super Boy legends (supplied by later apocryphal Gospels). Rather, they presume an ordinary upbringing with no signal messianic markers. Jesus the Son of God had a more or less normal human life as a Jewish boy and young man in the backwater town of Nazareth.

Except for the temple incident where the twelve-year-old Jesus does flash a certain brilliance and flaunt a special relationship with God. Unknown to Mary and Joseph, Jesus is not among the caravan of returnees to Nazareth after Passover. When they discover his absence, it takes them three days to find him "in the temple, sitting among the teachers, listening to them and asking them questions" and dazzling them with "his understanding and his answers" (2:41–47). The prodigy emerges.

When Jesus's anxious parents finally discover him, their relief is mixed with astonishment and anger at his callous disregard for their feelings (any parent who's ever had a child go missing knows these feelings well). And he only compounds their frustration by his dismissive response, "Why were you searching for me? Did you not know that I must be in my Father's house [or about my Father's interests]?" (2:49). Whatever his awareness before this episode, Jesus now knows he has a close filial bond with God that supersedes his human family (certainly his stepfather Joseph). He puts his earthly parents in their place, which they, especially Mary, should have been expecting. As Jesus reaches puberty and maturity, it's time to step out and fulfill his divine calling. What a great press story this temple incident would make to launch Jesus's messianic mission. The public loves child phenoms.

Except the story quickly changes in a markedly unspectacular direction. After the twelve-year-old wunderkind asserted himself to Mary and Joseph in the Jerusalem temple, he promptly "went down *with them* and came [back] to Nazareth, and was *obedient to them* [or set under their authority (*hypotassomenos*)]" for eighteen more years, until he's "about thirty years old" (2:51; 3:23). Say what? If he can impress the temple scholars, what more does Jesus have to learn from his pedestrian parents? Apparently a great deal, and much more besides from his divine Father. A sharp mind is one thing, social-emotional intelligence and mature wisdom, another. Luke frames the temple account with announcements of Jesus's continued *growth* in "wisdom . . . and in divine and human favor" (2:40, 52).

Stop the presses. No big messianic campaign story to write about yet. Just another lost-and-found kid in the big city ushered back to a small hometown up north. Who cares—other than Mary who keeps stewing over these things (2:52) but likely not saying much to anyone else? What would be the point? She barely understands what's going on herself (2:50). Couldn't Gabriel keep her updated about God's unfolding messianic plan for Jesus?

BLESSED IN SONG

Even so, Mary knows more than any other human character about Jesus's God-appointed mission—and not just because of Gabriel's conception announcement. Throughout her pregnancy she continues to ponder God's will, and at one poignant moment she bursts forth in prophetic song about God's destiny for her, her son, and her people. Soon the Holy Spirit inspires two other people, both elderly men, as it happens—Zechariah the priest and Simeon the prophet—to erupt in additional songs related to Jesus's nativity. You could call them the first Christmas carols, along with the "first Noel the angels did say to certain poor shepherds in fields as they lay" (cf. 2:13–14).

The nativity hymns, unique to Luke's Gospel, are far from little children's ditties about good cheer and cozy warmth. They voice good news, to be sure, but at a rousing tempo with robust lyrics that range across a spectrum of emphases: at once theological, political, and emotional.[9] Nothing stirs the imaginations and actions of audiences like compelling music. It's no surprise that pulsating popular songs blare at modern political rallies, pumping up the crowds for candidate speeches and campaign support.

We may chart Luke's three main Christ hymns as follows:

Title/Text	Setting	Singer/Audience	Theological Themes	Political Points	Emotional Elements
Magnificat (1:46–55) "My Soul Magnifies the Lord"	Judean home of Zechariah and Elizabeth in early months of Mary's pregnancy	Mary of Nazareth praising God before her pregnant relative, Elizabeth	Mighty, merciful Savior God who helps the poor and lowly	Dethroning the arrogant powers Reinforcing the covenant with Israel	Joy Fear Pride (of oppressors) Pity/Mercy
Benedictus (1:68–79) "*Blessed* Be the Lord God of Israel"	Judea (maybe Zechariah's home) soon after the birth of John the Baptizer	Zechariah the priest and father of John the Baptizer praising God before general audience	Mighty, merciful Savior God who forgives sins and provides peace	Rescuing from enemies Reinforcing the covenant with Israel	Hate (from enemies) Fear Pity/Mercy Peace
Nunc Dimittis (2:29–32) "Now You Are Dismissing Your Servant in Peace"	Jerusalem temple during baby Jesus's dedication	Simeon the prophet praying to God in the presence of Mary, Joseph, and the Christ child	God of salvation for all peoples, Jewish and gentile	Falling and rising of many in Israel opposing the Christ child (see 2:34–35)	Peace Psychic (*psychēn*) pain

---

9. See Streett, *Songs of Resistance*, 59–75 (focused on Mary's Magnificat).

With God on Our Side

In the antiwar era of the 1960s, Bob Dylan wrote and recorded the satirical song "With God on Our Side," a sweeping indictment of America's tendency to justify military aggression as God's agent. Joan Baez also recorded duet (with Dylan) and solo versions of the popular protest anthem. Obviously, one's response to such a provocative song depends on one's political viewpoint. But it also depends on one's *theological* perspective, one's perception of how God operates in human affairs.

All of Luke's prophetic singers robustly affirm God's active involvement in people's lives, especially poor, lowly, and vulnerable folk. The powerful God is on the side of the powerless, the merciful God on the side of the disfavored, the saving God on the side of the lost, the forgiving God on the side of the sinful. The young Mary, pregnant with God's Son, proclaims in song both the personal and communal dimensions of God's work. The mighty, merciful God "has looked with favor on the lowliness of his servant"—that is, on *her*—and "done great things *for me*" by choosing her to bear Jesus Messiah (1:46–49). But far from crowing about her own exceptionalism, she regards her experience as exemplary of God's gracious attention to all "the lowly" spanning "from generation to generation," from "Abraham and to his descendants forever" (1:50–55).

Make Israel Great Again

In its long biblical history from Abraham to Jesus, Israel enjoyed little time on the big geopolitical stage. It was repeatedly conquered and exiled by neighboring empires. The major exception to this pattern came in the golden age of Israel's United Monarchy in the tenth century BCE under David's and Solomon's successive reigns. As this period became increasingly idealized in memory, it fueled hopes for a restored glorious kingdom under God's Davidic-messianic son. Such hopes could run in various directions, one of which was militant or at least used martial language to characterize the defeat of Israel's enemies, as the warrior David did in his day.

In his prophetic hymn, Zechariah highlights this martial messianic image, as he exults in God "rais[ing] up a mighty savior for us in the house of his servant David . . . [so] that we might be saved from our enemies and from the hand of all who hate us" (Luke 1:69–71). "Mighty savior" is more literally "horn of salvation" (*keras sōtērias*), evoking images of bulls' and rams' butting and battering horns ("battering rams") in Davidic military victory songs (2 Sam 22:1–4; Ps 18:1–3). Such language could obviously be appropriated for a strongman Messiah-Warrior who would revive Israel's golden monarchical age and defeat Israel's enemies. In the first century CE, that would mean toppling the Roman Empire. A tall order, to put it mildly, and not all Jews at this period expected a militant Messiah and superpower kingdom.

Does Luke have such expectations, voiced through Zechariah's song? Perhaps for some apocalyptic grand finale associated with Jesus Messiah's future reappearing on earth ("second coming"), but not during his or his forerunner John the Baptizer's (Zechariah's son) lifetimes. They both recruit students (disciples), not soldiers. They lift no finger to attack anyone. They are both executed by imperial authorities (Luke 9:7–9; 23:23–25, 32–33). Jesus blows everyone's minds by advocating *love for enemies* and *praying that God forgive his torturers* (6:32–36; 23:34).

This is *not* to say that Jesus's ministry is salvation-lite, nice and helpful as far as it goes, but not earth-shattering. As we will see, the saving work of Luke's Jesus is explosive, liberative, world-changing in its own substantive way—just not the voracious, violent way of tyrannical worldly powers.

Notably, Zechariah sings his combat victory anthem in a *covenantal* key, specifically trumpeting the "holy covenant . . . [God] swore to our ancestor Abraham" (1:72–73). This Abrahamic-covenantal theme also resounds at the end of Mary's song (1:54–55). From ancient times, God chose the descendants of Abraham as a beloved, favored people whom God would love "forever" (1:55) with steadfast commitment. God did not, however, elect this people of Israel to be a pet nation of privilege but rather a partner community with God in blessing the world. In the original covenantal pact, God promised Abraham "to make of you a great nation . . . and make your name great" (MAKE ABRAHAM GREAT ALWAYS)—"*so that* you will be a blessing . . . [*so that*] in you *all the families of the earth* shall be blessed" (Gen 12:1–3). Note well: *not* so all other peoples will be cursed and crushed under Israel's boot but so that all families worldwide will be blessed and enjoy the bounty of God's salvation.[10]

In his swan song in the temple at the infant Jesus's dedication, the elderly prophet Simeon highlights the universal scope of God's saving mission: "My eyes have seen your salvation [embodied in the Christ

---

10. For a incisive discussion of biblical election "for the sake of—for the very life of—the world," see Clapp, *Naming Neoliberalism*, 130–38 (131 for the quoted phrase).

child], which you have prepared in the presence of all peoples, a light for revelation to the Gentiles and for glory to your people Israel" (2:31–32). Simeon brings in a significant Isaiah strain into the messianic symphony (Isa 42:6; 49:6; 60:1–3). Salvation for all peoples, Jewish and gentile. Thus streams a steady biblical chorus in the Law, Prophets, and Gospels, from Abraham to David to Isaiah to Luke.

To Fear or Not to Fear?

Compelling songs, both spiritual and political, hymnic and patriotic, aimed to move people to action and devotion, must stir people's hearts and minds. Ancient and modern psychologies stress the vital nexus of emotion-cognition-action, with emotion functioning as the primary (primal) trigger—e/motivating thought and deed.[11] Two emotions—one positive, the other negative—prove critical in political persuasion: *joy* and *fear*. Charismatic politicians trade in whipping up crowd support by mixing these thrilling and threatening emotions into an intoxicating brew. Get people feeling elated and scared at the same time, and they're poised for zealous action!

Luke's Spirit-charged prophets, Mary and Zechariah, both inspire joy and fear in their messianic songs. They naturally rejoice as unexpectedly blessed parents of God's agents of salvation (Luke 1:47–48, 68–69; cf. 1:41, 58). Their expressions of fear, however, are distinct. For her part, Mary emphasizes God's merciful dealings with "those who fear him," that is, fear *God* (1:50). Although modern interpreters often tone down God-fearing to God-respecting or reverencing, a fearsome, phobic (*phobeomai*) element remains in biblical theology: trembling in anxious awe before the "Mighty One" (1:49), the ineffable God of the universe. To be sure, it's the proud, prosperous earthly rulers who have the most to fear from God if they oppress the lowly and poor whom God most favors (1:52–53). Yet regardless of one's station in human society, all mortal beings are called to maintain a healthy, humble (not cowering or cringing) fear of the immortal Creator God. Even so, Mary says nothing about fearing her son Jesus and gives no hint that he will use fearmongering—exaggerating fear of either God's punishment or enemies' predation—to get people to follow him.

---

11. See Spencer, *Passions*.

Zechariah knows God's fearsome side well. When the angel appears to him in the temple, he becomes "terrified and fear overwhelmed him" (1:12). And though the angel attempts to assuage Zechariah's fear with the promise of "joy and gladness" at the coming birth of a son (John), he's not so assured and winds up throttled with an inability to speak throughout his wife's pregnancy (1:18–20). On the eighth day after his birth, when Zechariah writes on a tablet that the boy should be named "John," as the angel had ordered, finally "his tongue freed, and he began to speak [again], praising God." Yet the result is not all warm, fuzzy feelings. "Fear (*phobos*) came over all their neighbors" and throughout the community (1:59–66).

All this drama proves to be as unsettling as it is inspiring, as spooky as it is special. But that's not a bad thing. Fear has its vital uses, and not just in triggering a jump-and-run flight from potential danger. In his classic work on rhetoric, Aristotle instructs public speakers in strategies of audience persuasion, not least playing on people's emotions. With respect to judicious use of fear (*phobos*), Aristotle counsels that it must leave room for "some hope of salvation . . . concerning the matter over which they anxiously contend. And there is a sign of this. For fear renders people apt to deliberate, yet no one deliberates about hopeless things."[12] Fear, rightly directed and in modest proportion, prompts considered thought and action—quite the opposite of fearmongering crowds into mindless, marauding mobs.

To his credit, Zechariah turns his terrifying encounter with the angel—tempered by nine months of silent contemplation—into a rousing, hopeful song of salvation. He's not naïve. He knows that the fearsome inimical Roman Empire is still going strong and that the fearsome God of Israel holds his people accountable for their covenantal responsibility and calls them to courageous service. Yet Zechariah works through this fear—even as God's creative Spirit works wondrously through Zechariah's wife Elizabeth and her relative Mary—to a remarkably hopeful, peaceful resolution. He goes so far as to rejoice in God's raising up a "mighty savior" (Jesus, 1:69) and preparer (John) of "his ways" (1:76) "to grant us, that we, being rescued from the hands of our enemies, might serve [the Lord] *without fear* (*aphobōs*)" (1:76). From fear to fearlessness; from

---

12. Aristotle, *Rhet.* 2.5 [1385a].

panic to peace (1:79)—a healthy emotional evaluation of God's stunning ways, a deeply felt and thought-out vote of confidence.[13]

BAPTIZED TO CONFIRM

Thus far Luke's two opening chapters have heralded grand promises of salvation through Jesus the "Savior, who is the Messiah, the Lord" (2:11). That's what campaigns do: make promises to curry people's favor and win power. Fulfilling those promises is another story.

Commentators routinely note Luke's emphasis on promise and fulfillment.[14] Luke's Jesus fulfills the lofty destiny charted for him from his conception and birth, though not always in the most popular or conventional ways. Moreover, as we've seen, Luke does not rush Jesus into messianic "office." Whatever sense of divine commissioning Jesus had at age twelve continued developing over the next two decades under his earthly parents' wings (2:49–52; 3:23). It would be wonderful to have Jesus's daily diary from ages twelve to thirty. But we don't. Christopher Moore's cheeky novel, *Lamb: The Gospel according to Biff, Christ's Childhood Pal*, which cleverly fills in the gaps of Jesus's "hidden" years, makes for fascinating reading—as pure fantasy.

When the adult Jesus finally ventures outside Nazareth, Luke does not characterize him as self-consciously embarking on a messianic mission *until* he has a fresh encounter with his heavenly Father and the Holy Spirit. Before that happens, however, in the Judean desert area near the Jordan River, a messianic buzz begins to swirl around the prophetic reform movement launched by Jesus's maverick cousin John, calling the people to "repentance for the forgiveness of sins," lest they fall under God's judgment. Such repentance is evidenced in doing righteous acts and submitting to John's baptismal rite (3:2–14). Increasingly "the people were filled with expectation, and all were questioning in their hearts concerning *John*, whether *he* might be the Messiah" (3:15).

John promptly sets them straight. There's "one who is more powerful [stronger, *ischyroteros*] than I . . . coming; I am not worthy to untie the thong of his sandals." I'm not the one you're hoping for. My baptizing with water is a drop in the bucket compared to his "baptiz[ing] you with

---

13. See McKnight, *Bible*, 16: "Luke turns the wheel for the peaceful imagination before the other evangelists" (cf. 16-18).

14. See, e.g., Tannehill, *Shape of Luke's Story*, 105–24; Johnson, *Prophetic Jesus*.

the Holy Spirit and fire" (3:15–16). John does not name anyone, but we readers know he's referring to Jesus.

Right on cue, here Jesus comes, but not with the fanfare we might expect after John's setup. And, for that matter, not with any word from Jesus: he simply shows up at the Jordan "when all the people were [being] baptized." John doesn't single Jesus out, and Luke only describes Jesus as (silently) "praying," without providing any content (3:21). How is anyone going to know Jesus is the Messiah? Does he even fully know himself at this point, or is still growing in self-understanding (cf. 2:40, 52)?

Jesus's first public act since his impressive performance in the temple is an act of submission to John's campaign and submersion in baptismal waters with sinners. We assume that Jesus endorses John's mission, but Luke doesn't tell us why Jesus seeks John out. Is the older John Jesus's mentor? If Jesus has an inkling that he is God's Messiah, no one else in the crowd has a clue. Again, John does not openly identify Jesus as the Stronger One, and Jesus engages in no self-promotion.

Yet Jesus's personal awareness of his divine calling crystallizes at his baptism. In his prayerful state, Jesus palpably senses God's presence. He sees and feels the anointing Holy Spirit upon him "in bodily form like a dove" and hears the assuring voice of his heavenly Father, "You are my Son, the Beloved, with you I am well pleased" (3:21–22).[15] The last phrase conveys more than paternal delight; it is better rendered, "You I am *pleased to choose (eudokēsa),*"[16] with a strong *elective-service* component: Jesus's divine Father officially certifies his Son as the *Chosen One* to lead God's people as servant-ruler in "the way of peace" (1:79). Caesar may rule with an iron fist under the military banner of the eagle. Jesus Messiah will rule under the peaceful wings of a dove.

Jesus emerges from the Jordan River with a strong sense of solidarity with the people God has called him to serve, with finite and flawed beings like those *with whom* he was baptized. No longer the immature standout impressing the temple teachers and pulling away from his earthly parents, the mature Jesus now *stands with* the people, indeed, immerses himself in the human condition. As much as he is the son of David in the royal dynastic line, Jesus is "son of Adam, son of God" (3:38)—the son of everyone.

---

15. Luke presents this as Jesus's private revelation. No one else sees or hears anything extraordinary.

16. See the careful argument by Peppard, *Son of God*, 106–12.

And what becomes of John the Baptizer, in whom many had invested their messianic hopes? For the most part, John and Jesus part ways after Jesus's baptism. John's movement remains stationed in the Judean wilderness, while Jesus will conduct an itinerant mission throughout Galilee before journeying to Jerusalem. Both have their own corps of disciples (5:33; 7:18; 11:1; cf. Acts 18:25; 19:1–7). Whatever John may have thought about Jesus at his baptism, his understanding of Jesus's role later becomes shaky. While confined in Herod Antipas's prison, John dispatches two of his disciples to Jesus with the question, "Are you the one who is to come or are we to wait for another?" (Luke 7:18–20). Imprisonment seems to skew John's judgment; he's not yet or no longer fully convinced of Jesus's messianic calling.

But Jesus in no way holds this doubt against John. He tells John's messengers to report all the benevolent work they've witnessed Jesus doing: "Go tell John what you have seen and heard: the blind receive their sight, the lame walk, the lepers are cleansed, the deaf hear, the dead are raised, the poor have good news brought to them" (7:22). Then Jesus proceeds to commend John's career to the crowds as God's appointed prophetic forerunner of Jesus Messiah. No matter that John scarcely looked the part of a royal ambassador in his rough wilderness garb. All the better: plush robes and cushy palaces fit the exploitative economies of Herod and Caesar, not the redemptive realm of God for the disabled, diseased, deceased, and deprived (7:22, 24–30). Accordingly, in Jesus's book, "Among those born of women no one is greater than John; yet the least in the kingdom of God is greater than he" (7:28). God's salvation thrives on straight, level ground where high and low, smooth and rough people, places, and paths meet (3:4-6; 6:17-49).

Jesus is not remotely anxious or jealous about competition from John or John's disciples. That may not make him a very good campaigner. But he's not running against anyone to win the "office" of Messiah. He's already got the job. God has chosen him. The Holy Spirit has fully endorsed him. There is still the hard, persistent work of persuading the people that he has come to lead them in God's way of salvation and justice. But he gladly welcomes others who run in that same direction. To the extent that John might be a rival, intentionally or not, with a different mission "style" (which Jesus doesn't try to change), Jesus wholly embraces John as part of a "team of rivals."[17]

---

17. Cf. Goodwin, *Team of Rivals*.

Testing the Candidate

> **Strategy 2**
>
> *Make sure you're running for the right reasons—principled reasons focused on honoring God and meeting people's needs rather than on boosting personal wealth and status. From the start, critically assess your ego-structure and self-awareness, and honestly confront temptations to misuse power for personal gain.*

As Jesus emerges from baptismal waters convinced of his God-ordained mission, the time seems ripe to get on with the work. Conditions are getting no better in Roman Galilee and Judea; the need for helping the needy, lifting the lowly, and feeding the hungry remains urgent (Luke 1:52–53). And Jesus himself is getting on in years. While being "about thirty years old" (3:23) seems young to us—one must be at least thirty-five to run for president in America—average life spans in Jesus's day ran about *forty* years.

But Luke continues to track a deliberative messianic campaign—urgent, yes, but not reckless. All in due time, in God's time. Before he preaches a single word or performs a single deed, "Jesus, full of the Holy Spirit, returned from the Jordan and was led by the Spirit in the wilderness" (4:1). We might say that the Spirit arranges a pre-campaign retreat in the desert to get organized, though today candidates and staff prefer a nice mountain or beach getaway.

As it happens, however, Jesus is not led to some desert resort, and he has no associates. Those will come later, but now it's just Jesus and the Spirit—oh, and *the devil*. And *no food* for *forty days* during and after which the devil confronts him! This is Messiah boot camp, testing Jesus's mettle for the race he's about to run. The sweet dove-Spirit acts more like a drill sergeant. This is round one of a long contest with the opposition, the real opposition: not with hostile teachers or leaders (those debates will come), but with malevolent cosmic forces of evil spearheaded by the devil or Satan.

This is bigger than running for a local position in Nazareth or higher office in Jerusalem: the Holy Spirit, Jesus's campaign manager, thrusts him into an intense period of contemplating God's realm and confronting diabolical spirit-forces infecting "all the kingdoms of the world" (4:5). The fate of the world is at stake. If that seems over the top for our modern sensibilities, it wasn't for Luke or Jesus. Increasingly it's dawning on us how all politics is not only local but also global, interconnected through time and space in root and branch. And there's no shortage of evil influencers. However limited Luke's geography and cosmology might otherwise be by modern standards, his holistic perspective deserves our respect. In Luke's narrative, tiny backwater Judea and Galilee, at the southeastern rim of the Roman Empire, is deeply embedded in wider Caesarean politics (2:1–4; 3:1–2) and creational ecospheres encompassing heaven and earth.

BEWARE THE TRAPS

The extended test represents a power contest between Jesus and Satan, centered around the critical issue of how Jesus will *use* his messianic power. The devil eggs Jesus to flaunt his power to the max—for self-centered and devil-supportive aims. Satan is a full-blown bully and authoritarian, which also means at root he's an insecure coward and conniver. He knows he's no match for Jesus on a fair playing ground. So he plays dirty and sneaky.

The devil catches Jesus at a vulnerable point during and after his forty-day desert fast, which he undertakes to concentrate wholeheartedly on the demanding mission to which God has called him. Forty days! An abnormal period of fasting, reminiscent of Moses's and Elijah's stints of fasting over the same timeframes (Exod 34:28; Deut 9:9, 18; 1 Kgs 19:8). Such an extended fast assumes supernatural sustenance, not superhuman strength. We presume Jesus's increasing hunger pangs and physical draining that also sorely test his mental and spiritual mettle. Is part of the goal to emerge stronger from this extreme ordeal? Perhaps, but if so, this goal by no means lessens the excruciating process.

Satan strikes Jesus when he's down with tempting propositions, *if* he would just use his intimate connection with God to nurture his body and bolster his name: "*if* you are the Son of God" (Luke 4:3, 9). The devil has no doubt about Jesus's filial relationship with God. But he dares Jesus to prove himself by using his power *for himself* alone, others be damned, and thus show himself unworthy of being the Son of the loving God. To paraphrase Satan's gambit, "*Since* you're the Son of God, you deserve to be honored and glorified by the world, not languishing out here in the desert. You've got the power, man, so use it. Enjoy it. Let it rip!" The devil seeks to lure Jesus into three specific power traps.

Bread Machine

Around 100 CE the poet-satirist Juvenal laments the loss of the Roman Republic to an empire ruled by autocratic Caesars who appease their beleaguered subjects with periodic dispensations of "bread and circuses," which they greedily lap up.

> But what of the Roman Mob? They follow
> Fortune, as always, and hate whoever she
> Condemns . . . if the old Emperor had been surreptitiously
> Smothered; that same crowd in a moment would have hailed
> Their new Augustus. They shed their sense of responsibility
> Long ago, when they lost their votes, and the bribes; the mob
> That used to grant power, high office, the legions, everything,
> Curtails its desires, and reveals its anxiety for two things only,
> Bread and circuses. (*Satires* 10)

Notice that the people whom Juvenal derides as a "mob" used to *vote* for their leaders and "everything" else governing society. But they've long since "shed their responsibility" for self-determination and succumbed to jonesing for their twin obsessions of "bread and circuses," face-stuffing and eye-popping indulgences.

Seventeen centuries later, the French philosopher and social critic Jean-Jacque Rousseau mocked the snooty insensitivity of aristocrats to the plight of the poor who needed daily bread: "At length I recollected the thoughtless saying of a great princess, who, on being informed that the country people had no bread, replied, 'Then let them eat pastry!'" We're used to hearing this as, "Let them eat cake!" (*Confessions* 6). In French it's actually, "Let them eat brioches." Pastry, cake, brioches—the point is the same: "As long as I have my luscious goodies, what do I care if the masses are scrambling for breadcrumbs?" Or from another angle, "Give the rabble enough sweet delights now and again to mollify them. They'll eat it up. They'll love me forever and otherwise let me get away with murder."

Speaking of murder (on Fifth Avenue, maybe)[1] and cake, to bring the matter up to current American politics, consider former President Donald Trump's infatuation with "the most beautiful piece of chocolate cake you've ever seen" served at his Mar-a-Lago resort, as he told a reporter, to cap off the dinner he was hosting for China's President Xi Jinping. Oh, by the way, while entertaining Xi, Trump managed to authorize a missile strike on a Middle Eastern airbase. When the reporter commented on the "brilliant" strategy of deploying "unmanned" missiles, Trump blithely replied, "It's so incredible, so brilliant" (almost as good as the chocolate cake). "We've just launched fifty-nine missiles heading to Iraq, and I wanted you to know this," Trump said in the interview. "And [President Xi] was eating his cake. And he was silent" (evidently so engrossed in his culinary experience). The interviewer (a Trump fan) gently suggested that he meant to identify the target country as Syria, not Iraq. "Yes, heading toward Syria," Trump continued (without apology), hastening to add that Xi ate every bit of his chocolate cake.[2] A dilettantish engagement in world politics, oblivious to life-and-death consequences.

Such is the narcissism of autocratic strongmen, which the devil knows well and seeks to exploit in Jesus Messiah, the Son of God. He starts with bread (the circus trap comes later) and plays it smart, tailoring his temptation to Jesus's situation. It would be futile to ply Jesus with some exotic delicacy. Nazareth fare was more bread and fish than pastry and pheasant. Plus, the desert offers limited menu options. Satan simply nudges Jesus to turn one of the dusty rocks at his feet into a loaf of ordinary bread (no stones to scones) (Luke 4:3). Clever move—not to tempt Jesus to eat something (Jesus had completed his fast)—but to tempt him to use his God-given power to satisfy his own basic needs.

Yet what would be wrong with that? Why does Jesus resist this action? Because he knows, as Satan knows, that this would be the first step to authoritarian exploitation. Start with special powers to satisfy yourself. People on the lower rungs of the social ladder love seeing nobodies climb

---

1. See Dwyer, "Donald Trump: 'I Could Shoot Somebody.'"
2. Oh, "Trump Brags."

to the top. At the same time, however, feelings of envy and scorn toward someone who gets "above their raising" creep in. It's a mixed bag but becomes easier to carry if the celebrity promises to pave the way for others' success and throws a big banquet now and then for everyone to enjoy.

Jesus will in fact later feed a huge crowd *in the desert* (9:10–17). Is the devil just trying to jump-start this ministry? Hardly. As a matter of principle, Jesus confirms from the start that his messianic mission is about service to God and others, not about self-gratification or -aggrandizement. He maintains this commitment to the end: "Who is greater, the one who is at the table or the one who serves? Is it not the one at the table? *But I am among you as one who serves*" (22:27; cf. vv. 24–26; 9:46–48; 12:35–38; 17:7–10). Luke's Jesus fills a dual host-servant role, feeding the hungry masses, which the authorities neglect and even Jesus's own disciples would rather turn away (9:12). He enacts this feeding ministry both miraculously and modestly, as odd as that combination seems.

Jesus uses his creative power to multiply scant resources into a superabundance of food, with twelve baskets of leftovers after "all ate and were filled" (9:17). But he orchestrates no downpour of manna from heaven, no zapping of desert sands and stones into an all-you-can-eat buffet. Taking the meager five loaves and two fishes the crowd offers, he calmly "looked up to heaven, and blessed and broke them, and gave them to the disciples" to distribute. Somehow more and more pieces of bread and fish keep coming, more than enough for the whole throng. Jesus lets his skeptical, stingy disciples have a helping hand in this dinner on the desert grounds. Perhaps others in the crowd begin sharing foodstuffs they've been guarding.[3]

In any event, this spontaneous banquet no doubt boosts Jesus's messianic reputation. But Luke's Jesus is not seeking the spotlight. The very next scene features Jesus "praying alone" with his disciples nearby. He then asks his followers what the people think of him (9:18–20). He takes a poll, as it were, of public opinion, which we will explore in strategy 9. For now we simply note that Jesus is not seeking popularity as a miracle worker. He devotes his mission to serving and suffering with the poor and needy, in solidarity with them, not superiority over them. In John's Gospel, the satiated multitude reacts by acknowledging Jesus as "the [true] prophet who is to come into the world" (that's good) and by scheming "to make him king" (not so good). In this scenario, Jesus

---

3. See Theissen, *Shadow*, 119–24.

"withdr[aws] again to the mountain by himself" (John 6:1–15). He has no intention of being a Bread (or Burger) King or Celebrity Chef, which is not to say that people's material needs do not matter to him, just that they are not all that matters.

Further, Jesus has no intention of playing on people's *fears* of scarcity in order to commend himself as their sole savior. "Savior"—properly understood—is a significant part of the Lukan Jesus's profile. But Jesus comes "to seek and to save the lost" through *redemptive love and forgiveness*, not repressive lordliness and fear (Luke 15:1–32; 19:1–10; 22:24–27). Dostoevsky's Grand Inquisitor pierces to the heart of Satan's desire to create pernicious messianic megalomaniacs: "Do you see these stones in this bare, scorching desert? Turn them into bread and mankind will run after you like sheep, grateful and obedient, though eternally trembling lest you withdraw your hand and your loaves cease for them." The duped, dread-filled masses will do anything for their bread: "Better that you enslave us, but feed us."[4] That's what Satan wants—enslavement, not nourishment. He wants the world eating out of his and his autocratic agents' hands. Jesus promotes the way of freedom, true freedom born of love, not fear.

Big Deal

Next the devil goes for broke. Nothing subtle or incremental about this test. Somehow, he whisks Jesus to a mountaintop. Cooler, cleaner air up here, perhaps bracing for Jesus after his desert depletions. But more importantly for Satan's aims, it affords the better vantage point to appeal to Jesus's highest worldly aspirations. From this perch, Satan flashes "in an instant" an eagle-eye view of "all the kingdoms of the world" (4:5). He tries to emblazon this surreal, "virtual" image on Jesus's mind. He trades less in practical politics (Realpolitik) than in psychological programming (brainwashing), with the singular goal of recruiting Jesus to Satan's dark side. Here's the Faustian deal the devil proposes to Jesus: "To you I will give [these kingdoms'] glory and all this authority; for it has been given over to me, and I give it to anyone I please. If you, then will worship me, it will all be yours" (4:6–7).

Satan makes the grandiose claim that he is the world's master-ruler, the ultimate supervillain to whom all earthly rulers must answer. There's enough truth in this claim to be dangerous. It's hard to deny that many

---

4. Dostoevsky, *Brothers Karamazov*, 252–53; cf. May, *Freedom*, 199–200.

political leaders seem in league, wittingly or not, with nefarious forces. Ironically, Jesus, Luke, and Satan would all agree that Caesars Augustus, Tiberius (2:1; 3:1), and successors, despite claiming divine authority, promote devilish, death-dealing activity. Caesar is Satan's man, not God's. Though Israel's God ultimately stands as the true "Lord of heaven and earth" (10:21), in the present age God has allowed Satan and his minions, both demonic and human, considerable free rein. God's righteous and peaceful kingdom, though operative in the world, is still to "come" fully (11:2).

Whether or not Satan has the will or power to make the deal he promises Jesus is beside the point. It's enough if he can get Jesus to think it's possible: "Look at all this territory, man! Caesar thinks it's his. But I can make it all yours! I can make you Caesar of all." Just one hitch: "*You have to bow down to me, worship me. Acknowledge me as your God!* But you'd be #2, the global Viceroy with unimaginable power at your disposal (not some token vice president). What a deal! Sign here and now."

Few politicians, even those of good character, would not pause a moment or two to consider such a tempting offer. Political life inevitably involves power plays. To use power benevolently to help people still requires gaining and staying in power; the powerless don't make the rules. Further, those who desire to lead, for good or ill, typically have a robust ego; they'd be eaten alive without one.[5] The astonishing thing about Jesus, who will demonstrate amazing power and authority to heal and save, is that he cares little about following standard rules of politics. Not because he's an arrogant, autocratic rule-breaker, but because he's first and foremost an obedient servant of God. Jesus's pledge of allegiance, with which he answers the devil's bargain, couldn't be clearer: "Worship the Lord your God, and serve only him" (4:8).

Big Top

With that stark rebuff, the devil takes one more swing at Jesus. Since the reward of world dominion doesn't work, he presents another singular

---

5. See the astute comment of Naím, *Revenge of Power*, 211: "For many [autocrats], ego is a powerful driver. All politicians of any vintage share a marked tendency toward narcissism. In this respect, however, autocrats are often more explicit in letting the world know that they possess special and unique talents, marking them out from the rest of humanity." Autocrats are "deluded by the belief that they are destined for the world stage, that their genius and historical weight are too vast to be contained within a single country."

option with a sneaky-smart addendum. Satan plays a *religious* trump card, which he's very adept at doing. He chooses the perfect setting, now staging Jesus at the pinnacle of the Jerusalem temple, at the highest "wingtip" (*pterygion*) on the temple wall perched over a long drop to the valley below. If Jesus doesn't care to be king of the world, maybe he will be tempted by a high-priestly role, a literal high-*flying* act off the temple "wingtip" escorted by angels, God's parachutes. The people will go crazy with excitement.

Far from making a wild proposition, Satan evokes a *scriptural promise*: "For it is written, 'He will command his angels concerning you, to protect you,' and 'On their hands they will bear you up, so that you will not dash your foot against a stone'" (4:9–11). Yes, that's really "written" in Psalm 91:11–12; the devil knows his Bible (better than most Christians today).[6] Of course, there's this little matter of *context*, which the devil conveniently ignores. More on that in the next section.

For now, we focus on the aim of Satan's test. Is he trying to finish Jesus off, lure him into suicide before he starts his messianic campaign? Doubtful, because Satan knows, remember, that Jesus really is God's Son under God's protective care. Of course, on the off chance the angels are busy with other business when Jesus jumps, the devil would be thrilled with Jesus's demise. Yet Satan doesn't need Jesus to die at this point to ruin his mission. The diabolical plan will work just fine if Jesus performs this stunt—which is exactly what it is—a self-serving, people-pleasing aerial stunt worthy of the Ringling Brothers, Barnum, and Bailey's Circus under the big top and Evel Knievel's motorcycle jumps and rocket launches over buses and canyons—both insanely popular with twentieth-century American audiences.[7] The Roman emperors would've gladly sponsored these extravaganzas. They would have feted Mr. Knievel as the top supergladiator (until he crashed and burned), the star of the "Evel Empire."[8] And then there's Russia's President Vladimir Putin who revels in his own high-flying acts. As Masha Gessen comments, "Whether [Putin]

---

6. Cf. Whitaker, *Even the Devil Quotes Scripture*.

7. See Kolbert, "You Can't Make It Up," including the eerie foreshadowing of Trump: "[Barnum] welcomed any imbroglio that would be noticed by the press. (Many times, he staged controversies for the express purpose of generating coverage.) He made a fortune, then lost it. While broke, he gave speeches on 'the art of money-getting'; improbably enough, these proved extremely profitable. Toward the end of his life, Barnum toyed with the idea of running for President."

8. I couldn't resist the pun, but I can't take credit for it. See Neveu, "Evel Empire."

is attending a summit, piloting a plane, or hang gliding with Siberian cranes, it is the spectacle of power that interests him."[9]

To return to the ancient world, the late second-century apocryphal Christian work known as the Acts of Peter features a fantastic flight by the popular wonder-working charlatan, Simon Magus, who presented himself as the "Great Power of God" (the "Greatest Show on Earth" centuries before Barnum). The New Testament book of Acts recounts Simon the "Great's" spellbinding influence in the city of Samaria, which Philip the evangelist and Peter the apostle boldly resist in winning the people to Christ. Simon even (supposedly) believes in Christ and submits to baptism, but his ulterior motives drive him to uncover the missionaries' miracle-working secrets for his own advantage. The story ends with Peter's vehement charge to Simon, "Repent . . . of this wickedness of yours, and pray to the Lord that, if possible, the intent of your heart may be forgiven you" (Acts 8:4–24).

Simon has no sincere desire to change, however. Bested by Philip and Peter in Samaria, Simon heads to Rome, according to the Acts of Peter, and mesmerizes the people with his magical arts, prompting many to wonder if he is the true Christ. His banner opening act is an aerial feat: "Tomorrow you shall see me about the seventh hour [1:00 PM] flying over the city gate in the form in which you now see me speaking to you." And so it happens, sort of. At the designated time, a smoky-fiery dust cloud appears in the distance and wafts toward the city; when it reaches the city gate it suddenly vanishes, unveiling Simon Magus standing in its place. Predictably, Simon's popularity soars after this extraordinary magical act (Acts Pet. 2.2.4).[10]

Simon seeks to cement his celebrity status by worming his way into the heart and home of Senator Marcellus, once beloved by the Roman masses for his charitable works in Christ's name. Under thrall to Simon, however, Marcellus turns against Christ, going so far as to erect a statue in his home dedicated "To Simon, the young God." As the poor Christians become wise to Simon's nefarious ways, they beg the apostle Peter to come and oust the meddling magician. Peter brings the duped Senator Marcellus back to his senses and begins to turn the tide against Simon (2.4.8-11). In turn Simon Magus engages in a series of showdowns with Peter, culminating in a flying contest on the Via Sacra, the main street

---

9. Gessen, *Surviving Autocracy*, 32.

10. Citations of the Acts of Peter are from Schneemelcher, ed., *New Testament Apocrypha*.

through Rome. After announcing to Peter, "I by ascending will show to all this crowd what manner of being I am," Simon takes off and flies "all over Rome, passing over its temples and its hills, while the faithful looked towards Peter," no doubt in dismay (3.32). Could Peter top that?

Peter doesn't try. While Simon zooms around overhead, Peter cries out in prayer, pleading for the "Lord Jesus Christ" to make himself known. Specifically, he prays for Christ to bring Simon plummeting to earth. Accordingly, Simon crash-lands, breaking his legs in three places. Adding insult to injury, the people then "stoned him and went to their homes; [and] from that time they all believed in Peter" (3.32).

Leave the flying to the birds and the angels. All would-be messianic aeronauts are destined to fail and fall.

FOLLOW THE SCRIPTS

Successful political campaigns must stay on message, stick to the script(s). Too much waffling and flip-flopping makes people nervous and distrustful. People want to know what you stand for and stand by. While riffing and rabbit-chasing can be effective to maintain interest, a little goes a long way, *except* for demagogues who specialize in ear-tingling rants and rabble-rousing, sometimes—especially hardscrabble times—to the thrill of beleaguered crowds desperate for change. "Throw the bums out of office," "drain the swamp," etc. ad nauseam. Autocratic demagogues hate scripted speeches and teleprompters.

We will explore Jesus's public speech throughout this study, but it's important to note from the start his staunch commitment to foundational scripts—the Jewish Scriptures. He rebuts each of the three tests the devil presents with "It is written,"[11] followed by quoting specific texts. He simply recites three concise verses: no elaborative sermon, no extended debate with the devil—just a straightforward declaration of his Scripture-rooted convictions.

It's no accident that Jesus derives all three quotations from the same biblical book, Deuteronomy, which represents Moses's review of the Torah God had given the Israelites at Mount Sinai on their forty-year desert journey from foreign enslavement to the promised land. In Deuteronomy, Moses urges the new generation to be truer to the covenant with

---

11. *Gegraptai* in Greek, a single word in the perfect tense, implying, "It has been written and its authority stands."

God than were their parents, almost all of whom died in the wilderness. Only by being faithful to God could they expect to flourish in a new land. For his part, Jesus stands in solidarity with fellow Israelites, whom the Torah images collectively as God's "firstborn son" (Exod 4:22–23). Jesus seems to envision his messianic mission, beginning with a desert test, as retreading—and redeeming—Israel's covenantal journey through the wilderness. His threefold recitation of Deuteronomic scripts suggests his (and Luke's) deep engagement with the broader scriptural contexts and concerns of the lines he quotes.[12] Three key attitudes emerge for navigating God's challenging way: humility, loyalty, and security.

Humility: "One does not live by bread alone" (Luke 4:4; Deut 8:3)

The statement about bread in Deuteronomy 8 recalls the Israelites' experience of hunger during "the long way that the LORD your God has led you these forty years in the wilderness, in order to humble you, testing you to know what was in your heart, whether or not you would keep his commandments" (8:2). God does not lead the people out of slavery to starve them to death! God provides daily "manna" from heaven in the wilderness to sustain them—but not *only* to sustain them physically. "One does not live by bread *alone*" (8:3); as necessary as bread is, it is not sufficient for full life. One needs a responsive (responsible) covenant relationship with the Lord of life nurtured by *humility*: God "humbled you by letting you hunger, then by feeding you with manna . . . in order to make you understand that one does not live by bread alone, but by every word that comes from the mouth of the LORD" (8:3).

While there is a place for healthy pride and self-regard in human flourishing,[13] pompous pride and self-glorification can be harmful. Not for nothing, it's the first of the so-called seven deadly sins: "Pride goes before destruction and a haughty spirit before a fall" (Prov 16:18; cf. 6:16–17). Corrosive pride is that which exalts one's achievements as entirely self-produced, with no aid from God or other people. "I alone can fix it" is the mantra of such "self-made men," beyond all common sense, much less spiritual insight.[14] Americans especially idealize such figures

12. See Evans and Sanders, *Luke and Scripture*, 1–13, 121–39; Boring, *Deuteronomy for the Church*.

13. See DeSteno, *Emotional Success*, 115–40, 166–67.

14. Cf. Richardson, *Democracy*, 145: "In [Trump's] now-familiar refrain, he claimed that the country was in chaos caused by his lawless opponents and that he alone could

who make their marks and fortunes against all odds with their dogged display of "rugged individualism." It's a false myth: no one has ever built a Fortune 500 company without infrastructures, materials, and services provided by *other* workers—to say nothing of good luck and even more critically, the natural resources of God's creation.[15]

Deep down, people know this, because in a tragic ironic twist, many disgruntled folks who have not made it on their own are taken in by charismatic super-achievers who promise to take care of all beaten-down unfortunates and pave their path to success. No one is truly self-reliant, including the putative strongman who, to compound the problem, only cares about what the masses can do *for him.*

In its own way Deuteronomy 8 amens the psalmist's confession that "The LORD is my Strength" (Pss 28:7; 118:14; cf. Exod 15:2; Isa 12:2), warning against presumptuous self-exaltation and independence:

> Do not exalt yourself, forgetting the LORD your God, who brought you out of the land of Egypt, out of the house slavery . . . and fed you with manna . . . to humble you and to test you, and in the end to do you good. Do not say to yourself, "My power and the might of my own hand have gotten me this wealth." But remember the LORD your God, for it is he who gives you power to get wealth. (Deut 8:14–18)

Even as God's anointed Son, Jesus acknowledges as a matter of first principle *his* dependence on God and on other human beings. He will host, feed, and serve others in thankful fellowship with God (Luke 9:12–17; 22:19–20, 24–30), even as he is regularly housed, served, and fed by other people (see strategy 5). He never demands a sumptuous feast or five-star service. Rather, he vividly exposes the folly of self-absorbed luxurious living in parables featuring narcissistic rich men (Luke 12:16–21; 16:19–31). One story drives home the foolish, self-defeating end of a wealthy farmer who thinks he has complete control over *his* ("my") prosperity and destiny, with no appreciation for the land and laborers, let alone the Lord, who helped him get where he is—or rather where he presumes he is—at the beginning of a long, lush retirement: "I will say to

---

solve the problem."

15. Brueggemann (*Ancient Echoes*, 70–72) notes the prophetic critique of Pharaoh's absurd arrogant claim to have created the Nile River: "I [the Lord God] am against you, Pharaoh King of Egypt . . . [for] saying, '*My Nile is my own*; I made it for myself'" (Ezek 29:3). Of course, the prophet's view is that God created the Nile and all the waters of the earth and everything in them (29:8; cf. Ps 24:1–2).

my soul [or self]: 'Soul [*Psychē*], you have ample goods laid up for many years; relax, eat, drink, and be merry'" (12:19). Turns out all this self-boosting talk is futile: far from having many years, his "life" (*psychēn*) is called to account by God "this very night," leaving behind all "his" riches for others' consumption (12:20–21).

Loyalty: "Worship the Lord your God and serve him only" (Luke 4:8; Deut 6:13)

While wise leaders welcome others' viewpoints and talents to complement and challenge their own, insecure autocrats demand absolute loyalty from their people; only sycophantic yes-men need apply. Alternatively, autocrats are happy to coerce loyalty, especially from rivals, through whatever means necessary. Of course, loyalty runs unilaterally *to* the autocrat, who always retains the right to turn *against* any staffer or supporter. To mix popular vehicular metaphors, it's "my way or the highway," where those who fall foul of the boss's favor or whom the boss needs to take the fall are "thrown under the bus."[16]

Authoritarian loyalty, however, perverts covenantal loyalty, based on mutual love, respect, care, and commitment. True loyalty does not oppose authority as such but rather seeks to use authority for benevolent purposes. In biblical terms, God is the rightful ruler of Israel and the world who initiates and delineates the covenant with God's people. But unlike tyrannical kings who squash their subjects into abject submission and subservience by oppressive laws and brute force, God woos Israel through redemptive love and constructive law (Torah) so that the people might flourish.

Most critically, God promises to remain loyal to Israel, supporting the people every step of the way in their covenantal journey, even in their slips, falls, and detours. Such steadfast love may require God's disciplining the people to get their attention and draw them back when they wander. But unlike other supposed deities, the God of Israel does not exercise

---

16. To anticipate Jesus's noncoercive campaign in Luke, see the comment by a leading Baptist ethicist Glen Stassen: "Baptists . . . committed . . . to following a thicker Jesus . . . insisted that the way Jesus made disciples was by teaching and persuasion, not by coercion. . . . The first defining characteristic of incarnational discipleship rules out coercion and so contributes to religious liberty" (*Thicker Jesus*, 66). Overall, Stassen advocates "a *thick, historically-embodied, realist understanding of Jesus Christ* as revealing God's character and thus providing norms for guiding our lives" (16, emphasis original). Cf. Gushee, *Defending Democracy*, 144-62.

authority capriciously, slapping loved ones around one day and making up to them the next, like an abusive father or husband.

God seeks the holistic well-being of the people, which God knows can only be realized in faithful covenantal relationship. The people have a vital role to play in their well-being by remaining committed to God and God's ways. As Jesus paraphrases Deuteronomy's mandate, "Worship the Lord your God, and serve him only" (Luke 4:8; Deut 6:13). That obviously means, "Don't worship the devil and follow his nefarious ways"—regardless of the earthly kingdoms he may promise you. Even if Satan could thus manipulate world politics, it would mean a raw deal for Jesus and everyone else. The power and authority Jesus might gain would ultimately be subject to Satan's evil aims to destroy God's good world.

Two dimensions of Jesus's response stand out. First, note Jesus's personal commitment to *serve God* as the faithful son. Jesus has no aim to usurp his divine Father's rule (as Absalom, for example, overtook father David's throne [2 Sam 15]); he has come to the world "as one who serves" (Luke 22:27). Second, Jesus makes no counteroffer: "Tell you what, Satan, how about you worship me—I am God's Son, remember—and I'll go a little easier on you and your demons." Jesus makes no deals with the devil. You don't negotiate with terrorists and tyrants.

It's also important to see how Deuteronomy 6 fleshes out what it means to worship and serve God. Such loyalty involves the whole person and community in dynamic cognitive, affective, and active responses of love, fear, and obedience toward God: "Hear, O Israel; The Lord is our God, the Lord alone. You shall love the Lord your God with all your heart, and with all your soul, and with all your might. Keep these words that I am commanding you today in your heart. . . . The Lord your God you shall fear; him you shall serve" (Deut 6:4–6, 13).

As common as it is to speak of loving and fearing God, of being God-loving and God-fearing people, these emotional attitudes toward God do not fit comfortably together. If you're scared *not* to love and be loyal to God because of what an angry God will do to you if you don't, is such love not suspect from the start? Forced love is fake love, as surely as an autocrat's claim that "my people love me because I love them" is fake news.

But God is no self-absorbed autocrat. God's very nature *is* love, self-giving "perfect love [who] casts out fear" (1 John 4:16–18). As the psalmist extols, "The Lord is my light and my salvation; whom shall I fear? The Lord is the stronghold of my life; of whom shall I be afraid?" (Ps 27:1). Well, we should still fear *God*, according to Deuteronomy, Psalms, and

Luke.[17] Yes, but that means we should revere, respect God, not cower in fear before God, right? Yes and no. By all means, give God due reverence and respect, love and loyalty. But *fearing* God in the Bible still carries a *fearful* dimension, a tinge of terror—not at God's temperamental volatility—but at God's unfathomable vastness, God's ineffable awesomeness.[18]

Security: "Do not put the Lord your God to the test" (Luke 4:12; Deut 6:16)

Tyrants commonly have a pathological craving to be loved and feared, adored and feted as demigods to compensate for their small-mindedness, vulgarity, and insecurity. One does not have to be a psychiatrist to discern the massive black hole at the ego-center of would-be strongmen's beings, which they obsessively seek to fill with grandiose claims and demonstrations.[19] On the flip side, this grandiosity is accompanied by a hyper-grievance mentality and paranoia, quick to blame any deficiencies on other parties, presumed to be jealous, corrupt, and out to get them. They are consumed by a "politics of resentment" against the establishment "system" that shuts them out and fails to credit their imagined superiority.[20]

As we've seen, the devil tries to goad Jesus into proving his greatness by flying off the temple pinnacle and landing safely on angels' wings. Apart from its misuse of Scripture (see above), the problem with this spectacular test is twofold. First, Jesus does not need to prove anything about his intimate relationship with God. As we saw in strategy 1, the twelve-year-old Jesus already has a strong sense of God's authorization *in the temple* (2:46-49). Yet he also learns not to be too full of himself, as he continues to grow "in wisdom and in years, and in divine and human favor" under his earthly parents' tutelage (2:51-52). Then, at his baptism some eighteen years later, Jesus receives further divine assurance of his beloved status (3:21-22). But he has no opportunity to strut because the Spirit promptly leads him to messianic boot camp in the desert. The fact is, Jesus needs no ego-coddling or constant affirmation; he remains secure in himself, in union with his loving Father.

---

17. See, e.g., Deut 6:13; 10:12, 20; Pss 2:11; 103:13; Luke 1:50; 12:5; 18:2.
18. See Spencer, "To Fear."
19. See Lee, ed., *Dangerous Case*.
20. Applebaum, *Twilight*, 29–33.

Second, this test of Jesus is really a presumptuous test of *God*, as Jesus makes clear: "Do not put the Lord your God to the test" (4:8; Deut 6:16). The proposed daredevil act provocatively tests God's love for Jesus that God has already revealed. The story of God's dealings with ancient Israel remains significant. God provided abundant evidence of loving faithfulness by redeeming the Israelites from slavery and by guiding, protecting, and providing for them in the wilderness. Yet the people dared to test God's covenantal commitment "ten times" (Num 14:22), which is to say, too many times.

Deuteronomy 6:16 (the text Jesus quotes) pinpoints Israel's early provocation of God "at Massah ['Test']," as Moses designated the place in the Sinai desert. Exodus 17:6 adds another name, "Meribah ['Quarrel'], because the Israelites quarreled and tested the LORD, saying, 'Is the LORD among us or not?'" (Exod 17:6). How quickly they forget God's parting the sea for their escape to freedom (14:15–30) and perpetual presence with them in "a pillar of cloud by day . . . and in a pillar of fire by night (13:21–22). How quickly they begin to grumble against God, specifically griping at Massah/Meribah about the limited water supply, as if God brought them out of slavery so they would die of thirst (17:1–3)! Grievance trumps gratitude. Moses thunders at the people, "Why do you quarrel with me? Why do you test the LORD?" (17:2). On this occasion, God resolves their complaint with a gush of water from a rock. At other times, God will not be so patient with the people's thankless whining (see Num 11:33; 21:4–9).

Again, Jesus will have no part of testing God's love or patience. Jesus remains grateful for all God has given him and rests content in his vocation as God's servant (see Luke 9:46–48; 10:21–22; 22:24–27). He even pushes back at a respectful inquirer who addresses him as "Good Teacher," saying, "Why do you call me good? No one is good but God alone" (18:18–19)—directly echoing Deuteronomy 6:5 (cf. Luke 10:25–28).

As for Psalm 91:11–12, which Satan flippantly offers as a prooftext (see above), Jesus undoubtedly knows the full hymn, not just a couple of cherry-picked verses. This psalm could well be titled, "The Lord Is My Refuge" or "My Shelter," "My Shadow," "My Fortress" (inspiring Martin Luther's famous composition, "A Mighty Fortress Is Our God"):

> You who live in the shelter of the Most High,
> > who abide in the shadow of the Almighty,
> will say to the LORD, "My refuge and my fortress;
> > my God in whom I trust."
> You have made the LORD your refuge,
> > the Most High your dwelling place. (Ps 91:1–2, 9)

Notably, the psalmist addresses "you" who *presently live/abide* in God's refuge or, more precisely, in the Refuge that *is* God. No need to seek out or run to—still less *fly to*—God's protective presence when it's all around you! And speaking of flight safety, God has everything covered "with his pinions, and under his wings you will find refuge" (91:4). It's only when God's children try to fly out on their own from under God's wings—exactly what Satan is daring Jesus to do—that they court disaster. Later, Luke's Jesus envisages himself as a mother hen lamenting that his chicks (the people of Jerusalem) spurn his saving care: "How often have I desired to gather your children together as a hen gathers her brood under wings, and you were not willing!" (Luke 13:34).

Abiding under God's wings from where he in turn extends his wings to shelter God's children, Jesus has no intention to launch off the temple wing to prove God's love or promote his own greatness. Jesus Messiah operates under God's sacred canopy, not under the devil's circus tent.

Launching the Campaign

> **Strategy 3**
>
> *Begin with your home base, but don't pander to their most parochial interests. Push them to follow their better intentions of hospitality to strangers and aliens as well as family and neighbors. Lay out your basic approach to domestic problems and foreign policy. If the home crowd rejects your mission, move on to more receptive audiences.*

ON JUNE 16, 2015, Donald Trump launched his presidential campaign with a golden escalator ride to the ground floor of Trump Tower (where he lived and worked) on Fifth Avenue in New York City. The journalist Tim Alberta aptly quips that such an image "would be the envy of Aaron's gold calf."[1] He followed with a rambling rant punctuated by denunciations of criminal Mexicans (rapists, murderers) he believed were flooding into America: a stunning mix of egotism and ethnocentrism. No one had ever seen anything like it, which is just what Trump wanted.

How a candidate launches a campaign sets the tone for the race and hints at how he would govern if elected. It certainly did in Trump's case, whose presidency favored the interests of wealthy Americans over poorer citizens and even more against poor immigrants. To put it mildly, Trump struck a different tone from Jesus's campaign announcement in Luke.

Recall that after the twelve-year-old Jesus made a splash in the Jerusalem temple—the magnificent gold-adorned complex renovated by Herod the Great—he returned with his parents to Nazareth until he started his messianic "work" around thirty years of age (Luke 3:23). Although

---

1. Alberta, *Kingdom*, 25.

he performed some prior (unspecified) ministry in Capernaum, about twenty miles northeast of Nazareth (4:23), he properly launches his mission in his home synagogue on an ordinary Sabbath (4:16). From a publicity perspective, this setting scarcely lights a candle to the Jerusalem temple at Passover. Jesus cares little about glitz and PR.

But he now has big, bold plans to announce, which create a stir among his hometown relatives and neighbors—and not the positive buzz he might have hoped for—as his audience ultimately stampedes him out of town (4:28–30). Regarding his brother Marcus Cicero's campaign for the Roman consulship, Quintus Cicero advised, "Do not overlook your family and those closely connected to you. Make sure they all are behind you and want you to succeed. . . . For almost every destructive rumor that makes its way to the public begins among family and friends."[2] In American elections, families can also drag down a politician's reputation. It's useful at least to put on a "happy family" face in public. Luke's Jesus does not care so much about playing to the crowd.

Jesus does not draw his messianic agenda out of the blue but rather from the "Spirit of the Lord" revealed in prophetic Scripture (4:18–19). There is much to unpack in Jesus's "good news" (4:18) program. But from the start, we should underscore that Jesus prioritizes meeting the needs of the *poor and oppressed* not only among his own people but among *foreigners and outsiders* as well. In other words, the opposite of the 2016, 2020, and 2024 Republican political platforms—which is *not* to align Jesus with the Democrats. Luke's Jesus is God's messianic prophet and member of no political party, ancient or modern. A true independent *and* solidarist.

DOMESTIC AGENDA

Jesus is not the leader of the Nazareth synagogue. He simply attends Sabbath services, "as was his custom" (4:16), as a member of the congregation. But ordinary members were often invited to read the Scripture lesson and comment on it. On the occasion in Luke 4, the synagogue assistant hands Jesus a scroll, which he unrolls to two passages in Isaiah that he combines in his reading (Isa 58:8; 61:1–2; Luke 4:16–19). He then returns the scroll, retakes his seat, and says, "Today this scripture has been fulfilled in your hearing" (4:20–21). No long sermon, no fanfare.

---

2. *How to Win an Election*, 17.

Just this one statement for now, inviting the people's responses. No big "I am the Messiah" announcement, at least not directly. But Jesus comes tantalizingly close to claiming to be the Spirit-"anointed" one forecast by Isaiah and to embracing the mission of Christ, the "christened" (*echrisen*) one. He dares to identify with Isaiah's profile of the Spirit's appointed servant-prophet:

> The Spirit of the Lord is upon me,
>   because he has anointed me
>   to bring good news to the poor.
> He has sent me to proclaim release to the captives
>   and recovery of sight to the blind,
>   to let the oppressed go free. (4:18–19)

Short and sweet as "good news." But serious and substantive, too, not to mention challenging and world changing, targeting three major "social gospel" issues: health care, prison reform, and debt relief.[3]

Health Care

There was no health care system, as we know it, in the Greco-Roman world, certainly no universal system as some countries have today. Hospitals, such as they were, in the Roman Empire were typically reserved for wounded and ill soldiers and slaves, not for charity's sake, but to get warriors and workers back into action to maintain state security and prosperity.[4] Treating and caring for infirm, injured, and disabled persons was left to family and friends, aided by local physicians with various levels of training and folk healers of varying reputations, including hucksters preying on desperate sufferers. Mortality rates were high, especially for the poor, undernourished, overworked majority; though overall life spans averaged forty years, many died much younger. To put it mildly, the public health crisis was dire.

Luke's Jesus advances no grand health care plan for his Jewish hometown or homeland. He's no professional administrator or political organizer. But he does advocate "recovery of sight to the blind" via Isaiah's prophecy (Luke 4:18/Isa 61:1 LXX). There was no shortage of totally blind and other sight-challenged persons and no optometric services as

---

3. For an assessment of the "social gospel" in American religious history and its aptness to Jesus's mission in Luke, see Spencer, *Luke*, 691–706.

4. Rhee, *Illness*, 212–13.

we know them: no Braille, guide dogs, or laser surgery. Various homeopathic eye salves brought limited relief.

In the Gospels of Mark and John, Jesus provides sight for a couple of men blind from birth, using mud, spit, and water in the process.[5] Near the end of his ministry, Luke's Jesus restores the sight of a blind roadside beggar simply by speaking the cure (Luke 18:35–43). Otherwise, Luke makes one brief reference to Jesus's giving "sight to many who were blind" (among other ministries) (7:21–22) and another to his challenging elite hosts to open their banquet tables to the blind (among other disabled persons) (14:12–13, 21). Though helping and healing blind persons is a vital part of Jesus's ministry, he does not carry out a campaign to cure all eye maladies in the land and founds no school or hospital for the blind. Though passionately dedicated to people's holistic well-being, Jesus does not go around acting like a super-healer of all ailments with a magic touch and bag of potions. Jesus has no more interest in selling himself as a healing guru than as a bread factory, simply to enhance his popularity and power.

Jesus's identification with Isaiah's Spirit-anointed, sight-restoring prophet "amazes" the synagogue audience. But amazement does not mean endorsement. They don't quite know what to make of Jesus's "gracious words . . . from his mouth" on this occasion. They've known Jesus his whole life, and this is not the way he normally talks. Is he just putting on airs, getting above himself ("Is not this Joseph's son?" 4:22)? Or has he had some recent genuine spiritual experience? He's starting to sound all mighty and messianic—very un-Nazareth. Of course, Mary knows about Jesus's special calling, but as we've seen, she's still struggling (understandably) to sort out the details.

Jesus knows his home folks are not convinced. He senses that they would like him to reprise an act or two from his recent performance in Capernaum they had heard about (4:24; Luke doesn't describe this Capernaum event). But Jesus doesn't play to the crowds any more than to the devil; he doesn't perform on demand and has no need to prove himself. He snaps at the Nazareth congregation, "Doubtless you will quote to me this proverb, 'Doctor, cure yourself!'" (4:23). In other words, "Let's see if you've got the messianic goods, Jesus. Let's see if this alleged healing power works for you—if it works *on you*." Sounds like, "If you can't feed

---

5. Mark 8:22–26; John 9:1–17; cf. the story of Tobit whose blindness was eventually cured by applying fish guts to his eyes, where previous ointments had proved ineffectual (Tob 2:10; 11:7–15).

yourself in the desert [Satan's first test], why should we expect you to help us?" Jesus has been down this road before.

The focal curative issue of bringing sight to the blind would be a little tough for Jesus to demonstrate on himself (he would have to blind himself first). But surely someone in the audience has an eye problem he could cure with a touch or a word (mud or spit optional). But would that be enough? Of course not. We're all like little children in these situations. Again, Jesus! Oh, do me next! My eyes are fine, but my back's killing me. Etc., etc. It's actually worse with one's own family and community. Less tolerance for strange behavior, less willingness to give new ideas a fair hearing. "Truly I tell you," Jesus continues, "no prophet is accepted in the prophet's hometown" (4:24). True indeed, though Jesus's pointing this out is not likely to endear him to the home folks (it doesn't, as we will see).

We might think that the Spirit-inspired mission to the blind focuses more on providing *spiritual* (in)sight, opening hearts and minds' eyes to understanding God's word. Luke and other biblical writers use optic metaphors for revealing and perceiving God's way. Jesus's tutelage of his disciples (students) involves enabling them to *see* God's way more clearly: "Blessed are the eyes that see what you see!" (10:23; he's not talking about the Galilean scenery). There are also times, however, when God's way remains hidden because people are not ready to see the light or refuse to follow the light they've been given (or for inexplicable reasons God only knows; see 8:16–18; 10:21–24; 18:34; 24:13–16, 25–31). Gaining and maintaining spiritual insight is not easy. Teaching, learning, and walking in God's ways are lifelong challenges.

Granting this vital spiritual dimension of bringing "sight to the blind" does not, however, diminish Jesus's concern for those suffering physical blindness or other eye disorders. Because illness is invariably multifaceted, affecting the whole person—including one's feelings, thoughts, viewpoints, actions, relations with others—full healing must likewise be multidimensional; in a word, holistic.

To be sure, in his campaign launch in Nazareth, Jesus does not elaborate on the broader eye-opening effects of his ministry. He will soon have more to say about the social-political ramifications of other types of healing. But we first explore two additional aspects of Jesus's domestic agenda derived from Isaiah.

Prison Reform

Two planks in the Isaiah platform Jesus adopts put the final accent on *freedom*. The Spirit has sent the anointed one "to proclaim release [*aphesin*] to the captives [Isa 61:1] . . . to let the oppressed go free [*aphesei*, Isa 58:6]" (Luke 4:18).

It's always good to campaign on freedom, and not just in America's "land of the free." It's even more important, though more perilous, to promote freedom in a land under foreign control, as in the exiled Isaiah's Judahite territory under the Babylonian Empire and in Jesus's homeland under the Roman Empire. No one runs on a "slavery for all" platform, though there always seems to be room for enslaving *some*, effectively if not explicitly. Our country has a checkered history on this score, granting only token (three-fifths) representation to enslaved persons at its founding and later splitting into two state-coalitions and spilling oceans of blood over whether such persons—or properties, as owners saw them—had any rights at all. The end of the Civil War scarcely ended the struggle for civil rights.

Neither Isaiah nor Jesus calls for a freedom fight against tyrannical rule on the battlefield, which would have been a suicidal disaster against imperial military juggernauts. So what kind of release/freedom does Jesus envision? Freedom-talk often amounts to so much popular jabber, empty rhetoric—"just some people talkin'" (cue the Eagles' "Desperado"), a high-sounding buzzword signifying nothing. But prophets like Isaiah and Jesus, who dare to speak God's inconvenient truth, don't waste words or engage in idle chats.

If Jesus is not lobbying for militant revolutionary freedom from Roman rule, then perhaps we should ask again if his aims are chiefly spiritual, in this case, setting people free from their *sins*. The freedom-term *aphesis* used in Jesus's Isaiah quotation can also mean "forgiveness." John the Baptizer proclaims "forgiveness of sins" or "release from sins" (*aphesei hamartiōn*, Luke 1:77; 3:3). The same terminology applies to Jesus's mediating God's forgiveness to a disabled man (whom he also heals) and a disreputable woman: "Your sins are forgiven (*apheōntai*)" (5:20, 24; 7:47–49). At the heart of the Lord's Prayer, Jesus teaches his disciples to petition the Father, "Forgive (*aphes*) us our sins (*hamartias*)" (11:4).

Jesus's religious culture not only believed that people required freedom/forgiveness from entangling personal sins (transgressions of God's law) but also freedom/liberation from enslaving diabolical spirits (demons, Satan's servants). Hence, Jesus's ministry will include exorcisms as evidence of the liberative character of God's rule: "If it is by the finger of God that I cast out demons," Jesus announces to skeptics and detractors, "then the kingdom of God has come to you" and Satan's "strongman" schemes have been thwarted (11:20–22).

As a case in point, in another synagogue Jesus encounters "a woman with a spirit that had crippled her for eighteen years," forcing her spine into a such a rigid bent-over posture that she "was quite unable to stand up straight." Upon seeing this woman, Jesus summons her and says, "Woman you are *set free* (*apolelysai*) from your ailment" (13:10–12). While modern orthopedists would diagnose her as suffering severe scoliosis, Jesus attributes her condition to demonic enslavement. When the synagogue leader quibbles with Jesus's choice to cure her on the Sabbath (performing nonemergency medical work), Jesus has the last word: "Ought not this woman, a daughter of Abraham whom Satan bound for eighteen long years, be *set free* (*lythēnai*) from this bondage on the sabbath day?" (13:16). Though using a different freedom verb, the point is the same one Jesus embraces in the Nazareth synagogue: God's Spirit has anointed him to "let the oppressed go free" (4:18).

Undoubtedly, then, Luke's Jesus aims to promote freedom from sins and demons, thereby reinforcing his holistic commitment to people's well-being. But does such a freedom focus preclude an auxiliary concern for *literal prisoners* physically bound in chains or confined to cells or another form of incarceration, like house arrest or surveillance? Might Jesus have a special interest in those unjustly imprisoned while also having compassion on those properly judged and jailed for true crimes?

It's doubtful that Nazareth had a local sheriff, police force, jail, or any patrolling Roman soldiers, for that matter. No major crime problem in this tiny village. But the threat of arrest and imprisonment for various violations—including nonpayment of taxes and debts—loomed across Roman Galilee and Judea. Jesus later refers to a common scenario involving a legal dispute between two parties, likely over property or inheritance rights. He advocates settling the dispute outside of court. Otherwise, "you may be dragged before the judge, and the judge hand you over to the officer, and the officer throw you into prison . . . until you have paid the very last penny" (12:57–59). Of course, this would place the prisoner in a double bind, especially if he's poor: how can he pay his fine or debt while locked up?

A higher profile case involves John the Baptizer's imprisonment by the Galilean ruler, Herod Antipas (3:19–20), who does not like John's increasing popularity and public denunciation of Herod's unlawful marriage to his brother Philip's wife (cf. Matt 14:3–5; Mark 6:17–18; Josephus, *Ant.* 18.116-19). Tyrants—including small fries like Antipas who only ruled a quarter-kingdom as tetrarch—do not take public criticism well, especially concerning their sex lives. Jesus continues to commend John as a great prophet (7:24–28) and reassures the imprisoned John that Jesus's messianic mission is flourishing. As proof, Jesus instructs John's messengers, "Go and tell John what you have seen and heard: the blind receive their sight, the lame walk, the lepers are cleansed, the deaf hear, the dead are raised, the poor have good news brought to them." Jesus says this just after he's "cured many people of diseases, plagues, and evil spirits, and . . . given sight to many who were blind" (7:21–22).

Although Jesus springs no one from a literal jail cell, concern for restorative justice and for meeting prisoners' basic needs naturally aligns with the broad evangelical agenda Jesus announces in the Nazareth synagogue. While prison reform is still desperately needed today, especially in the US, which has the highest incarceration rate in the world, modern prisons at least feed and provide some health care for inmates. But there were no cafeterias or infirmaries in ancient prisons; inmates depended on families, friends, or charitable volunteers for sustenance. Though not in Luke, I think Luke would heartily agree with Matthew's poignant expression of Jesus's intimate solidarity with prisoners and others in dire material need: "I was hungry and you gave me food, I was thirsty and you gave me something to drink, I was a stranger and you welcomed me, I was naked and you gave me clothing, I was sick and you took care of me, I was in prison and you visited me. . . . Just as you did it to one of the least of these brothers and sisters of mine, you did it to me" (Matt 25:35–36). Mentioning prison visitation last presumes everything that precedes, as if to say, "When you visit prisoners, bring them food, drink, clothes, and medicine they desperately need; let them know in their isolation that someone cares about them."

President Richard Nixon's so-called "hatchet man," Charles Colson, was the first of Nixon's coterie to serve time for his involvement in the Watergate scandal. He became a devout evangelical Christian, however, and devoted his life thereafter to prison reform and inmates' care in Christ's name through his Prison Fellowship organization. While he later promoted various Far Right social and political values, he never abandoned his commitment to prison ministry. Prison Fellowship International, as it's now called, is still going strong a decade after Colson's death in 2012.[6] While Colson might support some extreme right-wing politics in America today, it's hard to believe he would trumpet calls to "lock up" political opponents.[7]

Debt Relief

As mentioned above, incarceration was a common penalty for failure to pay one's debts in the ancient world (see Matt 18:23–30; Luke 12:57–59). Thus, prison release and debt relief converge. Once again, we acknowledge a sin-related issue, this time correlating debt relief with forgiveness or redemption. The Bible often images sin as debt.[8] The petition in the Lord's Prayer, "Forgive our sins (*hamartias*)," continues, "for we ourselves forgive everyone *indebted* (*ōpheilonti*) to us" (11:4); and Jesus reinforces his lavish forgiveness of the "many sins" of a woman who shows him "great love" with a parable about a creditor who cancels a debtor's sizeable financial obligation (7:41–43, 47–49).

But receiving forgiveness of one's moral-spiritual "debts" to God and one another, as vital as that is, would not keep one out of the poorhouse or count, by itself, as "good news to the poor" (4:18). Blessedness, according to Luke's Jesus, must extend not simply to the "poor in spirit" (Matt 5:4) but to "the poor" by any measure, certainly including those mired in material-financial poverty (Luke 6:20). Debt was a major source of poverty in Jesus's day.[9] Not, we should understand, because of ordinary people's boundless greed and reckless borrowing and spending habits. In a largely agrarian economy controlled by powerful land barons, many lived and worked as tenant farmers obligated to meet their landlords' production quotas. Deficits in production went on the books as tenants' debts due the landowner-creditors. Consequences for failed payment of these debts included eviction, enslavement, and imprisonment.

Jesus proposes no extensive New Deal (FDR) to lift people out of a Great Depression and declares no strategic War on Poverty (LBJ). But he

---

6. Mark and Banks, "Repentant 'Hatchet Man.'"

7. For non-"right" but equally Bible-based ministry to prisoners (and other unfortunates), see Ekblad, *Reading the Bible*.

8. See G. Anderson, *Sin*, 3–14, 27–94.

9. See Oakman, *Jesus*.

does endorse an old plan of debt relief from Israel's history, rooted in the Torah and Prophets: the Year of Jubilee. In all likelihood, this is "the year of the Lord's favor" in the last Isaiah line Jesus quotes in the Nazareth synagogue, since the biblical Jubilee is all about release/freedom (*aphesis*), not least from debt.[10]

Such debt release/relief was integrally tied to Sabbath rest. Complementing the weekly Sabbath every seventh day was the yearlong Sabbath every seventh year in which creditors "shall grant a remission of debts" held against fellow Israelites. "Of a foreigner you may exact [payment or penalty], but you must remit your claim on whatever any member of your community owes you" (Deut 15:1–3). Deuteronomy further warns against enacting the "mean thought" of calling in all outstanding debt payments *just before* the Sabbatical Year begins (15:9). The goal of such legislation is equality: meeting everyone's basic needs. The spirit is generosity: "Open your hand, willingly lending enough to meet the need, whatever it may be. . . . Give liberally and be ungrudging. . . . Since there will never cease to be some in need on the earth . . . 'Open your hand to the poor and needy neighbor in your land'" (15:8, 10–11).

Reinforcing the septennial cancellation of debt was a semicentennial super-sabbatical or Jubilee every fiftieth year (after seven seven-year periods), when "you shall proclaim liberty throughout the land to all its inhabitants" (Lev 25:10). This "liberty" (*aphesis*, LXX) is no mere rally word to make people feel good. It signals sweeping ecological and economic relief: (1) the land must not be actively cultivated through the Jubilee Year ("you shall eat only what the field itself produces," 25:12); (2) property must revert back to original owners and debts should be redeemed by close kin (keep it in the family); and (3) the poor who had sold themselves into slavery to survive must be set free, along with their children. Moreover, in the years preceding the Jubilee, debts must not be charged interest and land deals should be transacted fairly: "You shall not cheat one another" (25:14, 17). The overriding Jubilee principle coalesces with Creation and Sabbath: the land is *God's*, graciously entrusted to the people for their—and the whole world's—good.

What a wonderful freedom idea! But how realistic is it? Imagine the upheaval today if credit card companies and lending institutions were compelled to wipe the slate clean every fiftieth year. Pope John Paul II declared the new millennial year 2000 as the Great Jubilee. A nice gesture

---

10. See Long, "Debt"; Spencer, "Jubilee."

but one which few financiers took seriously, as greedy forces were already in motion for the Great Recession of 2009. Even in ancient Israel, while the Torah makes clear that Jubilee was not just a utopian ideal (Lev 27:16–25; Num 36:1–4), it's hard to know how regularly it was practiced. The constant drumbeat of the Hebrew prophets against prevailing patterns of social injustice suggest that Jubilee Year often went by the boards.

What, then, does Jesus intend by launching a fresh Jubilee campaign of debt relief? In a couple of parables, he refers to debt remission (Luke 7:41–42) or reduction (16:1–9). In another (noted above), he exposes a foolish rich man who thinks he has total control over his land, goods, and future to guarantee many years of easy retirement, only to die suddenly and forfeit all "his" gains. Jesus tells this tale to buttress his main point: "Take care! Be on your guard against all kinds of greed; for one's life does not consist in the abundance of possessions" (12:15–21).

Luke's Jesus is a Jubilee man. In today's America, he would favor Main Street over Wall Street, a back road over banker's row. But he's no economist or treasury official. He can challenge financial systems in Jerusalem and Rome (see 19:45–46; 20:20–25, 45–47; 21:1–4) but is in no position to change them personally. Yet he envisions a realm—the realm of God—where God's redeemed people could make a difference together—if they just would.

FOREIGN AID

As we've seen, Jesus's domestic agenda via Isaiah generates a buzz of amazement among the synagogue audience. Small-towners, then as now, had less access to medical and economic resources than urban elites. Thus, Jesus's proposed mission raises intriguing possibilities for the Nazarenes. Still, what gives Jesus the authority to make such grand claims? Aren't politicians always promising the moon yet delivering dust? What can this "son of Joseph" (4:22) really do about our everyday problems? He needs to explain himself.

Shockingly, however, his added commentary only makes matters worse. Far from winning his home folks over, he makes them mad to such an extent that they want to throw him over the cliff at the edge of town (a fate he mysteriously escapes [4:30]). We've already seen that Jesus lumps his family and neighbors with those who reject God's prophets

(4:24). Now he ratchets up the tension by appealing to other biblical-prophetic models: Elijah and Elisha (4:25–27).

On the surface, invoking two of Israel's greatest prophets—particularly Elijah, who's expected to return to earth and pave the way for the Messiah[11]—would seem to be a smart political move.[12] The Elijah-Elisha narratives of 1 Kings 17:2–9 feature numerous bold challenges to oppressive rulers and great miracles which benefit suffering Israelites. But Jesus singles out two incidents that display these prophets' ministry to needy *foreigners*: one, a destitute widow in Sidon (Phoenicia) aided by Elijah during a time of famine; the other, a Syrian official named Naaman afflicted with a skin disease who seeks and receives healing from Elijah in Israel. Jesus aims to strike a critical nerve by the way he highlights these incidents:

> There were many widows in Israel in the time of Elijah, when . . . there was a severe famine over all the land, yet Elijah was sent to *none of them* except to a widow at Zarephath in Sidon. (Luke 4:25)
>
> There were also many with a skin disease (*leproi*) in Israel in the time of the prophet Elisha, and *none of them* was cleansed except Naaman the Syrian. (4:27)

What a stunning message to launch Jesus's campaign, as if to say, "I've got nothing for you all here. All this glorious talk of good news, freedom, Jubilee: it's all for outsiders across the border or those who cross into our land." Foreign aid before domestic aid. Try running on that platform in America these days. No wonder his Nazareth kinfolks run him out of town.

Jesus in fact exaggerates for effect—though maybe more effect than he bargained for. Elijah and Elisha spent most of their time in Israel working to help fellow Israelites, just as Jesus will. Soon he helps a distraught widow in the nearby Galilean village of Nain, raising her only son from his funeral mat (Luke 7:11–17). He also will cure a local man's skin disease (5:12–14) and heal a group of ten men's similar malady along the border between Galilee and Samaria. While one of these is a Samaritan "foreigner" (*allogenēs*, 17:18), the other nine are presumably Jewish. This Samaritan is the only one who directly praises God and thanks Jesus for

---

11. See Mal 4:5–6; Sir 48:1–11; Matt 17:10–12; Mark 9:11–13; cf. Luke 9:7–9, 18–19 (discussed in strategy 9).

12. American politicians on all sides routinely sprinkle biblical references into their campaigns. See Schiess, *Bible and the Ballot*.

healing him, thus implying that the "other nine" take Jesus's ministry for granted; but Jesus cures them all the same (17:11–19). Jesus has no intention of abandoning his needy countrymen and women. Nonetheless, he chooses to underscore in Nazareth his commitment to *foreign* aid. Charity may begin at home, but it doesn't end there in God's realm. Jesus makes that clear from the start of his messianic mission, regardless of the anger it incites and the "votes" it costs him.

Jesus's brief references to two well-known Elijah and Elisha episodes, punctuated by his barb that God seemed disinclined to help *any Israelite* widows or psoriatic sufferers at the time, are enough to enrage the Nazareth audience. A strange, risky move on Jesus's part. It's worth delving into these biblical precedents to help us understand their significance for Jesus's campaign.

Women and Children

The Elijah story launches his prophetic ministry. Elijah has no noble pedigree. He comes from the undistinguished town of Tishbe in the mountainous region of Gilead on the eastern edge of Israel's territory. In this marginal area, God calls Elijah during a time of famine to isolate himself by a local creek (wadi) called Cherith. Here the prophet learns to trust God for water during the drought and bread and meat brought by ravens, of all creatures, "unclean" predators who would otherwise be feasting on carcass casualties of the famine (1 Kgs 17:1–7).

Elijah goes to no prophets' school, stands on no ceremony, and cares nothing about appearances. He will prove to be a constant thorn in the sides of Israel's King Ahab and Queen Jezebel. And, as it happens, he represents the perfect prototype for John the Baptizer, Jesus's forerunner (see Luke 1:17; 9:7–8, 19).

After his retreat at Wadi Cherith, Elijah's first assignment takes him across Israel's northern border to the village of Zaraphath in Sidon, part of ancient Phoenicia (modern Lebanon), historically hostile territory to Israel and Israel's God. In Elijah's day, the Sidonian princess Jezebel who becomes Israel's queen by marriage aggressively promotes the Phoenician gods and prophets of Baal and Asherah (1 Kgs 16:31–34; 18:17–19). Yet God still sends Elijah to a destitute widow in Sidon as she and her son prepare to eat their last biscuit before they die. In the name of "the LORD, the God of Israel," echoing the meaning of Elijah's name, Elijah guarantees that her flour jar and oil jug will never go empty again (17:8–16).

Tragically, though, her son becomes terribly ill and dies. The mother thinks that Elijah and his God have tricked her by offering aid as a smokescreen for their murderous intent. In her worldview from the low end of society, you could never fully trust powerful gods, rulers, and their agents. But such is not the way of Elijah and his God. Stretching himself on top of the lifeless boy and crying out to God, Elijah channels God's resuscitative power. The child comes back to life, Elijah gives him back to his mother, and the mother confesses, "Now I know that you are a man of God, and that the word of the LORD in your mouth is truth" (17:17–24). A marvelous event, with notable parallels to Jesus's raising the widow's deceased son in Nain (Luke 7:11–17).[13]

The larger point here is God's special concern for poor women and children, widows and orphans, who represent the most vulnerable persons in patriarchal regimes obsessed with war, conquest, power, and possessions. Such victims become sacrificial pawns in political conflicts. Categories of "domestic" and "foreign" mean little to the poor and powerless who just want to survive. In God's book—attested time and again in the Law, Prophets, and Psalms—such least and little ones merit preferential treatment by God and God's people.

In addition to helping the desperate widow at Nain, Luke's Jesus advocates justice and mercy for exploited widows in a poignant parable (18:1–8) and in public teachings in the temple (20:45–21:4). He also proves to be a friend and minister to children from infants to adolescents, including raising another deceased child, this time a twelve-year-old girl, the only daughter of a synagogue leader (8:40–42, 49–56; see 9:37–43, 46–48; 10:21; 18:15–17). Powerless, "nobody" widows and children have nothing to offer Jesus politically.[14] And he does not use them for political ends and photo ops. This is real widow- and child-care advocacy and action. It's Jubilee time, the "year of the Lord's favor" to unfavored unfortunates.

---

13. See Brodie, "Unravelling Luke's Use of the Old Testament"; Evans and Sanders, *Luke and Scripture*, 76–77.

14. See Crossan, *Jesus*, 54–64; Caputo, *Weakness*, 30–38, 45–47 (cf. 1 Cor 1:26–28).

Enemies and Supremacists

Except for his "foreigner" status, which he shared with the Sidonian widow and mother from Zarephath, it's hard to imagine a figure more different from her than Naaman, the man featured in Jesus's second example of foreign aid, this time administered by Elijah's successor, Elisha. Naaman was a powerful, wealthy, male commander of the mighty Syrian (Aramean) army (2 Kgs 5:1). Yet even high-ranking elites get skin diseases. But when, like Naaman, they contract a serious malady, they have the clout and loot to procure better treatment than common sufferers do.

When Naaman learns from the Israelite slave-girl who attends his wife that a prophet in her country performs miraculous cures, he marshals all his influence and resources to acquire Elisha's services. Naaman's servants pack up a caravan load of "ten talents of silver, six thousand shekels of gold, and ten sets of garments" to accompany him on his chariot-trek to Israel. He also bears an official letter from his king to Israel's counterpart demanding that the latter "cure [Naaman] of his skin disease." General Naaman rolls up to Israel's royal palace with as much intimidation and entitlement to special treatment as he can muster. It scares Israel's king to death. He knows he has no power to heal anybody and frets that Naaman "is trying to pick a quarrel with me." If Naaman doesn't get his cure, what then? Wars have been fought over less (5:2–7).

Enter Elisha, who hears about his king's predicament and invites Naaman to come to him. And so it happens: "Naaman came with his horses and chariots and halted at the entrance of Elisha's house" (5:9). What a stir that must have caused in the neighborhood! Elisha does not live in fancy quarters. Nothing subtle about Naaman. But while happy to help this foreign officer, Elisha has no intention of kowtowing to Naaman's ego and sense of entitlement.

In an audaciously cheeky move, or rather non-move, Elijah doesn't so much as twitch a muscle to go out and greet Naaman but simply sends a prescription via a messenger that Naaman should dip himself seven times in the Jordan River. This makes Naaman apoplectic with indignation. How dare this Israelite prophet not rush out and perform some grand curative gesture worthy of his highness! And how dare he suggest that I dunk myself in Israel's measly, muddy Jordan River: "Are not Abana and Pharpar, the rivers of Damascus [Syria's capital] better than all the waters of Israel?" (5:12).

Naaman fulminates in his nationalist, supremacist bigotry against an inferior irritant, as he perceives this Israelite prophet. But as he stews over Elisha, Naaman stays in his psoriatic state. Only when Naaman's attendants urge him to give Elisha's remedy a whirl does he finally come down from his high horse, immerse himself seven times in the Jordan River, and, yes, come up "cleansed" from his skin ailment, "his flesh restored like the flesh of a young boy" (5:13–14).

Well, what do you know? Naaman learns a lesson in theology and humility. He returns to Elisha's house, stands with his retinue respectfully before the prophet, confessing, "Now I know that there is no God in all the earth except in Israel!" But he can't help adding an addendum—"please accept a present from your servant" (5:15)—payment to keep my dignity and keep me from being in your debt. Moreover, while Naaman promises to worship only Israel's God from now on, he asks Elisha for one indulgence, namely, to allow him to bow down to Syria's god Rimmon when he accompanies Syria's king in worship. Naaman is not about to jeopardize his power position for anybody. In response, Elisha adamantly refuses to accept any quid quo pro from Naaman but raises no objection to Naaman's occasional worship of Rimmon. Elisha is no religious pluralist, but he's not a hyper-dogmatist either. His final word to Naaman is a benediction: "Go in peace" (5:19).

Even historic enemies and avowed supremacists can change their hostile, bigoted attitudes toward God and God's people, find a place in God's kingdom, and receive the care of God's prophets. Luke's Jesus will soon rock everyone's comfortable world with the flat injunction, "Love your enemies and do good to those who hate you" (Luke 6:27; cf. 6:28–36).

He will also grant a Roman officer's request for healing for his desperately ill slave. But this foreign officer is notably distinguished from Naaman in several respects: he's of lower rank (a centurion, not a general); he seeks aid for a valued servant rather than for himself; while stationed in Capernaum to protect imperial interests, he proves to be benevolent toward the Jewish population, even building a new synagogue (7:1–5). But most strikingly contrasted with Naaman, the centurion refuses to meet Jesus or allow Jesus into his home *out of humble respect for Jesus's authority*. He deems himself "not worthy" to greet or host Jesus. Consequently, he sends word to Jesus through intermediaries conveying his faith that Jesus can deliver a healing command without making a house call (7:6–7). That's exactly what Jesus does: "When Jesus heard [the centurion's relayed message], he was amazed at him, and turning to the crowd that followed him, he said, 'Truly I tell you, not even in Israel have I found such faith'. When those who had been sent returned to the house, they found the slave in good health" (7:9–10).

The Roman officer in Capernaum turns the tables (1) on people's frequent amazement *at Jesus* (as in 4:22); (2) on powerful men's (like Naaman) arrogant, supremacist disdain toward underlings; and (3) on small towns' (like Nazareth) provincial, protectionist suspicions of outsiders. Jesus Messiah wholeheartedly seeks his people's salvation and flourishing. He even prioritizes helping them, with only occasional outreach to non-Jews, like the centurion in Capernaum. He could fairly be said to be "pro-Israel" and "Israel first"—but *not* exclusively, xenophobically. Hence he pushes his hometown synagogue to expand their circle of concern to fit the prophetic horizon of Elijah, Elisha, and Isaiah.

Jesus is no supremacist, separatist, or nationalist. He's first and foremost an embracive *gospelist*, embodying the good news of just and merciful rule, through which "*all flesh* shall see the salvation of God" (Isa 40:5; Luke 3:6; cf. 2:30–32). Since the twentieth-century World Wars era, various extremist versions of "American First" have been promulgated, including the America First Committee, led by powerful US senators, and the America First Party in the 1940s–50s, mixing a toxic brew of fascist, pro-Nazi, antisemitic, white supremacist, Christian nationalist, and isolationist-protectionist agendas. "First" meant *us and ours only and always—by divine right*. The trajectory from America Firsters to MAGA fanatics is not hard to track.[15]

Jesus's Nazareth kin and neighbors were not right-wing crusaders. They were too busy making ends meet and caring for their own people to care much about "national" or "international" politics. They would rather Jesus stay home, ply his father Joseph's trade, marry the girl next door, have kids, and support the local community, than traipse around Galilee in pursuit of some highfalutin mission. That's just good family values, and not only for clannish villages. The Stoic teacher Epictetus advised his elite male students not to become enamored with wanderlust and foreign adventures. If they must go away on business, they should come straight home as soon as possible:

---

15. See Hart, *Hitler's American Friends*, 160–87; Rothman, "Long History"; Roth, *Plot*, 13–14, 166, 229 (Roth's harrowing political novel imagines an America in which the infamous America-Firster Charles Lindbergh defeats FDR in the 1940 presidential election.)

> There are plenty of nice inns, and plenty of pretty meadows, too, but only as places on the way. You have a different mission—to return to your homeland and put an end to your family's fear, and to fulfill your duties as a citizen by marrying, raising children, and holding the customary offices. You didn't come into the world in order to go around picking out locations of the pleasanter kind, surely, but to live where you were born and where you've been enrolled as a citizen. (*Discourses* 2.2.37–39)

When Jesus pushes what appears to be a foreigners first-and-only agenda ("none" in Israel), scriptural or not, he steps way over the (border) line. The good folk of Nazareth have heard enough: if Jesus is so bent on helping everybody out there, we'll give him a quick boot out of town!

So sensitive, these Nazarenes. Maybe, but Jesus is also being provocative. As suggested above, his overemphasizing his border-crossing mission for effect proves *too* effective, almost pushing him and his whole campaign over the cliff. Surely he could've spoken more diplomatically. But not being a professional politician, Jesus is not given to rhetorical niceties to protect himself. He speaks the truth at his own cost. By contrast, autocratic strongmen are obsessively self-protective at others' expense. Jesus might escape Nazareth now, but soon enough Jerusalem authorities will execute him. Not that he angles to be a chaotic anti-traditionalist and go down in a blaze of martyrial glory.

As Jesus is by no means anti-Jewish or anti-Israel, he is not anti-family either. He simply has a broader family network: "My mother and my brothers are those who hear the word of God and do it" (Luke 8:19–21; cf. 11:27–28). And even those who don't first embrace God's word remain under God's nurturing wings and big tent, to reprise images from strategy 2. It turns out there's a lot of first-class room in God's realm; crazier still, the lowest, least, and last receive first-class treatment (see 1:46–55; 9:46–48; 14:7–24; 22:24–27).

Recruiting Staff

> **Strategy 4**
>
> Have an eye to spot great potential in ordinary people. Patiently teach and train recruits to serve with you as active participants, not adoring sycophants. Lead by example and instruction. Equip your team to carry on the mission in your absence.

ONCE MORE WE UNDERSCORE that would-be leaders with pathological messiah complexes tend to crow, "I alone can fix this," appealing to a sense of helplessness and victimization by desperate mobs: "Oh yes, great one, please fix this terrible mess, and we will love you forever." Of course, crowds are notoriously fickle when their bloated hero doesn't deliver the goods. Sooner or later—but in any case, too late to avoid damage—they see him for what he is: an empty suit, an emperor with no clothes.

The truth of the matter is that no one accomplishes anything worth doing alone. We collaborate—build on others' labors—whether we admit it or not. When I say, "I drove to the store to pick up some things so I could make dinner," I'm masking the truth to perpetuate my illusion of self-control. What I should say is, "I drove in a car others manufactured, fueled by gasoline produced by drillers and refiners, on streets paved by road crews, to a store built and staffed by many workers to procure foodstuffs grown, harvested, and processed by hundreds of hands, to prepare a meal in a home constructed by others . . ." You get the idea. We should all get the idea. But it's amazing how easy it is to fool ourselves, to play the "rich fool" (Luke 12:16–21).

Though Donald Trump never tires of boasting about his buildings and portfolio—"I've built a great company"—he still conceded that he needed others' help in his presidential campaign and administration. But rest assured, "I have all the best people," he trumpeted. Yeah, well. Maybe he did, though a good number of his "people" have been indicted and convicted for various malfeasances. Of course, in his mind, going after his lieutenants only proves the egregious injustice done to *him*, the principal target of the "witch hunt."

Luke's Jesus makes no claim to having the top people. He delights, it seems, in having ordinary, undistinguished people on his team—including "sinners"—though not to promote a criminal operation. He is passionately driven to *work with* those on the bottom to help them live better lives, to lift them up morally and materially. His last ministerial act in Luke, while lifted up on a cross, will be to secure a place in God's realm for a criminal hanging beside him (23:39–43). A strange way to end a messianic campaign (see strategy 11).

From the start, Jesus knows that he cannot carry out his messianic mission alone. This will be a team effort, not a solo flight. Who exactly are the not-so-best people he chooses to help him?

FIRST FOLLOWERS

We're used to hearing about Jesus's team of apostles and disciples, often assuming these are special Christian personnel. "Apostle," however, simply transliterates the Greek *apostolos* related to a common verb for "send" (*apostellō*); it thus designates any "sent one" (delegate, emissary) by a commissioner. "Disciple" translates *mathētēs*, related to the verb meaning "learn, study" (*manthanō*); hence disciples are "learners" or "students." Jesus thus acts as commissioner and teacher to his appointed followers and fellow ministers of God's realm. Yet this crew of student interns is not exactly cream of the crop by normal standards.

"Sick" Sinners

They need special "medical" treatment by Jesus for their "sin-sick souls."[1] Jesus's role as Spirit-anointed physician, alluded to in his Nazareth campaign speech (4:23), undergirds his companion roles as commissioner and teacher. One of his early curative acts, enabling a paralyzed man to

---

1. See the refrain in the African American spiritual, "There is a balm in Gilead to heal the sin-sick soul"; cf. Hawn, "History of Hymns."

walk, results from a surprising pronouncement: "Friend, your sins are forgiven you." When some religious teachers question his audacious claim to forgive sins, a prerogative reserved for "God alone," Jesus responds, "Which is easier to say, 'Your sins are forgiven you,' or to say, "Stand up and walk'?" (5:20–24).

Well, neither is easy, but Jesus's intimate relationship with his divine Father makes both possible. As we've seen, Jesus's mission prioritizes remission of sins (and other debts) and restoration to health. *Not*, let's be clear, that sin necessarily *causes* sickness, still less that sickness signals divine punishment for sin. But the human condition is beset by intertwined spiritual, physical, and other weaknesses requiring holistic repair.

Accordingly, it's natural for Jesus to develop further the medical metaphor for his work in another exchange with religious critics, this time related to his excessive fraternizing with sinners: "Those who are well have no need of a physician but those who are sick; I have come to call not the righteous but sinners to repentance" (5:30–32). In other words, Jesus is not aiming so much to help the self-righteous who don't think they need help but rather self-aware sinners who know they need to change their hearts, minds, and lives (repentance). Jesus is no private, pricey Harley Street physician but a folk healer—for ordinary folks—who makes house calls and eats and drinks with "sick" sinners, even daring to become their "friends," which only sends his critics into more of a tizzy (7:34–50; 15:1–2; 19:7–10).

Tending and befriending[2] sick and sinful people is one thing, remarkable in itself. But *recruiting* such folk as principal leaders of your campaign, and traveling and living with them, is another. That's exactly what Jesus does, however, calling his first apostles from two low-end social groups: fishermen and taxmen.

Fishermen

Fishermen were not notorious evildoers; they weren't smuggling drugs or slaves across the Sea of Galilee. But neither were they scrupulous religious law-keepers or Bible students; like most people, they spent most of their time working hard to eke out a living. Which didn't make them bad people but didn't especially commend them either. By necessity,

---

2. The lovely concept coined and developed by research psychologist S. Taylor, *Tending Instinct*, 20–29.

fishermen were generally rough, salty characters and creatures of the night, the most optimal time to ply their trade. They were ill-suited for government work and palace duty.

But that's not what Jesus is running for. A tradesman himself (see Matt 13:55; Mark 6:3), Jesus has no designs on "soft robes" and "royal palaces" (Luke 7:24-28)—or fancy modes of transport (Chariot Force One) to colossal stadiums to deliver his campaign speeches. Early on he walks to the Galilean lakeshore at Capernaum and stands there addressing those who gather to hear him. As the crowd gets larger, he steps into an ordinary fishing vessel that is moored on the shore.[3] He asks the boatowner Simon, who's mending the nets, to push out to sea a little so he has a better platform to see and teach the throng (5:1-3).

Jesus is no stranger to Simon. Recently Jesus visited Simon's home, healed his mother-in-law of a severe fever, and ministered through the night to a host of others who sought his aid (4:38-41). So Simon knows something about Jesus's identity and mission. But he's about to learn a lot more and have his own life turned upside down. After Jesus finishes his public teaching session, he tells Simon, "Push out into the deep water and let down your nets for a catch" (5:4).

Why is Jesus suddenly telling Simon how to do his business? Is Jesus wanting some private rest and recreation after his ministry to the masses? Following his nightlong healing work in Simon's home, Jesus sought respite in "a deserted/desert place"—but to no avail—as the people pressed after him (4:42). That would be harder to do in the depths of the sea! But that's not the point of Jesus's present business with Simon. He has bigger fish to fry.

Simon is skeptical but plays along: "Master [a respectful but not worshipful term], we have worked all night long but have caught nothing. Yet if you say so, I will let down the nets" (5:4). Simon owes Jesus the benefit of the doubt, but he has no great expectations, certainly not for the huge net-breaking haul that ensues (5:6). Still, one would think this is a happy event for Simon and his business partners, the Zebedee brothers James and John, who help manage the big catch (5:7). Jesus proves to be a great "master" to have around: great for business, great for healing, great for Israel. He locks in the fishermen's vote.

Yet Simon's first reaction is far from happy. The narrator adds the nickname "Peter (*Petros*)," meaning "Rock," to Simon's given name.

---

3. A modest working craft (no pleasure yacht). See Rousseau and Arav, *Jesus and His World*, 25-30.

Simon Peter now falls like a rock to his knees on the boat deck and pleads, "Go away from me Lord, for I am a sinful man!" (or "sinner-man" [*anēr hamartōlos*], 5:8). Simon upgrades Jesus's status to "Lord," though it's hard to know what he means by that title at this stage, except that Jesus is too much for Simon to handle, so much above Simon the sinner that he doesn't deserve to share the same space with Jesus.

Again, this doesn't mean Simon has a long rap sheet of crimes he's afraid Jesus will expose or punish. He's not worried that Jesus will throw him overboard. But out in this deep sea he now knows deep down how much he falls short of God's glory revealed in Jesus (to borrow Paul's classic language about *all* people's sinful state in Romans 3:23). If Jesus is the solid rock, Simon is sinking sand. Simon is way out of his depth, and he knows it. And that's just the kind of person Jesus wants to work with. Simon and his two fishing associates James and John will become Jesus's closest confidants, his inner circle of disciples.

But as disciples, they still have so much to *learn*. For now, though, Jesus simply says, "Do not be afraid"—that's reassuring; "from now on you will be catching people"—this part's not so clear (Luke 5:10). This won't be the last time Jesus speaks in cryptic figurative language. Though on the one hand he connects with their fish-catching business, on the other hand, Jesus suggests a complete retooling of their occupation to *catch people*. Not to catch fish for people to eat, but to catch people themselves! The analogy is not just puzzling; it seems grizzly. The only reason to catch fish commercially is to kill them, chop them up, cook them, make sauces out of them, and eat them. Certainly, Jesus is not advocating a slave-catching or cannibalizing mission. His mission is *for* the people, but exactly what that has to do with fishing remains to be seen. Luke's Jesus will become known for *seeking and saving lost sinners* (15:1–32; 19:10); fishing fits the "seeking" part but "saving" not so much.

In any case, Simon, James, and John know they've been summoned to a major career change. Upon returning to shore, they "left everything and followed Jesus" (5:11). The boatloads of fish, the boats, the nets, the whole kit and kaboodle—and whatever homes and families they have (see 18:28–29)—goodbye. They hit the campaign trail with Jesus Messiah, with little clue what lies ahead.

Taxmen

If we wonder whether these fishermen were the "best people" Jesus could enlist, his next recruit raises even more questions. After returning to shore, Jesus goes back on the road, walking around the Galilean countryside and in towns like Capernaum, healing one man's skin disease and another's paralysis (also forgiving his sins), and then "going out" to see a tax collector named Levi at his tax or tollbooth and summoning him, "Follow me" (5:12–27). Jesus does not call the cured psoriatic or paralyzed man to follow him and performs no miracle for the tax collector Levi—no windfall of coins to match the fish haul that got Peter, James, and John's attention. Which makes it more remarkable that Levi also "got up, left everything, and followed [Jesus]" (5:28).

Jesus's campaign now leaves behind a vacant tax booth along with abandoned fishing boats. These idle businesses may have been near each other. Tax booths ringed the shores of the Sea of Galilee to collect various tariffs and tolls on fish caught in the sea and fish products ferried across it.[4] It's intriguing to think that Levi might have collected fees from Peter, James, and John; in any event, they would not have been friends.

In Jesus's land, tax collectors were typically Jews working *for* the imperial Roman/Herodian government, collecting monies from compatriots to support the oppressive regime. They effectively operated as enemy agents. Moreover, as long as they met their quotas, they could overcharge the people and pocket the difference. John the Baptizer challenged tax collectors seeking baptism to "collect no more than the amount prescribed for you" (3:12–13; cf. 7:29). In Luke, tax collectors all but define "sinners" (see 5:30; 7:34; 15:1; cf. 18:9–13; 19:2–7).

One less tax booth in Galilee should be welcome news for both religious teachers and common laborers. But matters get more complicated when Levi throws a banquet for Jesus and invites a bunch of his former coworkers to celebrate his new career and meet his new "boss." But no evangelistic revival breaks out. Perhaps some of these taxmen find Jesus interesting, but we are given no indication that anyone follows Levi's lead and joins Jesus's movement. We may assume that most simply enjoy the dinner party with no intention of giving up their lucrative professions.

The bigger issue from the standpoint of Jesus's religious critics is why Jesus shares table fellowship—a particular mark of close communion in

---

4. See Hanson, "Galilean Fishing Economy"; Hanson and Oakman, *Palestine*, 106–10; Sawicki, *Crossing Galilee*, 27–30, 143–47.

this culture—with these "sinners." He's not recruiting a whole team of tax collectors (Levi is the only one he calls to follow him). He's not cozying up to them for a financial contribution. He's happy to meet, greet, and eat with all sorts of people—a good political strategy *unless* you spend too much time with the wrong kind of people. And this is what gets under Jesus's opponents' skin: most everyone agrees tax collectors are wrong for Galilee, wrong for Judea, wrong for God's people.

Jesus agrees with this moral evaluation but not with the social response of shunning these sinners. He believes that he can change and "cure" fraudulent taxmen of their harmful practices and allegiances. He calls them to repentance but not from a lofty pulpit or judicial bench. He makes house calls or receives "tax collectors and sinners" (5:30; 7:34; 15:1) in a guest house. He sits, eats, and talks with them, inviting them to change and accept God's rule without bringing down the scepter on them. Luke reports no great spiritual renewal movement among tax collectors, but later one chief tax officer named Zacchaeus welcomes Jesus into his home and testifies that he's given half his possessions to the poor and will provide quadruple recompense to anyone he's defrauded. The citizens of Jericho decry him as a "sinner." Jesus has another label: "Today salvation has come to this house, because he too is a son of Abraham" (19:1–10).

Dozing Dozen

Soon Jesus expands his campaign team from four to twelve "disciples . . . whom he also named apostles" (6:13). He chooses these dozen men after praying on a mountain all night "to God" (6:12). God's will remains primary for Jesus.

"Simon, whom he also named Peter" is listed first, signaling his role as the apostles' spokesman, first among equals, chief of staff, if you will. Jesus nicknames him "Peter/Rock" in hopes that he will emerge as Jesus's rock-solid right-hand man, after his rocky start in the boat (5:8). Peter will continue to vacillate, however, as we will see. Fellow fishermen James and John occupy the third and fourth slots in the list. Peter's brother Andrew, mentioned for the first time in Luke, takes the second spot, though he will not prove as significant as the big three of Peter, James, and John.

Surprisingly, Luke does not include Levi the tax collector, at least not by that name. Matthew's Gospel identifies the man Jesus recruits at the tax booth as *Matthew*, not Levi (Matt 9:9) and lists "Matthew *the tax collector*" among the twelve apostles (10:3). Luke places a "Matthew" in the seventh position but without designating his former profession. Still, Luke may conflate Levi and Matthew.

Filling out the twelve is another Simon, another James, and two Judases. Additional descriptors distinguish these figures but also raise new questions. The second Simon is "called the *Zealot*" and the second Judas, listed in the last position, is identified as "Judas Iscariot, who became a *traitor*" (Luke 6:14–15). "Zealot" suggests a violent political rebel, though not necessarily attached to an organized "Zealot" movement. No one knows what "Iscariot" means, but "traitor" is painfully clear, though the details of how Judas betrays Jesus's mission remain to be disclosed in Luke's story. Still, from the start, Jesus chooses his own traitor! Does he know or suspect at this stage what Judas will do?

Much remains uncertain about these twelve apostles' characters. But a ragtag group including fishermen, a tax collector, a revolutionary, a traitor, and God knows who else does not inspire confidence. Not close, it seems, to the "best people" Jesus might have enlisted; and risky to send out on a training mission armed with "power and authority over all demons . . . and all diseases," commissioned "to proclaim the kingdom of God and to heal" (9:1–2). What could possibly go wrong! Nothing on this occasion: their first mission is a glowing success (9:6). But this may just be beginner's luck; all twelve apostles (not just traitor Judas) will stumble and fall as they grow into their Christ-authorized vocations (see 9:37–55; 22:31–32).

Even on the last night of Jesus's earthly life—as he prays in agony that he might avoid execution and urges his disciples to pray for strength to survive the approaching "time of trial"—they choose to *sleep* rather than pray. They sleep "because of grief," which is understandable, but not the response of courage, commitment, and alertness the moment calls for (22:39–45). After Jesus comes through his prayer vigil to accept his own fate, he's not encouraged by his soporific supporters: "Why are you sleeping?" He repeats, "Get up and pray that you may not come into the time of trial" (22:46). Yet "while he was still speaking," Judas comes "leading" a large police force that arrests Jesus (22:47). So much for the twelve's leadership at this critical hour.

Frankly, appealing to Jesus as a managerial whiz or CEO amounts to special pleading. He doesn't fit the bill and doesn't want to. But some American Christians wedded to American capitalism cannot resist voting in Jesus as chairman of the board anyway, even though he never shows up for meetings and has other "business" to tend to. The famous statement from the twelve-year-old Jesus in the KJV of Luke 2:49—"Wist ye not [Did you not know] that I must be about my Father's business"—has nothing to do with corporate business,[5] managing staff, or making money and everything to do with God's work and making people whole.

But that didn't stop Bruce Barton from latching on to this felicitous "business" language, and lauding Jesus as the very model of a modern mercantile mogul. A preacher's son, advertising executive, US congressman, and staunch opponent of FDR and the New Deal, Barton penned a best-selling book, *The Man Nobody Knows: A Discovery of the Real Jesus* (1924), who just happened to be like Barton, though he would say he was just like Jesus. Here's the Jesus Barton "knows": "He picked up twelve men from the bottom ranks of business and forged them into an organization that conquered the world. . . . This is a man nobody knows. . . . someone [needs to] write a book about [this] Jesus. Every businessman will read it and send it to his partners and his salesmen. For it will tell the story of the founder of modern business."[6] And so Barton wrote the book, and the American public lapped it up.

And "Jesus wept" (John 11:35). (If Barton can take Jesus out of context, so can I.)

SUPPORTING STAFF

After appointing the twelve apostles on the mountain, Jesus "came down with them and stood on a level place, with a great crowd of his disciples and a great multitude of people" clamoring "to hear him and to be healed of their diseases" (Luke 6:17–18). While the twelve may be destined to become leaders, at present they remain part of a wider company of Jesus's disciples. Though Luke briefly reports Jesus's continuing work of healing (6:19), the principal focus falls on his extended *teaching* on this "level place" delivered to a large audience (6:20–7:1). We might say that Jesus promotes "public education" for all grade "levels."

---

5. There's no Greek word for "business" in Luke 2:49. A better translation would be, "I must be about the things [*en tois*] of my Father."

6. Barton, *Man*, 19–20. I first encountered Barton's work in Wiggins, *Evidence of Things*, 214; see also Du Mez, *Jesus*, 20; Keddie, *Republican Jesus*, 192–94; Sharlet, *Family*, 133–37, 141–42.

Recruiting Staff

At this stage, Jesus himself is the sole teacher. The twelve are not ready yet to graduate from learner to instructor. They need to go through basic leadership training. And as it happens, they're not the only recruits.

Working Women

When the twelve are next referenced in Luke's narrative, they are not the only close confidants of Jesus. As Jesus resumes his campaign travels "through cities and villages, proclaiming the good news of the kingdom of God, the twelve were with him, *as well as some women*" (8:1–2). Well, then. The Jesus team is not an exclusive men's club or male-dominated enterprise. Good to know, though too good to be true perhaps?

I mean, these "chosen" men can't be expected to cook and clean up for themselves on the road (ahem). They have important kingdom business to tend to. They need women helpers, right? Luke's opening two chapters feature two strong, vocal, Spirit-inspired women: Elizabeth and Mary, the mothers of John and Jesus, respectively. But between then and chapter 8, the only female characters Luke mentions are Herodias, Herod Antipas's unlawfully wedded wife (John the Baptizer is imprisoned and beheaded for criticizing the marriage [3:18–20; cf. 9:7–9]), and two unnamed women described in relation to male relatives: Simon's febrile mother-in-law (4:38–39) and a widow mourning her son's death (7:11–17). Jesus heals the first woman and raises the second one's deceased son. The only thing said about either woman after Jesus's interventions is that Simon's mother-in-law "got up and began to serve [*diēkonei*] them" (4:39). Fever's gone, all's well, now back to work!

Not surprisingly, then, the women attending Jesus were also beneficiaries of Jesus's healing ministry and "ministered to" or "served (*diēkonoun*) him and his male deputies" (8:2–3). But that's not the whole story. Three women are named and two ascribed relatively high social status: "Mary, called Magdalene . . . Joanna, the wife of Herod's steward Chuza, and Susanna." "Magdalene" designates a citizen of Magdala, a port on the western Sea of Galilee known as a fish-processing center (Migdal="Fish Tower"). Mary's identification by this demonym hints she was well-known in Magdala, perhaps as a businesswoman dealing in fish products. She may have run in the same social circle as Joanna, "the wife of Chuza, the manager of Herod [Antipas]'s household" (NIV) in the Herodian-Roman capital of Tiberias, about five miles south of Magdala.

Joanna was something of a court lady, accustomed to business in Herod's palace.[7] Apart from having John beheaded, this Herod (Antipas) also seeks to kill Jesus (13:31–33; cf. 23:6–12).

Even though Mary Magdalene and Joanna had benefited from Jesus's healing ministry, it's odd that they would leave their secure stations to tag along with Jesus and his band of not-so-classy men. Gratitude did not require uprooting their lives for Jesus's sake, and we have no record that Jesus called them to do so. Apart from the social demotion of joining the itinerant Jesus campaign, there was the potential for sexual scandal, if only imagined. But that's exactly what people do. They love a juicy political scandal. "High-class women—one of them the wife of a Herodian official—hit the road with Jesus and his gang of twelve crusty guys." The fabricated headlines write themselves. Add in "Susanna, and many others [*autais*, feminine pronoun]" (8:3) and orgiastic imaginations run wild.

Although Luke's brief report in 8:1–3 is sparse on details, it's noteworthy that the twelve and these women are placed on a par, linked by the simple word "and" (*kai*), as being "with him" (*autois*), that is, with Jesus. Of course, there are various ways to be "with" someone, on their side, supporting their work and campaign. Traveling with the candidate is one way. But in fact, from this point these women *are not mentioned again* until the end of Luke 23, where they witness Jesus's crucifixion "at a distance" (23:49) and visit his tomb three days later (23:56–24:10). Luke 8–23 is quite a gap of silence about Mary Magdalene and company. Belatedly, Luke covers his omission by describing the women at Jesus's cross and tomb as those "who had followed him from Galilee" (23:49, 55). So now we're supposed to assume the women had been traveling with Jesus all along? As silent, hidden partners? It feels a bit like scrambling to assure modern readers of the Declaration of Independence that, of course, "all men are created equal" includes all women, give or take a little time (150 years!) for women to get the vote.

In any case, doesn't the women's reported service to the Jesus movement imply their attending presence? Maybe but not necessarily. "Diaconal" (*diakon-*) language in Luke often applies to table service—preparing and serving food, busing tables and washing dishes—common work for women and household servants (male and female). As we've seen, Jesus turns this gender and class convention on its head by providing food himself for a hungry crowd and enlisting the twelve apostles as

---

7. See Sawicki, *Crossing Galilee*, 135–53, 179–84, 191–98; Sawicki, "Magdalenes"; Spencer, *Salty Wives*, 101–44.

servers and busboys (9:10–17). The standard of greatness in Jesus's book is humble service, identifying with and ministering to "the least" (9:46–48). The twelve struggle to embrace this role, up to the Last Supper they share with Jesus which he hosts and administers as "one who serves" (*ho diakonos*, 22:27). The Servant-Messiah is Jesus's ultimate vocation that he desires his followers—men and women—to carry on after his death.

Therefore, if Mary Magdalene and the other women provide food service for the Jesus campaign, they do so not because they are women but because they are *disciples* of Jesus following *his* example. Jesus dignifies and democratizes so-called "women's work."

But "diaconal" service can also involve *financial administration*, operating at a banker's desk or money table.[8] That seems to be the main service these women offer Jesus and associates: "minister[ing] [*diēkonoun*] to them out of their resources" (8:3), literally "the things belonging to them" (*hyparchontōn*): their monies, possessions, assets as wealthy businesswomen (like Mary Magdalene) or court ladies (like Joanna).[9] We will focus on fundraising for Jesus's campaign in strategy 5. For now, we simply acknowledge the important *contributions*, not least financial donations, women make to Jesus's mission. Again, we might wish Luke had given these women the press coverage they deserve rather than merely hinting at their significant work. But over two millennia later, we still struggle to give women their due, which is nothing less than equal opportunity and recognition. A quarter century into the twenty-first century and still no Madame President. How long, O Lord?

Dynamic Duos

Successful campaigns pay attention to numbers. Why does Jesus choose *twelve* apostles rather than ten or twenty? Almost certainly he evokes the twelve tribes of ancient Israel named after the twelve sons of Jacob, the founding fathers of Israel (see 22:28–30). By recruiting twelve deputies, Jesus signals his aim to restore Israel as God's faithful, flourishing people—focused on spiritual renewal rather than territorial reclamation (Jesus has no interest in reconstituting tribal boundaries). Even the

---

8. See Luke 19:23; Acts 6:1–2; Spencer, *Luke*, 204–5n204.

9. Cf. in Acts, Luke's second volume, businesswomen like Lydia (16:14–15) and Priscilla (18:2–3) and "women of high standing" (13:50; 17:12).

names of Jacob's second, third, and fourth sons (Simeon, Levi, and Judah) resonate with Jesus's apostles (two Simons, Levi/Matthew, two Judases).

The numbers game also highlights Jesus's *forty* days of testing in the desert as an echo of Moses's forty days on Mount Sinai during Israel's forty years of journeying to the promised land (see strategy 2). Recall, too, Jesus's inner circle of *three* apostles: Peter, James, and John. Three is a good "trinitarian" number and a frequent plot device in Luke's narrative.

In this numbers pool, we should not overlook the simpler number *two*. For Luke it often takes two—one man and one woman—to describe Jesus's story and mission. Starting with the juxtaposition of responses by John the Baptizer's aged father Zechariah and Jesus's young mother Mary to their sons' respective conceptions and births (1:5–80), Luke's two-volume narrative (Luke-Acts) features numerous pairings of male and female characters to various effects, at times, as with Jesus's mother, to the female figure's advantage.[10] The pairing of the twelve male apostles with Mary Magdalene and a group of female disciples fits this pattern. Moreover, soon after dispatching the twelve on their first training mission (9:1-6), Luke's Jesus deploys "*seventy-two* others . . . *in pairs* to every town and place where he himself intended to go" (10:1).[11] Thirty-six teams of two function as Jesus's advance reps. That's an impressive campaign organization for a small region like Galilee. Overall, the mission proves successful, as "the seventy-two returned with joy, saying, 'Lord, in your name even the demons submit to us!'" (10:17). However, Jesus is not as thrilled with their report, particularly their puffed-up attitude about being demon-slayers. It is God's power (not theirs) under the auspices of Jesus's name (not theirs) that releases those oppressed by evil forces. The seventy-two are simply God's servants in Christ, as he serves God (10:17–20). Still, Jesus's seventy-two emissaries do good work.

These seventy-two "others" further prove that Jesus's twelve apostles do not comprise a restricted ministerial cadre. The term for "others" (*heterous*), though masculine in form, may be taken generically, possibly including male-female teams of singles or married couples and even "sister" duos.[12] Again, it would be nice if Luke had been more explicit

---

10. See Spencer, *Gospel of Luke*, 41–44.

11. Some ancient manuscripts have "seventy" messengers; see Omanson, *Textual Guide*, 127–28.

12. D'Angelo ("Reconstructing 'Real' Women) suggests that Gospel traditions about Martha and Mary (Luke 10:38–42; John 11:1–12:8) reflect "the memory of two famous women who formed a missionary partnership" (108); cf. Rom 16:7, 12.

about women's participation in Jesus's campaign, but the climactic report that Mary Magdalene, Joanna, and other women were the *first witnesses* of Jesus's resurrection to the male apostles (who initially dismissed their testimony as an "idle tale") certifies the women's missionary credentials (24:1–11).

Apart from the possible gender mix of the seventy-two paired delegates, why does Jesus send out this particular number? Why seventy-two instead of sixty, a hundred, or another round number? Biblical connections again provide key clues, specifically two Torah texts: first, the world Table of Nations listed in the Greek version of Genesis 10 totals seventy-two; second, the group of elders Moses enlists in Numbers 11 to help him "bear the burden of the people" during the arduous wilderness trek starts with seventy but soon adds two more, Eldad and Medad (11:16–30).

Jesus's seventy-two missionaries suggests a wide, universal scope to his salvation campaign. Although he and this group stay mostly in Galilee, seeds are sown for outreach to "all nations" extending to the "ends of the earth" (Luke 24:47; Acts 1:8). Not that Jesus and his followers turn their backs on fellow Jews, even when many prove unreceptive, but that the Jesus group seeks to fulfill Israel's calling to be a "light to the nations" (Isa 42:6; 49:6; cf. Gen 12:1–3; Luke 2:32; Acts 13:47; 26:23). In numerical terms, Jesus's messianic mission targets the twelve "tribes" of Israel plus the seventy-two "nations" of the world, with matching numbers of leaders for each part of the plan.

The organizational precedent in the book of Numbers for seventy-two associates is illuminating. God first charges Moses to select *seventy* respected elders to help him lead and care for God's people—which reportedly number some six hundred thousand. And they're all hungry and unhappy about the bland bread God provides day after day for their nourishment. They even have the temerity to complain they had it better in Egypt because of all the free "fish we used to eat" there, along with "the cucumbers, the melons, the leeks, the onions, and the garlic." Never mind that Egypt provided this food to keep them working as slaves! The people wear out Moses out with their whining, and God hopes the seventy elders can help manage the crisis (Num 11:1–9, 21). But the Israelites keep complaining, and God eventually resorts to sterner measures to get them in line. Still, the principle of multiple, shared leadership over one-man, autocratic rule holds.

It gets more interesting during the installation ceremony for the seventy at the sacred "tent," when God places some of Moses's "spirit . . . on the seventy elders," enabling them to prophesy (11:24–25). Simultaneously, however, the same spirit blows into the wider camp and empowers two other individuals, Eldad and Medad, to proclaim God's word. Adding this pair now makes seventy-*two* elders—though this was not the original plan. What to do with these two mavericks? One of the seventy, Joshua, who becomes Moses's successor, strenuously objects to these independent upstarts: "My lord Moses, stop them!" Moses does no such thing: "Are you jealous for my sake? Would that all the Lord's people were prophets and that the Lord would put his spirit on them!" (11:26–30).

Seventy-two assistants, whether to Moses or Jesus, are not a fixed unit but a representative body of God's agents, serving *with* other anointed leaders. Again, we see that the dynamic work of God's realm is not a solo affair. The same spirit-wind that swept over the chaotic waters at creation (Gen 1:2) and gave breath to the first human beings (2:7) is destined to empower "all flesh"—young and old, female and male, lower and upper class—to bear witness to God's grace. The Spirit is an equal opportunity employer in God's realm (see Joel 2:28–29; Acts 2:16–18).

The charter twelve apostles in Luke, however, have trouble grasping this expansive vision. They quickly come to enjoy their "chosen" status, which naturally leads to jealousy about others' roles. Though they do not explicitly object to the seventy-two new recruits, between the two missions in Luke 9 and 10, the apostle John does his best Joshua impression, objecting to a maverick minister in Jesus's name, "Master, we saw someone casting out demons in your name, and we tried to stop him, because he does not follow with us" (9:49). He doesn't know our secret password. To make matters worse, John blurts out his complaint right after Jesus teaches the disciples, with a little child by his side, that "the least among all of you is the greatest" (9:46–49). Remember, gentlemen, it's not about making a name for yourself (cf. 10:17–20). This is God's work in God's name. "Do not stop" this one who is helping free the possessed and oppressed in my name, Jesus snaps back at John, "for whoever is not against you is for you" (9:50).

Speaking of not attacking others to protect your own turf, the next episode features Jesus's attempt to stay in a Samaritan village en route to Jerusalem in Judea. At this time, Jews and Samaritans were religious cousins who couldn't stand each other for various reasons, including disputes over ethnic purity (Samaritans were commonly slurred as "half-breed" descendants of Jews and Assyrians), sacred territory (Samaritans venerated Shechem/Mt. Gerizim over Jerusalem/Mt. Zion), and scriptural authority (Samaritans had their own version of the Pentateuch/Torah).[13] There's no feud like an intra-family religious feud. Jesus does not want to stir up trouble, so he sends some messengers ahead to make lodging arrangements. But the town wants nothing to do with this Jew and his travel party. Jesus plans simply to move on to a more hospitable place.

But John and his brother James have another idea. They want to go all Elijah on this rude village and "command fire to come down from heaven and consume them!" (9:51–54). Full of themselves much after their inaugural mission? At least they ask Jesus's permission to torch the place—which he by no means grants. In understated fashion, the best reading simply says that Jesus "turned and rebuked them. Then they went on to another village" (9:55–56). But I like the alternative reading in some manuscripts that fleshes out the spirit of Jesus's mission: "You do not know what spirit you are of, for the Son of Man [Jesus] has not come to destroy the lives of humans, but to save them." Pretty basic stuff, but still easily ignored by two of Jesus's closest apostles. Let all Jesus people beware.

---

13. See John 4:1–42; R. Anderson, *Samaritan Pentateuch*; Novakovic, "Jews and Samaritans"; Pummer, *Samaritans*.

Raising Funds

> **Strategy 5**
> Forget fundraising for personal advancement and interests. Live lean. Travel light. Challenge people, including wealthy people, to sell everything they have to give to the destitute, not to your campaign. Serve God, not Money.

MONEY TALKS. MONEY INFLUENCES. Money rules in American politics. Each election cycle sets new records for campaign financial contributions. Declared and prospective candidates must raise funds or fail. You don't necessarily have to raise the most money to win, but you have to raise a lot. You have to hit up your supporters for all they're worth through whatever legal (or not) means you can. Thank God (or not) for social media blitzes in recent years, however annoying they become even to staunch "friends."

Political Action Committees (PACs) perpetually pad their political war chests. Since January 21, 2010—when the Supreme Court decided 5–4 in favor of the plaintiff in *Citizens United v. Federal Election Commission*—corporations, unions, and other business entities may lawfully give unlimited funds to their chosen candidates, and nonprofit organizations may contribute to super PACs without disclosing their identities. So-called "dark money" now floods the campaign market.[1] Under the constitutional banner of "free speech," elections, which were never cheap, became much *less free*. The prospect of buying political influence, always a danger, became an epidemic with no vaccine in sight.

---

1. See Richardson, *Democracy*, 75–76.

On the candidate level, millionaires and billionaires who think they should run the country throw in huge chunks of their own money. It's unimaginable that a poor person, below the national poverty line, could be elected president in the US. We love a rags-to-riches story, but you better have long since ditched the rags. We, including many among the chronic poor, want successful leaders, which in American terms, means moneyed men who've made it financially, who excel in the "art of the deal," if only for themselves, the notion being that some of that wheeling-dealing bonanza will trickle down to us bottom feeders. A leaky notion at best, a cruel joke at worst.

By any Gospel account(ing), Jesus would have *zero* chance of winning an American presidential election, a number effectively matching his personal resources. Luke's Jesus has no financial portfolio, no property, no appreciable possessions, and no remunerative job after answering God's call. He calls disciples to leave everything behind to follow his way of life, not to sign over their worldly goods. He loses wealthy would-be followers because he demands they sell everything they have and give the proceeds directly to the poor (Luke 18:18–25)—not *to* or *through* Jesus—though he qualifies as a poor man. The only "deal" Jesus brokers is God's *covenant* with Israel and all people (22:20), a covenant of love and mercy based on God's forgiveness of sins and other "debts," including financial ones that unjustly crush the poor (see strategy 3).

As indicated in strategy 4, if you're looking for a successful CEO to manage the country's economy for maximum growth, especially for rich investors, Jesus is not your man. He doesn't pretend to be, doesn't want to be, which pretty much closes the books on fundraising. But I may be missing something, *discounting* something. Modern Christian candidates across the political spectrum do not feel they're being unfaithful to Jesus by raising funds to get elected and promote their good causes. And Luke's Gospel project may have been sponsored by a wealthy patron named Theophilus (1:3; Acts 1:1). It takes money to get the good word out, to publish books, including Bibles. It's worth probing more fully what Luke has to say about financing Jesus's campaign.

TRAVEL LIGHT

In the previous chapter, we noted that women of means like Mary Magdalene and Joanna supported Jesus and his followers with financial contributions (Luke 8:1–3). We don't know how much they gave, however, and are not told that they left everything behind to benefit the poor and follow Jesus. Though upper-class women enjoyed more freedom of movement than their poorer sisters, Joanna, as a married woman, would still need to consider the wishes of her husband (Luke identifies her as "the wife of Herod's steward, Chuza," 8:3). Even so, Joanna likely had control of some funds to manage as she desired, including helping the Jesus movement.[2]

What does Jesus do with these campaign contributions? The Fourth Gospel mentions a "common purse" mismanaged by Judas Iscariot, the thief and traitor of the group (John 12:6; 13:29). But Luke says nothing about this and provides no record of revenues and expenses. At any rate, Jesus and his emissaries have no travel budget (a big chunk of modern campaigns).

No Shoes, No Shirt, No Problem

Forgive the reference to Kenny Chesney's song (2002) if that's not your cup of tea. But this song title is apt for Jesus's campaign, even if the song's content is miles and eons removed. Chesney imagines himself barefoot and bare-chested on a Mexican beach dowsing his blues with a bottomless booze bottle. He's living footloose and fancy free, though presumably he pays for his drinks (unless Jimmy Buffett foots the bill).

Though Jesus spends time by the sea, he's no beachcomber. He combs for disciples and teaches the crowds. He enjoys a good party hosted by the tax collector Levi, but Levi then leaves his lucrative business behind to follow Jesus. When Jesus deploys the Twelve on their first mission, he sends them to mediate God's saving realm "with power and authority over all demons and to cure diseases" (9:1–2)—but with no material resources: "Take nothing for your journey: no staff, nor bag, nor bread, nor money—not even an extra tunic [undershirt]" (9:3). Similarly, he dispatches the seventy-two with these stark instructions: "Carry no purse, no bag, no sandals, and greet no one on the road [no roadside soliciting]" (10:4). For good measure, he also says, "I am sending you out like lambs into the midst of wolves" (10:3). How reassuring.

How are they supposed to survive to do the good work of deliverance and healing they've been assigned? In a word: *hospitality* (9:4;

---

2. See Spencer, *Salty Wives*, 101–44.

10:5–9). They must depend on the grateful kindness of those who welcome the missionaries' ministry. Jesus's deputies, like Jesus himself, do not charge a fee for their work and accept no monetary payment. Nonetheless, Jesus insists that the ministerial "laborer deserves to be paid" like other workers (10:7), except that Jesus's witnesses should be paid in food and lodging in a receptive home. Admittedly, the situation is still ripe for exploitation. The ancient world, no less than our own, had its share of unscrupulous traveling salesmen, including itinerant peddlers of various "gospels" and miracle "cures."[3] But Jesus imposes two key checks on his campaigners.

First, they must not rove from door to door, seeking to find the best bed and board or stockpiling the most goodies. If they find a welcoming place, they should "remain in the same house, eating and drinking whatever they provide" (10:7). This place, however humble, would then become a welcome center for the missionaries to receive interested inquirers. No hard sell, beat-the-bushes approach. Second, in the same low-pressure vein, if nobody in town seems receptive, don't keep hammering; don't browbeat anyone into God's kingdom. Lead with a message of "Peace" (10:5–6), and if that doesn't resonate, leave that town and go to another.

Yet all is not sweetness and light on the Jesus trail. On the way out of a resistant town, Jesus instructs his ambassadors to mount a protest: shake the street dust off their feet and announce one final time—"Yet know this: the kingdom of God has come near"—a not-so-peaceful kingdom now for those who reject it, as Jesus shockingly warns, "I tell you, on that day it will be more tolerable for Sodom than for that town" (10:10–12, cf. 9:5). Sodom and its wicked sister city Gomorrah were notoriously destroyed by fire and brimstone (Gen 19:12–29). What happened to Jesus's anti-fire policy concerning the inhospitable Samaritan village (Luke 9:51–56)? Just when we think we have Jesus all figured out, he reminds us to think again. There is a volatile side to this world-shaking messianic campaign.

But to return to our more immediate concern of fundraising, *why* is Jesus so adamant about neither soliciting nor accepting money for his campaign? Doubtless because of the human propensity to greed, which can engulf Christ-professing politicians and ministers as easily as anybody. Luke's Jesus flatly alerts his followers, "Be on guard against all kinds of greed" (12:15). Beware even the appearance of greed, it seems, for Jesus

---

3. See Acts 8:9–24; 13:4–12; 19:11–20; Philostratus, *Vit. Apoll.* 6.39; 8.7; Kee, *Miracle*, 252–79; Spencer, *Portrait of Philip*, 98–103.

and his messengers. Serve God and those in need, not Money (Mammon) and your own interests (16:13). The very integrity of the gospel rides on it. Billy Graham (and his organization) and some other modern evangelists have taken decisive steps to safeguard financial integrity; others, not so much as they fly around in their private jets, sail around in their posh yachts, and live in their palatial mansions—all to promote the gospel more widely and efficiently.[4] Uh-huh. Sure. Whatever you have to tell yourself, man.

Meanwhile, Jimmy Carter, God bless him—former president, peanut farmer, regular Sunday school teacher in his small hometown church, leader of the philanthropic Carter foundation, builder of Habitat for Humanity homes—lived most of his life in a modest 1960s ranch house in Plains, Georgia. He is a professed born-again Christian, lifelong Baptist, and once darling of American evangelicals. But no more, not for decades now, for various reasons political and theological, but maybe, too, because he just doesn't seem cool or charismatic enough.[5] Though brilliant and accomplished, he was also a genuinely *Plains* man who strived his whole life to live out the gospel of Jesus Christ, not least in Luke's Sermon on the *Plain*, as it's commonly called (see strategy 5), which opens with, "Blessed are you who are poor, for yours is the kingdom of God" (6:20) and then counterposes, "But woe to you who are rich, for you have received your consolation" (6:24).

No Place to Lay His Head

Speaking of politicians' houses, this became an issue in the 2008 presidential race between Barack Obama and John McCain, with the prize being who could paint the other as least in touch with average Americans' interests and thus least worthy of occupying the White House. The Obama campaign blasted McCain for owning multiple properties across the country. When asked by the press how many houses he owned, McCain pleaded ignorance and told the journalists to check with his staff.

---

4. See Beaty, *Celebrities for Jesus*, 23–41 (an excellent chapter on Billy Graham), 56, 78–89. This is not to make Graham into a monk or anti-capitalist radical. Far from it. Graham maintained close ties with the conservative American big business sector, as evidenced in his address to the American Association of Bankers (Honolulu, HI, 1974): "The Bible teaches you cannot serve the true God and another god called materialism, but you can serve God with materialism, if your heart is right toward God" (cited in Keddie, *Republican Jesus*, 98; cf. 97–103).

5. See Balmer, *Bad Faith*, 20–27; Balmer, *Redeemer*; Hendricks Jr., *Politics*, 193–94.

Not a smart response. Most of us don't have a staff and certainly don't need one to tally the single residence we own (or mortgage, more accurately) or rent (with a roommate or two to help pay the bills).

It didn't help that McCain had previously gigged the 2004 presidential candidate, John Kerry, for owning five homes with his wealthy wife, Teresa Heinz Kerry. Turns out that McCain and his wife had *seven* properties on the books, which Obama's team pounced on with an attack ad featuring a picture of the White House with the caption, "Here's ONE house Americans can't afford John McCain to move into." In turn, a McCain spokesperson snapped back, "Does a guy [Obama] who made more than $4 million last year, just got back from vacation on a private beach in Hawaii and bought his own million-dollar mansion with the help of a convicted felon really want to get into a debate about houses?"[6] Ah, the soaring, enlightening rhetoric of American campaigns.

The real estate mogul who became the forty-fifth president took the whole housing business to new heights with his raft of luxury hotels and other high-rent properties. He is the master Monopoly player and proud of it. No attempt to hide it; if anything, he exaggerates since many of "his" buildings simply lease his brand name.[7]

So what does Jesus say about his residence(s) and real estate holdings? Not much. Well, *nothing* actually: "The Son of Man" (Son of Humankind or Human One), his favorite self-designation, "has *no place to lay his head*." Even wild animals have it better, as Jesus informs a would-be follower: "Foxes have holes, and birds of the air have nests" (9:58). But not Jesus, the homeless Messiah. Try campaigning on that in modern America. The only places in Luke's story where Jesus in fact lays his head to rest are (1) a *manger* (animal trough) in Bethlehem, where Mary and Joseph were forced to go to register for the Roman census (2:1–7); (2) a *boat* on the Sea of Galilee during a raging storm (8:22–25); and (3) a "rock-hewn *tomb*" (more precisely, a rock ledge or slab inside the tomb) provided by a benevolent Jewish councilman (23:50–53). Neither Jesus nor anyone in his family owns any of these.

Again, Jesus and his campaign staff must depend on others' charitable hospitality—which they return as opportunity allows, as in a desert region where Jesus hosts his bread-and-fish dinner for five thousand people, starting with the meager available fare of five loaves and two fish

---

6. Martin and Allen, "McCain."
7. See N. Klein, *No Is Not Enough*, 13–60.

(9:12–17). Before nightfall Jesus dismisses the crowds to their homes—with full stomachs. Jesus's group either heads back to unknown lodgings in nearby Bethsaida (9:10) or camps out in the desert.

Jesus's team runs the risk of appearing to be drifters and moochers. One time his disciples help themselves to some crops in a grain field they happen to be passing through. Some religious teachers criticize their *timing*—doing harvesting-type work on the Sabbath—but not the action itself. Jewish gleaning laws stipulated that farmers should leave the edges of their fields unharvested so poor travelers could have something to eat (Lev 19:9–10; 23:22; Deut 24:19–22; cf. Ruth 2). Jesus defends his followers' Sabbath gleaning on this occasion, though he does not avail himself of the "walk thru" dining option and otherwise remains a faithful Sabbath observer (Luke 6:1–5).

Overall, the Jesus movement promotes *mutual sharing* or *general reciprocity*, in which everyone helps each other out, according to their ability and resources. The poor participate on both ends: giving as well as receiving. In fact, poor people often prove to be proportionately more generous than calculating, wealthier people.

TRUST GOD

Trusting God has long been integral to the rhetoric and media of the American economy, especially during times of crisis. In the throes of the Civil War, President Abraham Lincoln and his treasury secretary, Salmon P. Chase, led the Congress in 1864 to mandate embossing "In God We Trust" on all US coins. Despite President Theodore Roosevelt and others' discomfort in the first half of the twentieth century over melding God and Mammon/Money (cf. Luke 16:13), in the heat of the Cold War, Congress in 1955 extended the motto's imprimatur to all US paper currency.[8] To the present day, every cash transaction signals faith in God, gratitude for God's blessing, but also more problematically, God's presumed *approval* of how we earn and spend the money.

That's an audacious leap, if not a blasphemous one. Of course, it's just a symbol. We deal less and less with cash these days, and when we do, we scarcely care about the imprint on the money other than the number

---

8. See Begley, "'In God We Trust'"; Gibbs, Aikman, and Ostling, "America's Holy War," 64.

value. But symbols, images, icons *matter*: they are never "just" symbols; they profoundly shape our individual and collective consciences.

Though technology has advanced astronomically, social media is not a new thing. Roman coinage in Jesus's day featured images of Caesar's face and inscriptions touting Caesar as Son of God and Savior. All hail, Caesar, and here's your money back in taxes due you! Jesus later uses one of these coins—which he borrows from someone in the audience—to make a point about God, Caesar, and money (20:20–26). We'll have more to say about this in strategy 10.

Our current concern underscores Jesus's sincere trust in God to provide his and his followers' basic needs. As certified when Satan tried to induce him to dive off the temple wing, Jesus does not presume on God's care with a devil-may-care attitude. Yet he rests secure in God's watch care, which allows him to rest in a boat during a roaring tempest, as mentioned above.

Further, Jesus never resorts to trite "Don't worry, trust God, God will provide" platitudes for those in need. Yes, God provides, except when God doesn't, and people—including children and other innocents—die from starvation and destitution. *Not* that God chooses to neglect and kill them. Here God's sovereignty, interpreted in autocratic terms, crashes hard against God's sympathy, infused with love and mercy. It's outside the scope of this narrative-rooted political strategy manual to get too deep into the weeds of theological debate but suffice it to say that reconciling an all-powerful and all-loving God (or Messiah) in the face of persisting evil is a tough sell.[9] Trusting God and Christ is no transactional panacea. It is relational through and through, struggling together with God and Christ *through* the life's unpredictable journey in faith, hope, and love.[10] This trust relationship is dynamic and holistic, not static and individualistic. It pulses through a generative internet of cognitive, affective, and behavioral triggers and responses among God, humans, and the environment.

The affective flip side to trust/faith is fear/anxiety, which politicians commonly trade on in spades. Play to people's deepest fears, gin them up, and then persuade the people to trust you to come to their rescue. It's a well-known formula for exploitative strongmen. But in the hands of a true healer and caregiver, it can also be a genuine call to relief from

---

9. See the thoughtful works of Oord, *Death of Omnipotence*; Oord, *God Can't*; Oord, *Uncontrolling Love*.

10. See the major studies of early Christian faith/trust in Morgan, *Roman Faith*; Morgan, *New Testament*.

corrosive fear and worry, as Jesus offers in a major therapeutic session in Luke 12:1–34.[11] Here he flatly says to his disciples, "Do not worry about your life" (12:21). "Do not be afraid, little flock, for it is your Father's good pleasure to give you the kingdom" (12:32). That sounds like a sweet deal. That sounds like what a wealthy politician (or preacher) might say pushing a prosperity policy (or theology). "Don't worry, be happy, healthy, and wealthy. It's your birthright, your divinely ordained right!" It may sound like that because we want to hear that. A closer reading, however, strikes a rather different note.

Ravens and Lilies

Jesus's fuller statement runs, "Do not worry about your life, what you will eat, or about your body, what you will wear" (12:22). Fine, but food and clothes are basic to life. And beyond that, we prefer to eat well and look good! A large slice of the human economy deals in food and clothes. Think of the advertisements that bombard us daily. You are what you eat and drink, so enjoy that seven-layer cake and top-shelf champagne (you're worth it) while also maintaining a healthy diet (whatever the current fad). Dress for success; the clothes make the man/woman. You never get a second chance to make a positive first impression.

While Jesus enjoys a good party now and again, he's no socialite. Remember his policy to eat whatever is set before you and wear the same undergarment every day. Jesus is no foodie or fashionista. His philosophy of life is distinctly anti-consumerist, anti-commercial—which comes close to saying anti-American—though Jesus, we emphasize again, does not trumpet an anti-message against any people or culture. He is unabashedly "pro-life" in the fullest sense, though not in the way most Americans prefer when he makes pronouncements like "One's life does not consist in the abundance of possessions" (12:15) or "Life is more than food and the body more than clothing" (12:23). Try putting these statements on campaign banners and bumper stickers today and see how many yes votes they get. While we may give lip service to higher values, we love our bread and circuses (think gooey donuts and gory gridiron games). We like dressing up for fancy occasions, even if the ties squeeze and the shoes pinch.

---

11. See Spencer, "To Fear"; Spencer, *Luke*, 316–36.

Again, Jesus is not running a party-pooping, tight-laced, anti-everything campaign, and he certainly wants everyone to have enough to eat and wear to satisfy basic needs. But he also desires that we, whatever our economic levels, not obsess about acquiring stuff, not let consumerism consume us. Of course, that's easier to tell rich folks than poor ones who may not know where this day's food (their "daily bread," 11:3) is coming from. But Jesus also advises the poor not to be hyper-anxious about their provisions, any more than are the birds of the air or flowers of the field.

Great, Jesus turns naturalist, even something of a romantic naturalist: "Consider the ravens: they neither sow nor reap, they have neither storehouse nor barn, and yet God feeds them" (12:24). "Consider the lilies, how they grow: they neither toil nor spin, yet I tell you, even [King] Solomon in all his glory was not clothed like one of these.... God clothes the grass of the field" (12:27). Has he not heard of "nature, red in tooth and claw" (Tennyson) and "survival of the fittest" (Darwinism)? Choosing a raven as the prime avian example is puzzling since ravens are raptors that feed on other animals' carcasses! Lilies are the beauty contest winners of the floral world who don't work a lick (except for all that photosynthesis stuff), but they remain vulnerable to scorching sunrays and tromping hobnailed boots and highway crews (Rome loved its armies and roads).

More often than not, Jesus's designs his illustrations to stir the imagination, to provoke thought, to poke and prod—not to reduce complex ideas to a smooth polish. He speaks not as a biologist, economist, politician, or even professional theologian. No magnum opus from Jesus's pen; not even a pamphlet or any other writing (unless you count Jesus's doodling in the dirt in John 8:6). Others write their Gospel accounts. Jesus hawks no autobiography, ghostwritten or otherwise, like most major American politicians do, even arranging for their campaigns to buy up myriad copies to boost sales numbers.[12]

Jesus's theology—his view of God (*theos*) worthy of trust/faith—is again relational and creational more than propositional and doctrinal. Jesus invites us to live trustfully and hopefully as people of the creating God who deeply and widely "consider" humanity's God-imaged relationship with birds and flowers (and bees, too). His point about human beings having "much more value" than ravens and lilies is rhetorical rather

---

12. See Lovelace Jr., "Donald Trump"; A. Alter and Confessore, "Republican Party spent nearly $100,000." On similar problems surrounding books by high-profile Christian ministers, see Beaty, *Celebrities*, 95–115.

than mathematical (12:24, 28). He's not engaging in narrow speciesism justifying exploitative "dominion" over all other creatures. The point in Genesis 1 is about human responsibility in steward-partnership with God to care for God's good world (Gen 1:26–31). Of course, as God's "valued" stewards, humans themselves must receive God's care to do the creational work they've been tasked. We must trust God as God trusts us to do our part, though we too often let God and creation down.

In sum, Jesus's gracious and capacious theological perspective, as big as all creation, eases obsessive fears and anxieties. But he also asks a pragmatic question about worry, namely, what does it accomplish? Answer: in itself, *nothing*! You can't worry food on your table or clothes on your back. Worry doesn't work.

In addition to implying the futility of worry in matters of feeding and clothing (Luke 12:22, 29), Jesus exposes its irrelevance to longevity and growth.

Hours and Inches

"Which of you by worrying can add a single hour [*pēchyn*] to your span of life [*hēlikian*]" (12:25). In a footnote, the NRSVue admits an alternative reading, "Or *add a cubit to your stature*." The Greek *hēlikia* can mean either "age/lifespan" or "height/stature," but *pēchys* typically designates a "cubit" measure of space (not time), roughly eighteen inches. Yet Jesus's parallel reference to "so small thing as that (*elachiston*)" in the next verse (12:26) better fits a short age extension than a cubit growth spurt.[13] My modest height was a liability for my basketball aspirations (despite my mad shooting skills). I would've been thrilled with an extra inch or two, but the prospect of adding a foot and a half (cubit) is preposterous. Either way, small (one hour) or large (one cubit), Jesus's point stands: you can't worry yourself into living longer or growing taller.

Ironically, those already advantaged and accomplished seem to worry most about extending themselves further and higher. Silicon Valley titans Jeff Bezos and Peter Thiel, for example, aim to live to 120 via the most advanced health technology, which they can afford to access.[14] Image-obsessed politicians may use heel lifts (if the shoe fits) and camera

---

13. See Culy, Parsons, and Stigall, *Luke*, 424, 426–27; they favor "add a cubit to his height" and follow BDAG in interpreting the "small/minor thing" in 12:26 as "an exquisite bit of irony climaxing the hyperbole" (812).

14. Sample, "If they could turn back time."

angles to project a tall profile and demonstrate they're "up" to the job.[15] Conversely, those who are short by normal standards may overcompensate Napoleon style with authoritarian power grabs. I may be shorter than you, but I rule over you with my iron fist.

Biblical narratives surrounding Israel's first kings fit the pattern. The first king, Saul, whom God (reluctantly) appointed through the prophet-priest Samuel, stood "head and shoulders taller than any" other candidate (1 Sam 10:23). He was a natural, it seemed, to "reign over us" (11:12). To his credit, Saul did not seek the throne or tout his height. He had to be dragged from hiding "among the baggage" to appear before the people (10:22). But soon his regal authority goes to his head, and he begins to make power decisions on his own without God's approval (1 Sam 13, 15). He falls into a state of jealous madness, fixated on eliminating God's new chosen king—the young musician and giant-slaying shepherd boy David—before he officially takes the throne (16:14—18:30).

Surprisingly, Samuel almost falls for another tall candidate. After rejecting Saul, God directs Samuel to Bethlehem to find the new king, "a man after [God's] own heart" (13:13–14), among Jesse's sons. When Jesse presents his eldest son Eliab, Samuel jumps at this good-looking royal prospect. But God is not so impressed: "Do not look on [Eliab's] appearance or on the height of his stature, because I have rejected him [as I rejected Saul], for the LORD does not see as mortals see; they look on the outward appearance, but the LORD looks on the heart" (16:1–7). God is not any more satisfied with the next six sons Jesse parades before Samuel. As it turns out, God wants the eighth son, the youngest and smallest who is out tending the sheep. Character matters more than image in true leadership, though the narrator can't resist reporting that David "was ruddy and had beautiful eyes and was handsome" (16:8–13). And he's still growing and might shoot up to proper kingly height standards.

Whatever physical height he reaches (the Bible never says), David reaches soaring political heights and remains devoted to God's ways—except when he doesn't in spectacular fashion—committing both adultery and murder. He starts believing his own press and uses his power for his own self-gratification—and protection. But he repents of these crimes

---

15. Historically, Americans have preferred taller presidential candidates. See Stulp et al., "Tall claims?" cited in Robert Reich's incisive personal piece, "Why I'm so short." Reich is a leading economist and former Secretary of Labor in the Clinton administration.

and remains a faithful worshipper of God, while still suffering terrible consequences of his failures (see 2 Sam 11–13).

His son Solomon, Israel's third king, follows a similar arc, though ultimately weighted with idolatry and injustice that fuels a major kingdom split into rival northern and southern realms. But he starts off well, except for performing religious rituals at unauthorized places. At one of these offsites, however, God comes to Solomon in a dream with a genie-like offer: "Ask what I should give you"—one wish, not three, but the sky's the limit. In humble gratitude—confessing he is "only a little child" when it comes to ruling God's great people—Solomon makes his wish: "Grant your servant, therefore, an understanding mind to govern your people, able to discern between good and evil" (1 Kgs 3:1–9). In short, Solomon asks for God's wisdom to rule rightly. Thus begins Solomon's international fame as a paragon of wisdom, a royal sage (3:16–28; 4:29–34; 10:1, 6–7)—except when he wasn't—as his colossal power skewed his judgment (like father, like son).

Not surprisingly, God readily grants Solomon's model request. But then God adds two bonuses precisely *because* Solomon did not ask for them: (1) "I give you . . . riches and honor all your life; no other king shall compare with you" (2) "I will lengthen your life" (3:10–13; cf. Prov 3:13–16). So Solomon effectively gets three wishes after all, though this last one (longevity) is conditioned on walking in God's ways and keeping God's law (1 Kgs 3:14), which Solomon will fail to do and not repent of, as David did. Though he enjoys a long forty-year reign, Solomon doesn't make it to 120 years of age. Perhaps he could have lived longer *if* he had kept the terms of God's deal, *if* he had maintained the right heart for covenantal service.

But the Solomon story is not a game of "Let's Make a Deal." God's "deal" is already set, funded in wisdom and righteousness. Health and wealth may or may not come along as riders, but they are not what matter most. Don't worry so much about your body and bank account. Worry more about enhancing others' health and wealth, even at your expense. Remember that the true value of your life has nothing to do with your physical prowess or financial portfolio. Luke's Jesus is right. He grows "in years [or stature, *hēlikia*]" (2:52), as is natural for a young man at age twelve (worry has nothing to do with it), but Luke provides no physical profile of Jesus (no tale of the tape). Jesus also grows in "wisdom . . . and in divine and human favor"—spiritual and social intelligence—which Luke's narrative abundantly illustrates. Despite not having a penny to his name or a place to lay his head, Jesus ranks as "greater than Solomon" in the things that truly matter—like wisdom (Luke 11:31)—even as a field lily's more regally adorned than Solomon could ever dream (12:27).

TREASURE THE POOR

Jesus has more to say in Luke 12 concerning money and material assets in the "treasury" of God's kingdom. Nothing enhances the reputation of political leaders like boosting the economy and building a robust national treasury. Of course, this often enhances leaders' personal wealth, too. What does Jesus Messiah treasure?

After taking a broad-brush swipe at the "nations/peoples (*ethnē*) of the world" for seeking all the material "things" money can buy, Jesus tells his followers that *if* they seek God's realm first and foremost, then "these [material] things will be given to you as well. . . . For it is your Father's good pleasure to give you the kingdom" (12:30–32). In other words, God delights in sharing royal treasure with God's children.

This may surprise us in view of Jesus's disinterest in fundraising and wealth-building. Sounds like we're back to Solomon's deal, now focused on the money angle. Solomon became as renowned for his wealth as for his wisdom, amassing *daily* "thirty cors of choice flour and sixty cors of meal, ten fat oxen and twenty pasture-fed cattle, one hundred sheep, besides deer, gazelles, roebucks, and fatted fowl"—plenty to keep the pantries stocked for Solomon's twelve professional chefs to feed visiting dignitaries and keep the king's "forty thousand . . . horses for his chariots and twelve thousand horsemen" in tip-top shape. All of this goes naturally, it seems, with Solomon's three thousand proverbs and one thousand and five songs (1 Kgs 4:7–34). Solomon's numbers were exceptional. His treasury was the envy of the region. His stunning wealth and wisdom all but made the Queen of Sheba, a rich ruler in her own right, swoon from awe (10:1–10; cf. 10:14–29).

If God wishes, as Jesus says, to share all kingdom "things" with all of God's children, then are we not all destined to live as little kings and queens? A democracy of monarchs. Now there's a concept. Don't worry, just seek God's kingdom with Jesus and you'll be secure for life. If you sell that message effectively, you will win by a landslide.

But just as soon as Jesus appears to jump on the prosperity wagon, he goes and messes it up by tethering his assurance of God's royal blessing to his insistence that his followers must "sell [their] possessions and give alms [charity to the poor]." Try selling that! Jesus's logic? Earthly things are perishable and exploitable by thieves (and tyrants). They don't last; they're a bad investment. Better to invest in the "unfailing treasure of heaven" whose currency is a sincere, generous "heart": "For where your treasure is, there your heart will be also" (12:33–34).

Political leaders of all stripes commonly ask people to make sacrifices for the good of the commonwealth. But that's always risky. Whereas John F. Kennedy is widely praised for his inaugural summons, "Ask not what your country can do for you but what you can for your country," his successor Lyndon B. Johnson is widely blamed for sending thousands of soldiers to die for questionable American interests in Viet Nam. LBJ's legacy bears this stain even as it boasts landmark advances in civil rights. Politics are precarious. Back to ancient Israel's monarchic roots, when the people nagged Samuel, "Give us a king to govern us, like other nations." God warned from the start, before eventually ceding to their demands, that Israel's kings would do what other nations' kings do, namely, take your sons and daughters to serve, fight, and die to maintain the monarch's power, while he taxes your possessions to pay for it all, including his lavish lifestyle. Be careful what you ask for (1 Sam 8:1–22).

But Jesus promotes an entirely different program of sacrifice: one that he exemplifies rather than exploits, one that privileges the poor and lowly rather than the rich and powerful whom he calls to sell everything to help the poor (14:33; 18:22). He also commends the poor's extraordinary generosity, including one destitute widow's contributing her last "two small copper coins"—her whole meager livelihood—to the temple treasury in Jerusalem (21:1–4). That may be better than paying taxes to distant Rome, but it remains unclear how the widow is supposed to survive in her utter poverty. Will the temple system take care of her? Ideally, yes. But Jesus judges the current economic practices of temple officials as closer to robbery than charity (19:45–46; cf. 20:46–21:1; cf. Jer 7:8–11).

Though Luke does not report the widow's fate, we might assume that Jesus's hospitality principle comes to the rescue. She could depend on others' goodwill, as Jesus and his disciples do. But if all of Jesus's people follow his "sell all" advice, soon there will be nothing left for anyone to live on. While Jesus's heart is in the right place, his social, economic, and political vision seems shortsighted.

But remember: Jesus is talking about treasure *in heaven*. That's the blessed kingdom the poor will inherit (Luke 6:20). Jesus is not running for the political race of 30 CE. He's running for eternity, for perpetual pie in the sky rather than a slivery slice of cake here and now. He has a bigger, longer vision, right?

Yes, but Jesus's vision is big and long enough to *encompass* heaven and earth, for time and eternity. Luke's Jesus is more inclined to push boundaries than plot them on a map or timeline. He preaches, "Blessed *are* you who are poor, for yours *is* the kingdom of God" (6:20).[16] Jesus does not trade off this present world for a future kingdom. He mediates the saving blessings of God's realm "upon you" (11:20) "among you" (or "within you," 17:21)—persistently, inexorably—*as* he "endure[s] much suffering" on earth (17:25) with hurting humanity in order to bring God's realm to us where we are, in the trenches, not simply to take us away to some paradise outpost.[17] He plants small seeds in human "soils" to bear kingdom fruit (8:4–15; 13:18–19). The God to whom Jesus prays is the divine "Father, Lord of *heaven and earth*" (10:21). In this worldview, heaven is not a special place up there (with or without golden streets) or promised land down here (whether Israel or America) but rather the *holy sphere* of God's loving presence pulsing throughout the *whole (holos) world* to make everything whole.

All this is a lot to swallow. Heady stuff for a political campaign, not easily captured in sound and image bites. Back to the money business, Jesus makes no big ad buy promoting God's kingdom. No one can buy their way into God's realm. God's *holy-sphere*, God's *holo-sphere* (put that on your T-shirt) only comes as God's gift of grace. So why not sell everything you have and trust God? No worries—except that most Americans will think you're crazy.

---

16. Contrast Matthew's versions of this beatitude—"for theirs is the kingdom of heaven" (Matt 5:3, though Matthew uses "heaven" here as a circumlocution for "God," not as a celestial afterlife location).

17. Luke's Jesus only promises paradise to one of the criminals dying alongside him (23:43)—a last gasp hope, not a major campaign plank.

Making Speeches

> **Strategy 6**
>
> On the political stump, don't speak to make a name for yourself and boost your own popularity but rather to promote God's name and realm. Don't seek to excite and entertain the masses so they will adore you and follow your self-aggrandizing schemes, but rather seek to instruct and challenge people to be more authentic, faithful followers of God's ways.

AMONG ALL THE SCARY things in the world, the scariest for many people is, strangely enough, *public speaking*. Glossophobia, to use the technical term, ranks high among the phobias affecting the general population, even higher than fear of death, by some estimates.[1] It would seem disqualifying for elected political office, since campaigning and governing demand confident, persuasive oratory. How can a timorous politician hope to win over a fearful public? Supreme Court Justice Clarence Thomas might get away with years of taciturnity on the bench, but presidents and other leaders better speak up loud and clear (or at least loud).

But there have been notable exceptions. Israel's prototypical lawgiver and prophet Moses protested God's call to lead his people out of slavery: "O my Lord, I have never been eloquent, neither in the past nor even now that you have spoken to your servant, but I am slow of speech and slow of tongue" (Exod 4:10). While Moses might have been exaggerating his oratorical deficiencies to weasel out of God's commission, God takes him at his word, though doesn't give in. God assures Moses, "I will

---

1. Ebrahimi et al., "Psychological Interventions"; K. Dwyer and Davidson, "Public Speaking"; Croston, "Thing We Fear."

be with your mouth and teach you what you are to speak" (4:12). When Moses keeps demurring and pleads for God to find someone else, God becomes less congenial, downright angry in fact, but still accommodates the shy (or maybe just stubborn) Moses by calling his more rhetorically gifted brother Aaron to be his director of communications (4:13–16). Over the next forty or so years, Moses (with Aaron) becomes Israel's greatest leader (GOAT).

The Roman Republic consul and senator, Cicero, who became renowned for his political oratory, did not come by it easily, flatly admitting on one occasion,

> With what anxiety, O ye immortal gods! with what solicitude of mind! with what fear! Indeed, I am always very nervous when I begin to speak. As often as I rise to speak, so often do I think that I am myself on my trial, not only as to my ability, but also as to my virtue and as to the discharge of my duty; lest I should either seem to have undertaken what I am incapable of performing, which is an impudent act, or not to perform it as well as I can, which is either a perfidious action or a careless one. But that time I was so agitated that I was afraid of everything. I was afraid, if I said nothing, of being thought utterly devoid of eloquence, and, if I said much in such a case, of being considered the most shameless of men. (Cicero, *For Aulus Cluentius*, 51)

The chief author of America's Declaration of Independence and the nation's third president, Thomas Jefferson, made his mark with his pen more than his mouth. Reportedly, when Jefferson tried to speak forcefully in public, his "voice would 'sink in his throat,'" which explains why he delivered only two official presidential speeches—his two obligatory inaugural addresses.[2]

There is wisdom, however, not least for those who lead others, in being slow to speak, thinking long and hard before speaking, before running at the mouth and riling people up (see Jas 1:10; 3:1–12). Virtue, too, as Cicero's statement reveals—the virtue of humility and responsibility. Am I up to the task of meeting the political moment with honor and goodwill, of saying what is honest and true?

It's the loudmouths, the bloviators, the snake-charmers, the silver-tongued devils you have to watch out for, especially the charismatic demagogues who crave political power. "Demagogue" was originally a neutral term for one who "guides [*agō*] the people [*dēmos*]"—as a "pedagogue"

---

2. Kendall, *American Obsessives*, 21; Stossel, *My Age of Anxiety*, 99.

guides children and a "synagogue" brings congregants together for instruction and fellowship—in support of ancient Athenian democratic or Roman republican ideals. But the potential for misusing political power and rhetorical prowess always lurks.

Addressing his Roman imperial context by way of interpreting Rome's founding legends, the first-century-CE biographer Plutarch, a contemporary of Luke, introduced a distinction between an honorable statesman-politician (*politikos*) and two types of dishonorable leaders: the demagogue (*dēmagogōs*) and the tyrant-despot (*tyrannikos-despotēs*).³

> Although Theseus and Romulus were both statesmen [*politikōn*] by nature, neither maintained to the end the true character of a king [*basilikon*], but both deviated from it and underwent a change, the former in the direction of democracy [*dēmotikēn*], the latter in the direction of tyranny [*tyrannikēn*], making thus the same mistake through opposite affections. For the ruler must preserve first of all the realm itself, and this is preserved no less by refraining from what is unbecoming than by cleaving to what is becoming. But he who remits or extends his authority is no longer a king or a ruler; he becomes either a demagogue [*dēmagōgos*] or a despot [*despotēs*], and implants hatred or contempt in the hearts of his subjects. However, the first error [democracy] seems to arise from kindliness and humanity; the second [despotism] from selfishness and severity. (Plutarch, *Comparitio Thesei et Romuli* 2.1–2)

Notice that Plutarch is no more a fan of democracy than despotism. The "first error" (democracy) advanced by "demagogues" caters too much to the will of the masses; the second (despotism) rides roughshod over the people's needs. At least Plutarch's "demagogue" seems motivated by "kindliness and humanity" (indulgently so, but his heart is in the right place), whereas the despot-tyrant operates out of brute "selfishness and severity."

In more recent history, however, the "demagogue" has shed his kindly veneer and resorted to using a bully pulpit in true bully fashion, verbally beating masochistic crowds into submission. I can still hear the chilling rapid-fire voice of Hitler from black-and-white newsreels my ninth-grade history teacher constantly ran in class (instead of actually teaching us).

---

3. See Lane, "Origin of the Statesman"; Lane, *Birth of Politics*, 310–12.

JESUS ON THE STUMP

So much for a little demagogic history. How about some good pedagogy now concerning Jesus Messiah's speechmaking? We don't know exactly how he *felt* about public speaking, but in Luke he regularly withdraws from the madding crowds to pray and regroup in "deserted places" (4:42; 5:26; 6:12; 9:18; 11:1). He doesn't seek the spotlight and megaphone. Today's voracious twenty-four-hour news cycle would doubtless drive him crazy. When he does speak publicly in Luke, he rarely refers to himself and his interests: he's all about proclaiming the reign of *God*. The moment he becomes popular with the crowds, he runs away. That's no way to run for public office.

Moreover, Jesus's speeches in Luke are relatively short. No grandstanding or rattling on. No hogging the stage or stump. To be sure, he speaks authoritatively as one who has something important to say (which is not the same thing as authoritarian bloviation). And he aims to command attention and capture the hearts of audiences (which is not the same thing as emotionalist manipulation). But Luke's Jesus, though no statesman, no spokesman for any *state* power, is even less a demagogue, whether in the Plutarchan "kindly" sense pandering to people's tastes or in the modern sense of strong-mouthing the masses into adoration and submission, thus melding demagogue and despot.

Jesus eschews the demagogue's pedestal for the pedagogue's perch, which is no cushy academic chair but whatever's handy on the trail, like a moored fishing boat or a bare piece of ground, or better yet, speaking on the road *while* walking (keep up if you can). In any case, Jesus prefers to instruct rather than incite. He's a *teacher* of disciples (students), not a browbeater or self-promoter.

But he's also a prophet, one who speaks for God to challenge the people to repent (5:32; 13:1–5), to change their attitudes and actions to align with God's right-making realm. Yet he's less of a threatening revivalist than a tantalizing parabolist, spinning subtle short stories on the campaign trail (especially during the central travel narrative in Luke 9:51—19:44) that pack their own dizzying punch but at more of a glancing blow than a knockout. Jesus is no smashmouth. He's a *storyteller*, a truthteller through provocative stories.

PLAIN-SPOKEN TEACHER

"Plain-spoken" can be taken in different ways. It usually suggests homespun common sense, nothing fancy, the kind old men share in rocking chairs with their grandkids on the front porch (or so the myth goes). Mister Rogers had some of the vibe, though his sweater and sneakers did not quite fit the part, to say nothing of his Rollins College and Pittsburgh Seminary degrees. Though Luke's Jesus speaks to common folk, often using everyday earthy images to illustrate his points, he doesn't fit the aw-shucks profile. Remember, he has no home to sit in, with or without a front porch.

Straight Talk

"Plain-spoken" can also reflect straightforward speech, telling it like it is—plainly, pointedly, pulling no punches and pandering to no one. Flattery will get you nowhere, as the saying goes—except with narcissistic politicians and fair-weather friends (and Mae West). Here's Cicero again:

> It is not virtue I am talking about but a reputation for virtue. For many wish not so much to be, as to seem to be, endowed with real virtue. Such men delight in flattery, and when a complimentary speech is fashioned to suit their fancy they think the empty phrase is proof of their own merits. There is nothing, therefore, in a friendship in which one of the parties to it does not wish to hear the truth and the other is ready to lie. (Cicero, *De Amicitia*, 98)

True friends will always be frank with one another, offering constructive criticism—"speaking the truth in love," to switch to Pauline mode (Eph 4:15; cf. 4:16–5:1)—even if costs you a true friend's temporary anger (he'll come around and thank you later), or a few social media "friends," or a lot of votes!

The first-century-BCE Epicurean philosopher Philodemus, whose name incidentally means "friend of the people," addresses the political side of frankness versus flattery, characterizing the model frank speaker as one who "bears goodwill and practices philosophy intelligently and continually and is great in character and indifferent to fame and *least of all a politician* and clean of envy and says only what is relevant and is not carried away so as to insult or strut or show contempt or do harm, and does not make use of insolence and flattering arts" (Philodemus, *On Frank Criticism* Col. Ib).[4]

Civil, respectful debate among thoughtful citizens. Honest, constructive criticism among genuine friends. Intelligent, careful investigation among wisdom-loving women and men of goodwill. Remember those good old days? Neither do I.

This second form of plain-speaking comes closer to the mark with Jesus. He doesn't trade in flattery, whether dishing it out or soaking it in. While loving intelligence and wisdom, he doesn't privilege the intelligentsia or sophists. He speaks plainly enough so that the little ones may understand and follow the ways of God as well as, if not better than, the bigwigs (Luke 10:21–24).

On the Level

Another angle on Jesus's plain speech considers the leveling effect of his discourse in Luke 6:20–49. The content parallels the "Sermon on the Mount" in Matthew 5–7, but in more concise form. More distinctively, Luke's version of this "sermon" is set on "a level place," a flat-footed plain (*pedinos*)—hence the common title, "Sermon on the Plain"—after Jesus *comes down* from the mountain where's he just prayed and chosen the twelve apostles. As mentioned in strategy 4, Jesus teaches not only the Twelve but also "a great crowd of his disciples and a great multitude of people" from neighboring areas (6:17). Rather than sitting down to teach, as he does on the mountain in the more customary authoritative posture of the day (similar to judges "sitting on the bench" today, before whom we "all rise" to honor), Luke's Jesus *stands* to speak, not to stand over the people but to stand "with them" (*met' autōn*, 6:17) in solidarity, on solid ground level, on common footing, as one who *understands* their lives.

Further and right in line with speaking plainly on the plain or on the level, as we say, Luke's Jesus speaks in this "sermon" about leveling the playing field between standard social and political tiers, between the rich, full, happy, admired highbrows in the box seats and the poor, hungry, sad, hated lowlifes in the bleachers (6:20–26; cf. 14:7–24). Equal opportunity for all. A great idea, which still plays well in American politics rhetorically, though not so realistically.

---

4. Cf. Austin, *Living for Pleasure*, 66–79.

But Jesus's plain speaking goes further still. Proposing a better deal for the destitute and depressed is one thing but funding it the expense of the wealthy and healthy—asking them not only to pay a little more tax but to trade places with the down and out—that's a whole other deal. Not only, "Blessed you who are poor, for yours is the kingdom of God. Blessed are you who are hungry now, for you will be filled" (6:20). But conversely, "Woe to you are rich, for you have received your consolation. Woe to you who are full now, for you will be hungry" (6:21).

Is that necessary, fair, just, or even smart? Isn't that just flipping social reality, leaving us right back where we started, except with different occupants in social locations? Isn't that just a recipe for puffed up nouveau riche kings of the hill to give the old ruling guard the same hell they used to give out? Revenge is sweet. On the flip side, won't the deposed power brokers just be incensed at the interlopers for taking their good jobs they worked so hard to earn (maybe) or feel entitled to? Replacement is bitter.

It happens all the time. Power corrupts, and new power makes worse tyrants than its predecessors. On the other side, loss of status embitters, makes more resentful victims out of the perceived losers. It's those vile immigrants' fault for taking our rightful places and positions, abetted by bleeding heart liberals aiming to boost their own power. It's time to "take our country back," "lock up" the whole usurping lot, and make them pay.

Former trade minister of Venezuela and executive director of the World Bank Moisés Naím describes the autocrat's standard strategy as milking populist resentment and lust for revenge to the last drop: "Autocrats . . . know that aggrieved masses propel to power those offering not just redress but revenge. They've grasped that the people most eager to sweep them into power are the most aggrieved: those whose identities revolve around feeling victimized in their own societies. Aspiring autocrats have relearned the old insight that nothing creates a visceral bond with followers like speaking directly to a deep sense of having been wronged."[5]

Has the true triumphal Jesus Messiah suddenly burst out of his shell to forge his bombshell path to the throne? Is he shifting course to advocate the chaotic, anarchic, autocratic goal of God's kingdom—less level ground than disheveled heap, blown up with no place to stand? Or is he suddenly auditioning for the part of the world's strongest strongman, the biggest bully on the block, the only macho man left standing, the whiniest self-styled victim of all (no one's ever been treated so unfairly) finally

---

5. Naím, *Revenge of Power*, 37.

sticking it to the man, particularly his abusive or callous father? Certainly not, though Jesus seems to have some explaining to do after his walloping Sermon on the Plain intro. That's no way to get anywhere in authentic, holistic messianic politics: that's just plain messy. Once more, I think the way forward is to profile Luke's Jesus as more poet than politician or policy wonk. He's not rewriting the constitution, reducing (or inflating) the bureaucracy, draining the swamp, claiming that everything will be different in "my administration."

Jesus is more interested in *character* or *virtue*, in right ways of thinking, feeling, acting, and relating—not right (or left!) political posturing. The rule that guides his messianic vocation is the Golden Rule—"Do to others as you would have them do to you" (6:31)—which has nothing to do with gilded thrones (or toilets) and everything to do with doing good to everyone as you wish they would do to you.[6] We might imagine his campaign rallies festooned with "Love Kindness Mercy" banners (all three words feature in 6:35–36) and "Be Kind" signs and stickers, with Glen Campbell blasted over the loudspeakers before Jesus's speeches: "You've got to try a little kindness / then you'll overlook the blindness / of narrow-minded people on a narrow-minded street."

But we know better by now than to reduce Jesus's campaign to nice and sweet sound bites. We expect more real bite. And Jesus delivers it here in stunning fashion.

> Love your enemies.
> Do good to those who hate you.
> Bless those who curse you.
> Pray for those who mistreat you.
> If anyone strikes you on the cheek, offer the other also.
> Give to everyone who asks of you.
> If anyone takes away what is yours, do not ask for it back again.
> Love your enemies [yes, he repeats this!].
> Do good, and lend, expecting nothing in return.
> Be children of the Most High, for he himself is kind to the grateful and the wicked.
> Be merciful, just as your Father is merciful. Forgive. And you yourself will be forgiven. (6:27–37)

---

6. One of Norman Rockwell's most famous paintings depicts multiple peoples of the world and the inscribed text of the Golden Rule. It appeared on the April 1, 1961 cover of *The Saturday Evening Post*; in 1985, a mosaic version was installed in the United Nations headquarters in New York, where it still hangs. See Perry, "Something Serious."

Thus Jesus frames and fleshes out the Golden Rule (6:31). Not so golden after all. Where's the recourse, the reckoning—the revenge! Isn't this just draining the moat (forget the swamp) and inviting the enemies to storm the castle to set up their own wicked realm under their Godless Rule? Where's the Pax Romana (Caesar), the "Peace through Strength" (Reagan)? Seems like Jesus's foreign policy and defense strategy are not much stronger than his domestic social and economic agenda. He sticks with strength of *character* in the loving, being-kind, forgiving, mercy-dealing image of God the Father (more on the "Fatherland" below). He's betting his life on this "Strength through Weakness" campaign[7] to repair and restore the world to God's right and good purposes. Good luck with that, Jesus.

This straight love-your-enemies talk on a Galilean plain seem miles and millennia away from John McCain's signature "Straight Talk Express" presidential campaigns in 2000 and 2008—with the tour bus and whole shebang.[8] McCain was known for his straight-shooting talk, not infrequently laced with angry outbursts. He was a military man's man, having endured brutal years as a POW *without talking* (no betrayal of state secrets) and advocated for a strong military in his long postwar political service. He infamously joked in a Beach Boys parody about his aim to "Bomb-Bomb-Bomb-Bomb-Bomb-Iran."

But for McCain, serving one's country with honor was not just about military honor but also about honest speech and action. When a woman at one of his campaign town hall meetings tried to get him to endorse the "birther" conspiracy theory about Obama, McCain politely but plainly set her straight, "No ma'am, [Obama's] a decent family man, citizen, that I just happen to have disagreements with on fundamental issues, and that's what this campaign is all about." After the results were in on Election Day, he graciously conceded the race and congratulated Obama on his victory, and early in Trump's presidential term, McCain broke with his party and gave the thumbs-down verdict to repealing the Affordable Care Act—or Obamacare, as it's commonly known. McCain remained a crusty straight talker to his dying day. Whatever his flaws, he strove to do and say the right thing, not the convenient, expedient thing. McCain was "not [so] far from the kingdom of God" after all, as Mark's Jesus told one of the

---

7. See Paul's "weak," cross-centered gospel (1 Cor 1:17—2:5) and personal motto, "Whenever I am weak, then I am strong" (2 Cor 12:10); cf. Caputo, *Weakness*; Spencer, *Seven Challenges*, 35, 70–78, 145–46.

8. See Wallace, *McCain's Promise* (including Weisberg foreword).

"scribes" (a typical opposition group in the Gospels) after he commended Jesus for being "right" about the two greatest commandments: love God and love your neighbor (Mark 12:28–34).

We may also again salute the plain-spoken Jimmy Carter of Plains. Like McCain, Carter was a graduate of the US Naval Academy, though with a considerably higher student ranking.[9] Carter undertook "graduate work at Union College in reactor technology and nuclear physics and served as senior officer of the pre-commissioning crew of the Seawolf, the second nuclear submarine."[10] Quibble all you want with various policies and decisions during his one presidential term, but it's hard to argue with his better-than-average character and accomplishments. While remaining a devout, Bible-teaching Baptist his whole life in the Deep South, he was never afraid to buck racist, anti-feminist, anti-social-gospel, and anti-environmentalist strands, even within his own Baptist tradition.[11] His non-segregationist bona fides were established from childhood in respectful engagements with black friends in rural Georgia classrooms, playgrounds, and farm fields. Carter's commitment to women's equal rights and opportunities in church and society, local and global, is well-documented in his *A Call to Action: Women, Religion, Violence, and Power* (2014). The motto of the Carter Center, the NGO established in 1982 after his defeat in the 1980 presidential election—"Waging Peace. Fighting Disease. Building Hope."—is not just slick branding. It reflects many good, nonpartisan political actions and projects over forty years and counting. Not a bad legacy for Jimmy of Plains following Jesus's Sermon on the Plain.

PARABLE-SPINNING STORYTELLER

Why does Jesus supplement his straight talking with storytelling, with so many more parables than sermons or lectures? The short stories serve an instructional purpose, illustrating propositions and principles concerning God's realm with vivid images and vignettes. That's good pedagogy. But Jesus's parables also have a way of teasing and frustrating the student, delivering more than a simple moral lesson, something more disruptive

---

9. Carter graduated "with distinction," sixtieth out of 821 in 1946, while McCain graduated fifth from the bottom, 894 out of 899, in 1958.

10. Carter Center, "Jimmy Carter."

11. See Balmer, *Redeemer*; K. Bird, *Outlier*; Eizenstat, *President Carter*.

and less definitive. If they "pay attention to how [they] listen" (8:18)—and it's easy not to because the stories seem so simple on the surface—hearers (and readers) of Jesus's parables frequently find themselves shaking their heads and shaking off inconvenient challenges that come through.

Even so, before Jesus's parables sink in, they spark interest. They do not simply parrot the same old trite party lines. That's good rhetorical strategy on Jesus's part. People become weary of career politicians (and theologians) in their bureaucratic bubbles saying the same things year after year and doing blessed nothing. Maybe this strange new guy with his tantalizing stories will stir things up. But not too much. Don't ask too much of us. Tell us more about luscious pastries and crazy circus acts.

That's not Jesus, though. He stirs things up plenty, but he does so through everyday stories that challenge the status quo, to be sure, but only if attentive hearers are willing to change *their* ways rather than blame everyone else for their troubles. If not, Jesus doesn't care about renegotiating terms of disciples, recasting his prescription to make the medicine go down more easily. He even says, echoing Isaiah, that he speaks "in parables, *so that* 'looking they may not perceive and hearing they may not understand'" (8:9; cf. Isa 6:10). He's not trying to make it easy. He's not trying to win votes.

What's going on here? What's the "secret" (Luke 8:9) of Jesus's parables? What is a parable event in Jesus's campaign, thinking of "event" in the more loaded sense used by some modern philosophers, meaning "not . . . simply 'what happens' . . . but *what is going on in* what happens . . . *what is really happening in* what happens."[12]

Ground Levels

The first major parable Jesus tells comes with explanation (unusually) and prepares the ground for understanding (Jesus still wants understanding) all his parables and indeed his entire mission. Some scholars aptly call it "The Parable of Parables."[13] Get this one, and you're on your way to getting at the core of Jesus's campaign. It comes not long after his ground-leveling Sermon on the Plain, and not incidentally foregrounds *four grounds*—wayside, rocky, thorny, and fertile soils. The parable of the soils is about different grounds yielding different crop levels—including

---

12. Caputo, *What to Believe*, 111.
13. Snodgrass, *Stories*, 145; Herzog, "Sowing," 187-88.

no crop at all—from the same seeds sown by the same farmer (8:4–8). Which is to say it's about different *heart-level receptions and responses to God's dynamic word* (8:11–15). It's a parable about how to hear and heed, read and receive Jesus's other parables and proclamations.

It's not very encouraging. In three of the four cases (75 percent), the word-seed is wasted: either by (1) hardhearted, close-minded know-it-alls resistant to new insight, in whom the word gains no entry, as if sown on hard-packed ground; or (2) superficial, shallow enthusiasts ready to give anything a whirl, just not for long with any depth, as if the word were sown on rocky ground; or (3) worn down, overcommitted worrywarts too entangled to give the word a fighting chance, as if sown on thorny-weedy ground. What's worse, these wasteful soil samples may represent not only callous, careless, and cluttered groups of respondents but also comparable parts of individual persons: the hard, rocky, thorny parts lurking in each of our hearts. Let the hearer beware, but not despair. "If you have ears to hear, then hear!" (8:8).

Cultivate the good ground (level four) deep within you and your social and political groups that welcome gospel truth, even when its challenges you to change. When God's word, endorsed and exemplified by Jesus Messiah, reaches you, strive to "hold it fast in an honest and good heart and bear fruit with endurance" (8:15). In other words, be responsible receptors and diligent doers of the word, not hearers only, thereby establishing a firm foundation on which to build flourishing lives and communities (see 6:46–49; 8:21; Jas 1:21–22).

Still, if you're on Jesus's public relations team, trying to get his good word out, prepare to be ignored, misunderstood, and disappointed a good bit of the time, around 75 percent. That's not a propitious polling number.

Slant Talk

Taking his cue from Emily Dickinson's poem, "Tell all the truth but tell it slant," Eugene Peterson, author of the popular Bible translation, *The Message*, titled his book on Jesus's speech *Tell It Slant: A Conversation on the Language of Jesus in His Stories and Prayers*. Jesus's parables particularly qualify as slant talk. Again, we ask, why not keep with straight talk?

For the same reason, I suggest, that baseball pitchers don't simply throw the ball straight over the plate. Where's the challenge for the hitter (respondent) in that? At root, the Greek compound term for "parable" (*parabolē*) means something that is "thrown beside" (*ballō* + *para*). Jesus throws out (pitches) these provocative stories to keep his hearers on their toes, to keep their eyes and ears sharp (you can hear the projectile's swoosh), to be alert to a surprising curve, drop, slide, rise, or changeup in velocity or vector. By throwing parables beside his target audience, Jesus is not trying to hit them or knock them out. But he's very much aiming to brush them back and keep them off-balance. Best to hear/read Jesus's parables well equipped with hard-shell, foam-lined helmet (and ear extension), leather elbow and shin guards, and any other protective gear you can find. Jesus is throwing "filthy stuff," as they say in baseball lingo. Seriously? Filthy stuff in these pithy little everyday stories?

Case in point: the famous parable of the good Samaritan that Luke's Jesus delivers early in his long campaign trek to Jerusalem (Luke 10:30–5). Though no one I know knows any Samaritans (there are only a few hundred left in the world), the image of the "good Samaritan" has become prototypical of one who stops and helps a stranger in distress on the side of the road or more generally aids anyone in need. Pretty straightforward. Be kind to others as you'd like to be treated (back to the Golden Rule). Play nice. Any kindergartner can understand this story.

Not really. Not the way Jesus means it. He never labels this parable or its main character "the good Samaritan." This traditional title misses the plate by a mile (a wild pitch) because Jesus's Jewish audience would never call a Samaritan "good" (and vice versa). We've alluded previously to the fraught relations between Jews and Samaritans in Jesus's day. Though sharing borders and both claiming to be true worshippers of Israel's God, they hated and mistrusted each other. Remember that Jesus begins his final journey to Jerusalem talking down the Zebedee brothers who propose calling down fire on an inhospitable Samaritan village (Bomb-Bomb-Bomb-Samaria, 9:54–55). While there might be some nice Samaritan grandmas, the prevailing Jewish prejudice officially acknowledged no good Samaritans, to which the Samaritans would say, right back at you no-good Jews! In Jesus's culture, a "good Samaritan" was an oxymoron.

But Jesus dares to differ, even as he cheekily plays on this ethnoreligious prejudice. In this story he throws out to a Jewish religious legal expert who asks, "Who is my neighbor" that I'm bound to love? (10:27–29; cf. Lev 19:17), one of his "filthiest pitches" that locks the batter in frozen shock before he buckles to the ground. Or if you will, Jesus brings a journeyman Samaritan out of the bullpen to throw an incredible changeup that changes the whole ballgame. We expect the players and fans to rush together in the mother of all brawls when a Samaritan takes the Jewish home field. But before that happens, the Samaritan steps off the mound to help the first base coach from the opposing team who's been struck with a beer bottle hurled by an angry hooligan. Okay, I know. Know when to stop the sports metaphor.

Back to plain talk: Jesus features a no-good Samaritan stopping on the highway and giving extraordinary aid (medicine, money, transport, lodging) to a traveler—a Jewish traveler, presumably—who's been highjacked and left for dead, while a pair of Jewish clerics "pass by on the other side" (10:31–32). All that is plainly shocking (and over-shaming, it should be said: most rank-in-file priests were doing the best they could to do good). Jesus seems to be making up new rules for the grand old game, though he would insist he's simply enforcing the rule of biblical law. As surely as the Torah says, "Love your neighbor as yourself" (Lev 19:17), it says later in the same chapter, "Love the alien [immigrant] as yourself, for you were aliens [immigrants] in the land of Egypt" (19:34).

But Jesus keeps it slant. He never directly answers his interlocutor, "See, the Samaritan is a neighbor you must love and care for, as surely as a fellow Jew." Rather, after telling his little story, Jesus asks the legal expert, "Which of these three [priest, Levite, or Samaritan], do you think, was a neighbor to the man who fell into the hands of the robbers?" (Luke 10:36). The answer is obvious, but Jesus wants the man to answer his own question that sparked the parable, though in fact Jesus *shifts the direction* of that question. Remember, the lawyer originally asked, "Who is my neighbor," whom I should love as myself? In this formulation, neighbor represents the *object/recipient* of active love. But after the parable, Jesus asks, "Which of these three was a neighbor to the [robbed] man?" In other words, who in the story acted *as* the true neighbor? Now neighbor represents the *subject/initiator* of active love.

Either way, the fill-in-the-blank answer is the same: the Samaritan. But the stunned lawyer can't bring himself to say this in plain terms. "Samaritan" sticks in his throat, so he goes with the circumlocution, "the one who showed [the assault victim] mercy" (10:37). He's been thrown for a loop—just as Jesus intended with his "nice" story about loving-kindness and mercy. Whichever way it goes, whoever is on the giving or receiving end of neighborly care—Jew or Samaritan (or fill in any other either/or blanks)—*love* rules. If a Samaritan's in the ditch (or a muddy gully on either side of the Rio Grande), love, help, aid him or her any way you can. Who knows, you might get stuck yourself one day and need a Samaritan's helping hand. If so, be gracious if she or he offers help and receive it gratefully. How about that for a border policy![14]

Fatherly Advice

Father language is loaded with authoritarian, strongman freight; it's a nicer way of saying patriarch or king of the castle in male-dominated cultures like America, though the founding fathers are increasingly showing their age. The nineteenth amendment to the Constitution, passed by Congress in 1919 and ratified by the states in 1920, granted women the right to vote. That's good news and bad news: good that it allowed women's direct involvement in the democratic process; bad that it took over a century from the nation's founding and bad that we're still struggling over a century later to realize women's equal participation in government, business, and yes, the church, too (the Southern Baptist Convention recently doubled down on barring ordained female ministers).

Grandfathers, if we're lucky, have a slightly better rep than fathers. We mellow with age and are forgiven for telling more stupid jokes and forgetting things. But there can be a serious political downside. The opposition does not refer to our oldest president as Grandpa Biden with affection. Move aside, old man, if you can still move. If not, we'll steamroll over you.

"Fatherly advice," grand or not, is taken at best with a grain of salt, at worst with an eye roll. It too often comes across as patronizing counsel to women and children, more admonitory than advisory, more my way or the highway. This is not to bash all fathers and grandfathers; many of us are trying to be better guys, and we enjoy the loving support of the women in our lives, even as we strive to love and affirm them (the Golden Rule again). But we do no one any favors, including ourselves, by whining about male-bashing or glossing over the interminably long

---

14. See the trenchant critique of Trump's anti-immigrant "parables" that were "mainstays of his rallies" in Sharlet, *Undertow*, 54–57. The most egregious example is the one Sharlet dubs "The Bullet," a fictional account (which Trump passes off as history) featuring General "Black Jack" Pershing's execution of forty-nine Muslims accused of terrorism in the Philippines with bullets dipped in pig's blood. The historian Daniel Immerwahr (*How To Hide an Empire*, 104–7) also debunks Trump's mythical tale and provides a more critical account of Pershing's work in the Philippines in the early 1900s.

run of abusive patriarchal history. On the political front, "Fatherland" (*Vaterland*) evokes those Hitlerian chills again. Our founding fathers deserve our respect for what they accomplished, but not our worship. They loved their power and authority as much as the next guy, while trying to safeguard against tyrants and demagogues. "First Lady" may be the most patronizing label of all time. Abigail Adams merits as much attention as John Adams, not least for writing to her husband, "In the new code of laws which I suppose it will be necessary for you to make, I desire you would remember the ladies and be more generous and favorable to them than your ancestors. Do not put such unlimited power into the hands of the husbands. Remember all men would be tyrants if they could."[15] John was not amused.

The image of God as Father continues to dominate Christian America. It has solid biblical warrant, not least in the fact that Jesus teaches his followers to pray to his Father, as he does, "I thank you Father, Lord of heaven and earth" (10:21–22; cf. 11:1–4; 22:41–42; 23:34, 46). But we should not ignore the fact that Jesus never calls *himself* Father (or Führer). Matthew's Jesus amplifies this point by imploring his followers to "call no one your father on earth, for you have one Father, the one in heaven." Further, "you have one teacher, and you are all brothers and sisters. . . . you have one instructor, the Messiah" (Matt 23:8–10). Of course, Matthew's readers know that Jesus is the Messiah, but he doesn't directly make that claim here. Instead, he lays down his main leadership principle: "The greatest among you will be your servant. All who exalt themselves will be humbled, and all who humble themselves will be exalted (23:8–12; cf. Luke 14:11; 18:14).[16]

Jesus, God's first Son, calls his siblings in God's family to reflect the Father's character, not flaunt patriarchal authority. Yes, we're back to character again—merciful, compassionate, forgiving character. And we're back to Jesus's Sermon on the Plain: "Be merciful, just as your Father is merciful" (6:36)—glossing the preceding Golden Rule (6:31). Clear enough but not slant enough to shake people out of calcified patriarchal thinking. Jesus needs parables for that.

---

15. Cited in Robin, *Reactionary Mind*, 14 (citing Adams, *Letters*, 148–49).

16. Cf. Clapp, *Naming Neoliberalism*, 196–97: "Centuries of Christian influence have installed humility as an admirable human trait so that many in our post-Christian society—not least after years of an egomaniacal narcissist in the White House—still regard humility as a desired characteristic of our leaders (and others)."

Farther down the road to Jerusalem, awhile after telling the story of the Samaritan helper, Jesus shares another shocking tale, the parable of the prodigal son, as it's commonly called (15:11–32). But this parable has also been misnamed, though not because the (younger) son in the story was not "prodigal"—he was exceedingly wasteful—but because he's not really the main character. Center stage, between the younger and elder sons, is the *prodigal father*, overflowing (wasteful) with *compassion* (*splanchnon*)—gut-level love, sympathy, mercy, forgiveness (15:20–24)[17]—for his wayward younger son who had squandered his life and inheritance in a distant land.

Once the boy had run through all his money and hit rock bottom in a pigsty, all he had left was to return home, confess his offenses against his heavenly and earthly fathers ("Father, I have sinned against heaven and before you"), throw himself on their mercy, and submit himself for slavish service, "no longer worthy to be called your son" (15:18–19). He had *no right* to any of this, but it was worth a shot.

The story's father, however, defies all expectations, breaks all the rules of traditional patriarchy. While the wayward wretch "was still far off, his father saw him"—willing him back home, whatever he'd done. Further, the father "was filled with compassion; he ran and put his arms around him and kissed" his filthy, smelly son. Running to, hugging, kissing a rebellious son: this is not how dignified, dominant fathers are supposed to act. When the son voices his prepared confession, the father pays no mind to it. Instead, he barks out orders for his servants to bring his son a top-drawer robe, ring, and sandals and prepare a party to end all parties to celebrate his return (15:21–24).

What? No repudiation, no probation, no plan to pay off the prodigal's debt (back to strategy 3). What a waste of a golden opportunity to teach this young man a lesson! What a waste of fancy clothes and fatted calf on this lowlife who had chosen his own slop-bed and should be made to lie in it! Where's the rule of law? Where are the family values? What if the whole realm were run like this? Is this what the divine Father's righteous kingdom is all about?

In the parable of the prodigal father, Jesus aims to shake up dominant family and financial structures but not to replace them with other systems. Jesus is no systems analyst. On an earlier occasion, when a crowd member pleads with Jesus to settle an inheritance dispute with the man's

---

17. See Spencer, *Passions*, 184–90.

brother, Jesus shoots back, "Friend, who set me to be a judge or arbitrator over you?" (12:13–14). Jesus is not running for a place on the Supreme Court or for executive privilege to appoint judges. He's a plain-speaking leveler and slant-talking storyteller with a mission-critical concern to indict *systemic problems*, like patriarchy and hierarchy, and to inculcate *systemic principles*, like love and mercy.

In so doing, Jesus runs the risk of rankling the establishment ranks to no end, represented by the *older son* in the parable who has faithfully honored his father and family name his whole life. He about has a stroke in the field—where he's dutifully working as a good son should be—when he suddenly catches a whiff of roasting veal and a note of dancing music and realizes that his father is feting his no-good returning brother. Why this waste on this wastrel? (15:25–30)

The parable's father—the story's divine figure—is not playing favorites; he's not indulging the baby son over his firstborn. The older brother is most welcome at the party and still has the father's full love and blessing: "Son you are always with me, and all that is mine is yours." The older brother doesn't lose anything by this happy family reunion. In fact, he's gaining back a lost brother (15:31–32). This is not a zero-sum game, where one's gain is another's loss. This is the wastefully gracious realm of Father-God and Brother Jesus challenging conventional hierarchical (including patriarchal) systems.[18]

Another way of identifying the slant-talking storyteller Jesus is as a "theopoet" of God's kingdom, to borrow again from John Caputo, defunding the kingdom's usual surplus of "royalty and authoritarianism, power and patriarchy, even theocracy," and reinvesting it with counter "expectations, where offense is met with forgiveness . . . and we are asked to love our enemies." Caputo goes further, further than many American Christians prefer, but getting closer to the mark I suspect: "All the expected effects of power, authority, and hierarchical rule are *reversed*, resulting

---

18. We might still question the anti-patriarchal efficacy of a family story that mentions no mother, sister, or any other female figures (except for "prostitutes" the older brother accuses the younger brother of soliciting [15:30]) and reports work of household slaves. But again, Jesus's short stories are descriptive, not definitive; provocative, not prescriptive. As for women, Jesus gives female characters positive starring roles in three parables—including one immediately preceding the prodigal story (15:8–10; cf. 13:20–21; 18:1–8)—and also imagines himself in the role of a mother hen (13:34). See Reid, "Beyond Petty Pursuits"; Spencer, *Salty Wives*, 40–54.

in the rule of the unruly, the reign of the unroyal . . . a 'sacred anarchy,' as I [Caputo] like to put it."[19]

"Sacred anarchy"? Not sure I'm ready to put it that way, even less sure that Luke would sign on. But Jesus's parables do present a vibrant "theopoetic" commentary on God's realm—"the kingdom of God was [Jesus's] poem"[20]—more allusive and elusive than definitive, sure to knock the manifesto-blaring demagogues and strict constructionist constitutionalists off their strides, though these hardliners might get more votes.

---

19. Caputo, *What to Believe*, 134 (emphasis original).
20. Caputo, *What to Believe*, 31–32.

Working the Crowds

> **Strategy 7**
> Work to meet people where they are, as they are, in all their rich diversity and shared adversity. Seek to be truly "of the people" and "for the people" by being among the people: listening to them, not merely speaking at them; lending them a helping hand, not having your hand out for their votes and money; looking to serve them and their needs, not use them for your ambitious interests.

SPEAKING TO LARGE CROWDS in carefully curated public events and advertisements is optimal for an authoritarian candidate. Control the medium and the message as much as possible, always remembering that the "medium is the message," as Marshall McLuhan famously stated in 1964,[1] not coincidentally the first presidential election year after the 1960 campaign in which the photogenic John F. Kennedy outshone the five-o'clock-shadowed Richard M. Nixon in the first public televised debates.

Perhaps this is when Nixon began to develop his pathological penchant for secrecy and cover-up. Shed as little light on the subject as possible. Doesn't everyone look better in blissfully dim mood lighting? Keep a tight lid on details (that's where the devil lurks). No one likes leakers (tattletales, snitches, dirty rats). These tapes and papers are mine anyway; you can't hear or see them unless I let you. So don't come poking around my office, study, garage, or bathroom witch-hunting for classified stuff I might have kept and declassified with my mind, or not, but in any case, it's none of your business.[2] Let the "silent majority," to whom Nixon ap-

---

1. McLuhan, *Understanding Media*, 7–21.
2. I might have drifted here from Nixonian to Trumpian territory. Trump constantly

pealed with great effect, keep silent (I'll speak for you, tell you what you need to know) and stay in the shadows (it's cooler there, I'll show you the way to follow).

Making formal speeches is one thing. Meeting people face-to-face is another. Demagoguing is one thing. Synagoguing—coming together in common fellowship—is another. Of course, retail politics—shaking hands, kissing babies, chatting and chowing in local diners and fairgrounds—can pay big political dividends if you can pull off being one of the guys, the kind the average Joe wants to grab a beer with.[3]

Populism is the first of Naím's 3P's (his designation) in the standard autocratic playbook (the other two are polarization and post-truth).[4] Though it focuses on *people*, populism as a political strategy is not really "of the people, by the people and for the people." It's all about the *politician*, what's of-by-for *him*. It's all about stirring up disaffected people to believe he's their last hope and salvation. But you shouldn't spend too much time with the masses. Don't let them get to know you too well. Keep the mystique alive. Autocratic strongmen prefer hiding out with a few cronies and confidants in hotel suites and resort clubs, popping out for big spotlight events and then being speedily escorted by musclebound security back behind the curtain. Above all, they seek to control the flow of information as tightly as possible and brand all open criticism and investigation as "fake news."

How does Jesus's campaign in Luke fit this populist pattern? Poorly, I submit. Though Jesus is popular as an authoritative (again, not the same as authoritarian) teacher and healer, he's not a populist. He does not seek popularity; he does not pursue "clicks" and "likes" to boost his "influencer" profile. He routinely withdraws from the crowds to the deep sea or wild desert, as we've seen, but not so much to maintain his mystique as his integrity: he will not be mistaken for a super-messiah or egomaniacal strongman, however much the masses might want one. There is a "secret" slant to his parables (8:9) and a "hidden" or cryptic" dimension of his mission (8:17, *krypton*; cf. 9:45; 18:34)—not to cover up the truth,

---

bemoans the "witch hunt" against him, not least the FBI hunt that uncovered a stash of classified documents in a bathroom at his Mara-a-Lago home.

3. The so-called "Beer Question" (yes, there's a Wikipedia entry) began with the 2000 presidential campaign. George W. Bush won the question poll and the election over Al Gore; cf. Garber, "Who Cares?"

4. Naím, *Revenge of Power*, xv–105.

Working the Crowds

however—but to allow time for hard truths and realities (like his impending death) to sink in (see strategy 9).

Most importantly, even as Jesus retreats from clamoring crowds desperate to get a piece of him, he typically receives them with open arms when they track him down. He keeps teaching and reaching out to the people, walking and working among them as the Son of Humankind. Though no social butterfly or political schmoozer, he mingles with the masses out of compassion, not condescension, preferring their company over that of the rich and famous. He incarnates the love of God every step of the way at considerable cost, as it happens, to his personal advancement. In short, Jesus definitely works the crowds. But he does so in his peculiarly weak messianic way.

FEELING YOUR PAIN

One of the most famous political memes came to life in a Manhattan night club at a 1992 campaign rally for presidential candidate Bill Clinton. When an angry heckler peppered Clinton with accusations of ignoring the AIDS crisis, the Arkansas governor blurted back, "Let me tell you something. . . . You do not have the right to treat any human being, including me, with no respect because of what you're worried about. I did not cause it. I'm trying to do something about it. I have treated you and all the people who've interrupted my rally with a hell of a lot more respect than you've treated me, and it's time you started thinking about that." Forceful response but not as memorable as the next words he uttered: "*I feel your pain, I feel your pain.*" The meme is born.

No matter that Clinton followed these words of sympathy with more scolding: "But if you want to attack me personally you're no better than Jerry Brown [Clinton's primary rival] and all the rest of these people who say whatever sounds good at the moment. If you want something to be done, you ask me a question and you listen. If you don't agree with me, go support somebody else for president but quit talking to me like that. This is not a matter of personal attack; it's a matter of human wrong."[5] Clinton could counterpunch with the best of them.

But Clinton is most remembered for saying, "I feel your pain"—well, along with sexual scandals, being impeached, and a "Slick Willie" style. But you can't have everything, and that didn't stop him from being a

---

5. Specter, "1992 Campaign" (with verbatim).

two-term president and convincing folks that the hardscrabble kid from Hope (Arkansas), whose dad died before he was born, really felt their pain and aimed to do something to relieve it. He championed "hope and change" long before Obama, who was barely out of law school in 1992. Never mind again that Clinton had long left Hope for Georgetown, Oxford, Yale Law School, and back to Arkansas—as governor. A political path somewhat similar to (fellow Baptist) Jimmy Carter's, though Clinton is taller, slicker, and prefers a fancier lifestyle.

Was Clinton's sympathizing pain-sharing just a stunt then? Not entirely. By all accounts, Clinton had a remarkable capacity to relate to hurting people and give them hope. Even some silver-spoon elites can do that on a genuine level. Franklin Delano Roosevelt may be the most outstanding example of a truly sympathetic, even empathetic, aristocratic politician. His devastating polio diagnosis at age thirty-nine in 1921—before he became a (losing) vice-presidential candidate and the (winning) governor of New York and president of the US (elected four times!)—led him in 1927 to establish a polio rehabilitation center in Warm Springs, Georgia (about an hour's drive from Plains, as it happens), where he swam, played, and interacted with numerous children and other polio sufferers.[6] He sincerely felt their pain, which wound up serving him well in his political career, though at an excruciating cost (he was never cured).

We are thus reminded how much *emotions matter* in political life. Some would say emotions are all that matter: people, including intelligent and educated people, primarily vote with their hearts, not their minds. The psychologist Drew Westen analyzes political campaigns using the neuroscientific model of the brain as "*networks of association*, bundles of thoughts, feelings, images, and ideas that have become connected over time."[7] Cognition, emotion, imagination, and motivation closely intertwine.[8] Bill Clinton was a master orchestrator of the process, demonstrating "extraordinary emotional intelligence and gut-level, implicit horse sense."[9]

---

6. See the History Channel's three-part series *FDR* (2023), produced by Doris Kearns Goodwin, based on her *Leadership*, 39–67, 160–81, 273–305. Roosevelt built a modest home in Warm Springs. This "Little White House" became his favorite retreat spot through the years and the place where he died in 1945. Not incidentally, Jimmy Carter formally launched his presidential campaign here (J. Alter, *His Very Best*, 265).

7. Westen, *Political Brain*, 3 (emphasis original).

8. Cf. Maiz, "Political Mind."

9. Westen, *Political Brain*, 7.

Ethan Canin's novel *America America* focuses on the presidential run of a powerful US senator from New York named Henry Bonwiller. One of his aides comes to realize firsthand "the primacy of emotion in politics.... If I learned one thing over my time with Henry Bonwiller, it's that mass politics is an emotional struggle above all, a primal battle that is more charismatic and animalistic than either ethical or reasoned."[10] That perhaps puts the matter too sharply. I would like to think that charisma and passion can complement and enrich ethics and reason, but there's little doubt that much of the time, especially in politics, "the emotional tail wags the rational dog."[11]

How, then, does Jesus deal with this mass "emotional struggle" in his day? We've seen that Luke's Jesus is a straight-talking teacher of ethical principles. He may be fairly characterized as a coolheaded man of his word, the Word (*logos*) of God, a man of consummate logic. But that doesn't fully characterize him. He also has a penchant, as we've seen, for "slant" parables and paradoxes. And he's no pure rationalist. He feels plenty, as real humans do. And he's no Stoic guru who aims to keep all emotions on a short, tight leash. He knows that emotions matter, for good and ill. To riff on a well-known christological text from the KJV of John's Gospel, "The Word (*Logos*) became flesh and *felt* among us" (John 1:14).[12]

As with power, so with emotion, the critical issue concerns how Jesus *uses* emotions. Pathological, antipathetic (anti-pathos) strongmen prey mercilessly on vulnerable people's emotions to gain maximal power over them. (Act *like* you feel the people's pain, but never act *for* them, at least not much. That would just spoil them, the pathetic brats, and spoil your schemes for dominance.) But just as Jesus spurns the devil's strongman political power schemes (Luke 4:1–13, discussed in strategy 2), he eschews callous emotional manipulative strategies. On the positive side, he meshes his emotional energy with his Spirit-power "for doing good and healing all who were oppressed by the devil" (Acts 10:38). Emotions are powerful motivators of human behavior. Jesus uses his passions to drive compassionate ministry.[13]

Jesus's two signature parables in Luke, discussed in strategy 6, model intense inner feelings of sympathy that move (e/motivate) characters to extraordinary acts of care and mercy: the Samaritan traveler is "moved

10. Canin, *America*, 394.
11. Haidt, "Emotional Dog"; Haidt, *Righteous Mind*, 27–51.
12. Spencer, "And the Word 'Felt.'"
13. Spencer, *Passions*, 171–205.

with compassion (*esplanchnisthē*)" to go the extra mile to aid a Jewish victim of robbery and battery (10:33–35); likewise, the father is "filled [or moved] with compassion (*esplanchnisthē*)" to welcome his wayward son back home with a flurry of embracive activity (15:20–23). Elsewhere Luke applies this passion-action verb to Jesus's outreach to a grieving widow at the funeral of her only son: "When the Lord [Jesus] saw her, he was moved with compassion [*esplanchnisthē*] for her," prompting him to stop the proceedings, raise the son to new life, and restore "him to his mother" (7:13–15). Seeing-Feeling-Acting: that is the core network of Jesus's compassionate campaign.

In Mark's version of feeding the five thousand in the desert, Jesus is said to have "compassion [*esplanishthē*] on them, because they were like sheep without a shepherd" (Mark 6:34). Such fellow-feeling moves Jesus to teach and feed the vulnerable crowd, even as Jesus's apostles urge him to send them away. Though Luke's account of this incident lacks Mark's emotional and pastoral touches, Luke's Jesus later tells a short story about a shepherd who spares no effort in seeking and rescuing a lost sheep "in the wilderness," presaging the longer parable of the compassionate father who wholeheartedly welcomes home his wayward son (Luke 15:3–7, 11–32).

Though Jesus himself never marries or has children, is never robbed and abandoned on the roadside, and never works as an actual shepherd, he overflows with deep feeling for bereaved widows, mothers, and fathers; for imperiled travelers; and for wandering creatures and search parties off the beaten paths. What he lacks in direct empathetic experience, he makes up for in deliberate sympathetic action. The proof of true pathos is in performances of compassionate service.[14] Talk about "feeling your pain" is nothing but a cheap political move to lure voters if it doesn't motivate concrete actions and policies to alleviate pain.

PRESSING THE FLESH

Successful campaigns must reach out and touch people in ways they can feel deep down. This can involve literally shaking hands down the rope line, slapping backs at banquets and barbecues, pressing your case by

---

14. George W. Bush campaigned and won on a platform of "compassionate conservativism." The extent to which the Bush administration implemented this compassionate agenda may be debated, but its effective program to tackle the HIV crisis in Africa, launched in 2003 and still going strong, merits bipartisan support. See Schreiber, "Bush's anti-HIV program."

pressing as much flesh as possible (and socially acceptable). But such outreach can also be virtual. Though Franklin's Roosevelt disability did not stop him, as both candidate and president, from traversing the country to meet the people, it proved most practical—and effective—for him to enter the living rooms of millions of Americans via public radio, as if sitting and chatting with them and holding their hands beside their hearths. Through these famous "fireside chats," he galvanized the nation to deal anew (New Deal) with the ravages of economic depression and world war.

The potential for virtual campaigning has expanded exponentially with the revolution in social media technology. This proved especially valuable during the 2020 pandemic election, when physical contact was severely limited. Just as well, perhaps, given both presidential candidates' dicey reputations as touchers: Trump for being too "grabby," Biden too "handsy." It also suited Trump's media prowess and self-confessed germaphobia. He didn't win in the end (except in his own mind) but still managed to pull in over 74 million votes (give or take 11,780 votes in Georgia, wink-wink), almost 47 percent of the electorate. And most all Americans continued to "feel" Trump's influence, for good or ill.

In Jesus's world, Caesar was far and away the top influencer. His image was plastered on coins, statues, monuments, and plaques with captions touting his highness, majesty, kingship, and, of course, his gracious benevolence to the people. The historian Mary Beard notes the "reasonable guess" of 25,000–50,000 statues of Caesar Augustus alone scattered across the empire. The emperor brand extended to merchandise, including cookie molds and earrings designed to hang from the ear with Caesar's image upright.[15] Caesars and their cohorts controlled the media and the military, with few qualms about violently squashing free-spirited rebels and "free press" critics or "enemies of the people," as demagogues disingenuously call them.

While Jesus's words and actions advancing God's right-making rule may be fairly viewed as undermining Caesar's rule, Jesus never openly denounces Caesar and marshals no armed revolution. His famous response to a public question about tax policy (while holding up a borrowed coin stamped with Caesar's image)—"Give to Caesar the things that are Caesar's and to God the things that are God's" (20:20–26) may suggest a subtle jab along the lines of "Give Caesar his due—his just deserts!" But it's hardly a broadside attack on imperial authority. Over the

---

15. Beard, *Emperor*, 15–16; cf. 43–44, 325–43.

course of Christian history, religious and political authorities (naturally) have interpreted this statement as endorsing congenial "church and state" relations (see strategy 10). Be that as it may, by week's end in Luke story, Jesus is accused (falsely) of "inciting our nation, forbidding us to pay taxes to Caesar and saying that he himself is the Messiah," and duly crucified as an insurrectionist (23:1–2).

As we've seen, Luke's Jesus mounts no big publicity campaign, no glitzy media blitz. He generally shies away from the spotlight and grandiose claims about his messiahship. He does stage a final dramatic entry into Jerusalem and disruptive demonstration in the temple (19:28–48), but these are not as "triumphal" as often assumed (see strategy 11). Jesus is not very media savvy; he doesn't plan huge rallies and blockbuster events for mass appeal. But along the way, he does *touch* people at many levels—physically, emotionally, spiritually—at their critical points of need—and welcomes those who *touch him* to extract his healing power (6:18–19; 8:43–48) or express their loving gratitude for his ministry (7:36–50).[16]

Notice various occasions on the "campaign" trail where Jesus lays healing hands upon needy persons:

- When "a man covered with skin disease" approaches Jesus, begging to be healed of his skin malady, Jesus "*stretch[es] out his hand, touch[es] him*," and cures him. Jesus thus treats the man's physical infirmity and ritual (not moral) "uncleanness." Respecting the Torah's restorative process, Jesus urges the healed man to "go, show yourself to the priest, as Moses commanded." Moreover, Jesus commands him to tell no one about his miracle, which he understandably ignores. How could he help *not* testifying to Jesus's power! But again, Jesus does not seek publicity (5:12–15).

- In the funeral procession in Nain mentioned above, Jesus is motivated by compassion to step forward and *touch* the coffin of a widow's deceased son. He then commands the young man to rise up and restores "him to his mother"—alive and well (7:11–15). Not long thereafter, Jesus similarly resuscitates a synagogue leader's only daughter from her deathbed, "*taking her by the hand*" and telling her to "Get up!" He then issues another gag order, this time to the

---

16. To be sure, in 8:43–48 Jesus is first shocked by a bleeding woman's unauthorized touch from behind that draws out his curative power; but he soon welcomes her as "daughter" and commends her faith; see Spencer, "Woman's Touch."

girl's overjoyed parents. Little chance of that happening, but Jesus tries again to curtail public attention (8:49–54).

- Upon seeing a woman with a severely bent back in a synagogue on the Sabbath, Jesus summons her, *lays hands* on her, and enables her to right herself for the first time in eighteen years. This elective Sabbath medical operation provokes the synagogue to denounce Jesus as a Torah-breaker. But Jewish teachers routinely debated what did and did not count as forbidden work on the Sabbath.[17] In any case, no one seriously questioned the duty of leading working animals like donkeys and oxen to water or rescuing a child or ox from a ditch on the Sabbath (Jesus cites these examples in 13:15; 14:5). Accordingly, by restoring a scoliotic woman's health and releasing her from crippling "bondage" on the Sabbath (see 13:11, 16), Jesus reinforces God's first-order principles of creation and liberation for which the Sabbath was instituted (Gen 2:1–3; Exod 20:8–11).

Jesus thus presses the flesh and bones of afflicted persons—even dead persons—to benefit them, not to bolster his popularity. We might also note, however, that Jesus does not press himself *upon* people. Recall the incident in Luke 7:1–10 (discussed in strategy 3), where a Roman centurion wants Jesus to heal his beloved slave without coming to the house for hands-on therapy—not because the centurion is a snob but quite the opposite—because he does not deem himself and his household "worthy" of Jesus's presence. Jesus respects the man's wishes, commends his faith, and heals the ill servant long distance. He does not need to make some grand, high-handed entrance into the officer's quarters. He's willing to meet and help people where they're at, even if it means *not* meeting them directly.

KISSING BABIES

The odd electioneering habit of kissing babies has a rather odd origin, according to presidential campaign historian Paul Boller, with Andrew Jackson's stumping in New Jersey in 1833. Reportedly, at one stop a mother pressed her baby boy into the president's arms, prompting his remark, addressed as much to the crowd as the mother: "Ah! There is a

---

17. Cf. *m. Hag.* 1:8—"The rules about the Sabbath . . . are like mountains hanging on a hair, for [teaching] of Scripture [thereon] is scanty and the rules many" (Danby, *Mishnah*, 212).

fine specimen of American childhood! Note the brightness of that eye, the great strength of those limbs, and the sweetness of those lips." That's as far as Jackson was willing to go, but he sensed the political moment called for something more. He handed the baby to his traveling companion and Secretary of War John Eaton and ordered Eaton to "Kiss him!" as the president dashed away.[18]

This political puckery began to catch on as a campaign ritual, proving even more effective when a presidential candidate did the deed himself rather than passing it off. It wasn't everyone's cup of tea, however. Still sensitive about his 1960 loss to John F. Kennedy, owing in large measure to his dour image, Richard Nixon chose to spin his grim persona into a virtue during a *Life* magazine interview in 1968: "This is going to be an extremely intensive campaign. But I have a certain celebrity value. And I don't have to go from kaffeeklatsch to kaffeeklatsch. I won't wear a silly hat, or kiss a lady or a baby. I won't ski down a hill or do any stunting like that—I'd look like a jerk. A candidate must not be contrived."[19] He won the presidency this time and again in 1972—but lost the image battle for all time with his criminal stunts and cover-ups. Perhaps he should have kissed a few babies along the way.

Why has kissing babies become a campaign strategy? *Life* magazine answered in its July 4, 1960, issue: "There is only one excuse for baby kissing: it works. The aim, whether the pol is a machine-backed hack or a machine-bucking amateur, is to win the votes."[20] Thus American pragmatism has ruled: forget the whingey, sticky, drooly, germy tots—votes at all costs, baby!

Luke's Jesus kisses no babies. It wasn't a thing in his day, and remember, he wasn't a good campaigner anyway—which in no way casts him in Nixon's mold. In fact, though having no children and calling disciples to leave children behind to follow him (14:26; cf. 18:29; more on this jolting practice in strategy 8), Jesus proves remarkably embracive of infants, including sick children he heals and restores to their distraught parents.

One of the multiple times in Luke the disciples' egos swell, this time after returning from a successful exorcizing mission in Jesus's name (10:17), Jesus brings them down to earth by reminding them they would be nothing without God's wisdom and power. Fortunately, God delights in gracing the least wise and powerful, epitomized in helpless *infants*

18. Boller, *Presidential Campaigns*, 58; cf. C. Klein, "Election 101."
19. Wainwright, "One More Try," 62.
20. Capa, "Politics," 13; cf. Friedersdorf, "Why Do Parents?"

(10:21–24). Jesus had recently illustrated this basic lesson by placing a "little child . . . by his side" and urging his deputies to "welcome" this little one as they welcome Jesus himself and God who sent him. Jesus effectively says, "We're a package deal, this child, I, and God. We're in this together, side by side. You can't take one without the other two. This little one commonly regarded as 'least' is in fact 'greatest' in God's book." Jesus delivers this lesson to settle the disciples' foolish (childish) argument about which of them is "the greatest" (9:46–48).

Unfortunately, they make little progress in grasping this point. Toward the end of Jesus's ill-fated journey to Jerusalem, "people were bringing *even infants to him that he might touch them.*" This time the disciples don't simply overlook these little ones but "sternly order" their caregivers to stop bothering Jesus with baby business. We have bigger matters to tend to, stronger men's work to tackle. But it doesn't happen to be *Jesus's work*. As he calls the caregivers and babies "to himself" (connoted by the verb *proskaleomai*), he snaps back at the disciples, "Let the children come to me, and do not stop them!" (18:15–16).

Why? Not for a photo op, not for the appearance of caring about childcare (the kids can't vote but their parents and grandparents sure can!). Not for a sideshow to keep people's interest and create a little buzz. No. For Jesus, this *is* the main event, the main *kingdom* event no less, the whole point of politics in God's realm: "For it is to such as these"—these little ones—"that the kingdom of God belongs" (18:16). The kingdom of God *is* (*estin*) theirs. It is their domain, where they rule and thrive with God. Jesus's messianic mission is all about them. It's all *for* them and for those who identify with them as codependents on God's gracious love and care. Those who decline to identify "as a little child" need not apply for kingdom entrance (18:17).

Dividing the Electorate

> **Strategy 8**
>
> *Offer the people a clear choice to follow God's way wholeheartedly, even if such commitment sparks opposition from family members, friends, and associates. Do not seek to divide the electorate simply to create chaos and demonize opponents. But do expect considerable pushback from those threatened by reformative change, and do not dilute the "evangelical" message and mission—at once both inclusive and incisive—in order to win elections.*

AT THE RISK OF hyperbolizing and catastrophizing, I'll go ahead and claim that I've never seen American politics more divided along hard partisan lines than in the last decade. Of course, I wasn't around during the Civil War era, and my current judgments reflect my limited point of view. But they seem to be shared by many others. We may agree on little else, but we agree that we live in an extraordinarily polarized time.

For many of us, it gets personal, affecting our families, friends, and other fellowships. To keep us from crying, we joke about blowouts around the Thanksgiving dinner table and banning blowhard Joe or Jenny from the Christmas party. Such partisan politics increasingly invade our religious sanctuaries, too, turning these havens of rest into hotbeds of rancor. Safe places are hard to find outside tightly controlled echo chambers.

Polarization is the strongman politician's playground. It is the second of Naím's 3P's of autocratic rule (flanked by populism and post-truth):

> Polarization solidifies the 3P autocrat's grip over his followers. A polarized polity, where supporters can be expected to fall in line automatically, allows a leader to exercise power with far fewer

fetters than before. And, crucially, polarization can be sharpened unilaterally simply by heightening the rhetoric on one side of the divide and trusting the backlash on the other side to do half of the work. That's why polarization acts as such a centripetal force, concentrating power that would disperse and decay in its absence.[1]

Similarly, Ruth Ben-Ghiat comments, "Authoritarians hold appeal when society is polarized, or divided into two opposing ideological camps, which is why they do all they can to exacerbate strife."[2] *Divide et Impera*, Divide and Conquer, a classic Machiavellian campaign strategy in war and politics, in politics *as* war.[3]

Is polarization, however, the only path to political power? Must candidates, even those with more sensitive souls and compassionate aims, play dirty to win? That's just the nature of the game: politics as a blood sport. In her trenchant analysis of narcissistic, nationalist strongmen since Mussolini, Ben-Ghiat slips in an encouraging counterexample from Turkish politics.[4] Since 2014, President Recep Tayyip Erdoğan has held a strong right-wing grip on Turkish government, bolstered by a cadre of toady officials. But in the 2019 Istanbul mayoral election, an unlikely candidate pulled off a stunning upset. Ekrem Imamoğlu, a devout Muslim, brought his campaign of "radical love" that melded compassionate faith with liberal policies directly to the people of Istanbul and won over enough of them to defeat Erdoğan's handpicked candidate. In the wake of trumped-up allegations of voter fraud, the city board controlled by Erdoğan's cronies demanded a new election. President Erdoğan, himself a former mayor of Istanbul, called in all his chips and threatened to imprison Imamoğlu for slandering other politicians. Imamoğlu won this second round even more convincingly, garnering over 54 percent of the vote.

How did he do it? Imamoğlu's playbook was a fifty-page manual written by his campaign manager, Ates Ilyas Bassoy, entitled *Radical Love Book*, if you can believe it.[5] Sounds like an album from Woodstock. But

1. Naím, *Revenge of Power*, 32.
2. Ben-Ghiat, *Strongmen*, 8.
3. "A captain ought to contrive with every art to divide the forces of his enemy, either by making him suspect his own men in whom he confides, or by giving him a cause that has him separate his own troops and, through this, become weaker" (Machiavelli, *Art of War* 6.187); cf. Posner, Spier, and Vermeule, "Divide and Conquer," 431.
4. Ben-Ghiat, *Strongmen*, 219–20.
5. Ashdown, "'Radical Love Book.'"

Imamoğlu is no hippie protester or sappy politician. He simply practiced what he preached, calmly and consistently. Though "they want conflict from us, we will insist upon embracing each other," he pleaded. He eschewed the politics of fearmongering and wedge-driving in favor of promoting radical inclusion and compassion, "radical," that is, by comparison with the extremist exclusionary and divisive Erdoğan regime. Imamoğlu is clear-eyed about strongmen's aims to pit people against each other: "Polarization is a universal problem. All around the world, populism is used to divide and rule. But I believe we can turn this trend upside down."[6]

Good for him. God bless him. In his own way, Luke's Jesus advances a campaign of "radical love," including love of enemies, as we've seen. Yes, but. Yet again, Jesus ill fits designer labels, as he proves to be not only an embracive, magnetizing uniter but also a disruptive, polarizing divider—by intention as well as incidental consequence. This Messiah sent by God "to guide our feet into the way of peace" and bring "peace on earth" (1:79; 2:14) announces midway into his campaign, "Do you think that I have come to bring peace to the earth?" Well, yes, actually, that's just what we've been led to think so far. Yet he now answers the question in the negative, "No, I tell you, but rather division!" (12:51).

Is Jesus suddenly shifting strategy? He wouldn't be the first or last desperate politician to do so. No more Mr. Nice Guy. Weak doesn't win. Time to fight fire with fire (see 12:49). Peace through strength, brute bullish (bully) strength if necessary—and it seems necessary to get the job done. So much for radical love.

And so much for Jesus as a nonauthoritarian anti-strongman? I don't think so, not by a long shot. But we can't just bulldoze our way through counter-evidence. We must honestly confront elements of Luke's portrait of Jesus as a polarizing Messiah with corrosive effects on families and the wider body politic. For now, we need to pause the Kumbaya chorus and face the sharper music honestly and critically.

THE HOUSE DIVIDED

In the summer of 1858, the Illinois Republican State Convention in Springfield nominated Abraham Lincoln to be their candidate for the US

---

6. Cited in Ben-Ghiat, *Strongmen*, 219–20; cf. Imamoğlu, "How I won"; Ingleby, "Turkish Opposition Leader."

Senate against the Democrat Stephen A. Douglas. The burning issue of the time was whether slavery should be allowed to persist in southern states and allowed to expand into western frontier states and territories. The state of the Union, indeed, the fate of the Union, rested on the people's resolve to settle this bitterly divisive issue. Lincoln addressed the matter head-on in his convention speech:

> If we could first know where we are, and whither we are tending, we could then better judge what to do, and how to do it. We are now far into the fifth year, since a policy was initiated, with the avowed object, and confident promise, of putting an end to slavery agitation. Under the operation of that policy, that agitation has not only, not ceased, but has constantly augmented. In my opinion, it will not cease, until a crisis shall have been reached, and passed.
> "A house divided against itself cannot stand."
> I believe this government cannot endure, permanently half slave and half free. I do not expect the Union to be dissolved—I do not expect the house to fall—but I do expect it will cease to be divided. It will become all one thing, or all the other.[7]

One side or another must carry the day. We simply cannot survive such a bitterly divided polity. Lincoln lost the Senate battle but won the war when he assumed the presidency in 1861. Rather, he began to win the war—a terrible full-scale war that tragically erupted between the states—ill-named the Civil War, a bloody testament to rank incivility. The Union held, but Lord, at such a cost: over 600,000 American lives, including Lincoln's, which ended in assassination a little over a month after Lee surrendered to Grant at Appomattox. Officially divided no more, but barely standing. We're still trying to find common ground today.

"A house divided against itself cannot stand." Lincoln and everyone who heard him knew he was quoting red-letter words of Jesus from the Gospels (Mark 3:25; cf. Matt 12:25; Luke 11:17). Jesus was embroiled in his own battle against enslavement in his era. Not, we must admit, against the widespread institution of slavery in the Roman world.[8] Jesus never directly calls for abolition of slavery, still less a slave revolt. His parables feature various household slave scenarios illustrating various points about God's kingdom—including a more reciprocal point about masters

---

7. Lincoln, "House Divided."

8. On slavery in ancient Rome, see Joshel, *Slavery*; in early Christian practice, see Glancy, *Slavery in Early Christianity*; Glancy, *Slavery as Moral Problem*.

serving slaves (Luke 12:35–38; cf. 15:11–32; 16:1–13; 19:11–27)—all the while allowing the slave system to stand.

This ambivalent perspective on slavery in Gospel literature has complicated Christian America's politics, as Lincoln candidly lamented in his Second Inaugural Address in Washington, DC, March 4, 1965 (a month before Appomattox and then six more days to Ford's Theater): "Both [sides] read the same Bible and pray to the same God, and each invokes His aid against the other. . . . The prayers of both could not be answered. That of neither has been answered fully."[9] Unwittingly and unconscionably, President Trump parodied this message, claiming there were "good people on both sides" of the conflict that erupted in the summer of 2017 over the removal of Confederate monuments in Charlottesville, Virginia, even though only one side—white supremacists under their "Unite the Right" banner—resorted to violence, including murdering (by vehicular assault) a counter-protester.[10]

We might wish that Luke had cast Jesus in a bolder abolitionist role. Nevertheless, as we've seen, his commitment to a broad liberative agenda is evident from the start of his campaign (4:16–21; see strategy 3). And in fact, the conflict that sparks his "divided" realm comment (11:17) focuses on a prominent dimension of his emancipatory mission: freeing victims of *demonic* enslavement. Up to this point, Jesus has demonstrated his authority over evil spirits that afflict one man in a Capernaum synagogue and many others in the area (4:31–37, 40–41), a man in the Gerasa region driven mad by a "Legion" of torturous demons (8:26–39), and a boy who suffers terrible demon-induced convulsions (9:37–43). In the present case, Jesus expels a demon that throttles its victim's voice (11:14).[11]

In Jesus's culture, physical and mental illness were commonly attributed to demonic infection. Accordingly, healing operations often necessitated exorcisms. By ousting demons from their positions of malevolent control over people's lives, Jesus releases the sufferers and restores their health and well-being. Who could object to that? There's always someone ready to make a vice out of a virtue, a villain out of a savior, especially if that savior gets too popular and influential. The crowds' amazement over Jesus's restoring speech to the demon-choked man signals a boost in Jesus' political power, even though that's not what he seeks. But those who covet popularity and authority can't let Jesus go unchecked.

9. Lincoln, "Second Inaugural."
10. See Richardson, *Democracy*, 111–16.
11. See Klutz, *Exorcism Stories*.

Since Jesus's critics can't argue with the results of his actions—every sound and word from the formerly mute man testifies to Jesus's benevolent power—they attack the means and motives behind his actions, throwing in malicious deviant-labeling for good measure: "He casts out demons by Beelzebul, the ruler of demons" (11:15). Quick, turn the tables, cast suspicion, attack the apparent demon-deliverer as a demon confederate and co-conspirator—even worse, Demon-King Beelzebul's (a.k.a. Satan) right-hand man (11:18)! Demonizing your rivals, casting them as dangerous extremists, is a classic strongman strategy. Blunt your own extremist ideology and agenda, make it seem normal, by branding others as the real invidious outliers.[12]

We enlightened moderns might think we're beyond crass rhetoric invoking mental illness and demonic influence. Think again. Soon after Donald Trump was indicted by a federal grand jury (August 1, 2023) on multiple counts related to defrauding the American public about the 2020 election results, he ripped into Special Counsel Jack Smith (leading the prosecution) and Congresswoman Nancy Pelosi (former Speaker of the House) on his social media account. He continued brandishing his chosen moniker for the special prosecutor as "Deranged Jack Smith," and in response to Pelosi's gibe that he looked like a "scared puppy" after the indictment was handed down, Trump blurted,

> I purposely didn't comment on Nancy Pelosi's very weird story concerning her husband,[13] but now I can because she said something about me, with glee, that was really quite vicious. "I saw a scared puppy," she said, as she watched me on television, like millions of others, that didn't see that. I wasn't "scared." Nevertheless, how mean a thing to say! She is a Wicked Witch whose husband's journey from hell starts and finishes with her. She is a sick & demented psycho who will someday live in HELL![14]

I'm not the Devil [no one said you were]—you are! Calling Smith or Pelosi "Beelzebul" (if he knew the term) would have added an apt flourish, especially in all caps.

Jesus counters the "Beelzebul" charge with his own sharp rhetoric based, however, more in logic and evidence than in lashing out and

---

12. See Snyder, *Tyranny*, 99–102.

13. Her husband Paul Pelosi was brutally attacked in his San Francisco home on October 28, 2022 by a right-wing extremist who intended to take Speaker Pelosi hostage (she wasn't home).

14. *Truth Social* website, August 6, 2023.

name-calling. To be sure, he bolsters his defensive argument with a divisive rally cry: "Whoever is not with me is against me, and whoever does not gather with me scatters" (11:23). Yet Jesus's ultimate goal is not to divide the world—divided social and political systems *cannot stand*—and his vision encompasses the whole world of the Creator-Redeemer God. Jesus seeks not to carve out his own little fiefdom but to bring the world into restorative harmony with the very "kingdom of God" (11:20). Notice how Jesus fleshes out his case in Luke 11:17–22.

Wielding God's Finger to Reinforce God's Kingdom

Again, Jesus's case rests on logic and evidence, not on labels and lies. He starts by exposing the nonsense of the calumny that he expels Satan's demonic agents *by* Satan's authority. That makes no sense. Satan may be sinister, but he's not stupid. Why would he deliberately defeat his own forces? "If Satan . . . is divided against himself, how will his kingdom stand?" (11:18). If Jesus were Satan's loyal chief officer, as his accusers claim, why would he attack Satan's realm and liberate Satan's prisoners?

Moreover, Jesus reminds his prosecutors that they support their own network of exorcist-healers (11:19), whom Jesus is also happy to support, under whatever label. Health care should not be a partisan battleground. Earlier when Jesus's disciples bristle about some outsider who was appropriating Jesus's name to cast out demons, Jesus shoots back, "Do not stop him, for whoever is not against you is for you" (9:49–50)—a notable, embracive counterpart to his more divisive "whoever is not with me is against me" remark in the present incident (11:23). This follows Jesus's deft turning of his accusers' charge of Satan-dalliance back on their own heads: "Now if I cast out the demons by Beelzebul, by whom do *your exorcists* cast them out? Therefore they will be *your judges*" (11:19). Sharp, effective counterpunch, to be sure, but not mean and abusive: Jesus values his opponents' healers and judges rather than vilifying them as witches and psychos.[15]

On the evidential side, Jesus calls his interlocutors to consider his exorcising track record. The deliverance cases mentioned above may be offered as Exhibits A-D (we may add the subsequent case of freeing the back-bent, Satan-bound woman [13:10-17] as Exhibit E). All of these

---

15. More literally, the text reads, "your *sons* [*huoi*] who cast out demons" (11:19), using the respectful "sons," not "bastards" or some other derisive label.

demonstrate Jesus's dynamic advance of the *saving realm of God* overcoming and outstripping the enslaving realm of Satan. These are local, specific cases with national, cosmic effects.

This is the stuff of exodus, indeed, the historic exodus of God's enslaved people in a new key. "If it is by the finger of God that I cast out the demons, then the kingdom of God has come upon you" (11:20)—a kingdom of liberating salvation not dominating oppression. The arresting *finger of God* image derives straight from Exodus and Deuteronomy, casting Jesus in a Mosaic mold.

> And the magicians said to Pharaoh, "This is the finger of God!" (Exod 8:19)
>
> And the LORD gave me the two stone tablets written with the finger of God. (Deut 9:10)

The first reference comes in the context of Moses's demand that Pharaoh release God's people from bondage. To shake Pharaoh out of his stubbornness, Moses inflicts plagues on the land, starting with turning the Nile River into blood, followed by unleashing a horde of frogs. However, Pharaoh's "magicians" match both acts by employing "their secret arts" (Exod 7:22; 8:7). But the third plague—a dust storm of gnats—proves more than Egypt's wizards can handle, prompting their admission that Moses wields the true *finger of God* that Pharaoh must not cross (8:16-19). Effectively, the God of Israel has more power in his finger than Pharaoh can muster in his entire realm. Yet Pharaoh continues to resist. He still has his army and weaponry, not that they accomplish much in a gnat storm! Or in a fly, thunder, or locust storm, as subsequent plagues generate.

But the point is not a power showdown revealing who has the biggest finger or strongest thumb under which to crush one's enemies. The point, again, is the *goal* and *use* of power. Strongman Pharaoh uses his power to conquer, destroy, and enslave. That's how he builds his kingdom. But Moses's God only uses lethal power against Egypt as a last resort (12:29-32; 14:1-31). The ultimate goal is freedom for God's people, freedom to worship God and live peacefully under God's benevolent rule (3:18; 7:16)—not conquest of Egypt or any other earthly realm.[16]

---

16. Admittedly, biblical history does not always live up to this pacific ideal, most notoriously in the genocidal conquest of Jericho, supposedly ordered by God, in Joshua 6. Also, the tenth plague—even as a last measure taken against an obdurate tyrant—raises a hard theological and ethical question: Is God justified (theodicy) in killing "all the firstborn in the land of Egypt" (Exod 12:29)?

The second reference comes from Moses's review of God's dramatic revelation at Mount Sinai after freeing the enslaved Israelites. Here God gives the Torah, the way of life for God's redeemed people, which Moses receives in the form of "two stone tablets written with the finger of God" (Deut 9:10).[17] In this mode, God's mighty finger enacts and enforces the *rule of law*. But this is not crushing, enslaving law, trading one tyrant's strong-arm control for another's. To the contrary. Though, again, God has more raw power in his finger than Pharaoh has in his whole body, God's finger etches a *liberative rule of law* rooted in love of God (6:5) and love of neighbor. Though not abolishing slavery and household servitude, the law insists upon compassionate treatment of enslaved persons. Notice the centerpiece of the Ten Commandments:

"Observe the Sabbath day and keep it holy as the LORD your God commanded you. Six days you shall labor and do all your work. But the seventh day is a Sabbath to the LORD your God; you shall not do any work—you, or your son or your daughter, or *your male or female slave*, or your ox or your donkey, or any of your livestock, or the resident alien in your towns, so that *your male and female slave may rest as well as you*. Remember that *you were a slave in the land of Egypt*, and the LORD your God brought you out from there with a mighty hand and an outstretched arm (Deut 5:12-15)"—and an *uplifting and right-guiding finger*, we might add.

Jesus counterpunches with a laser finger, not an iron fist. He strategically wields the finger of God like a surgeon, cutting out malignant demonic tumors afflicting vulnerable people so that people might *stand together* in God's free and flourishing realm.

Storming the Strongman's Castle to Secure God's Kingdom

Complementing Satan's role as ruler of a diabolical kingdom is his image as a "fully armed" *strongman* with demonic guards stationed to protect his "castle" and "property"—his *stronghold* (11:21). This portrait accentuates Satan's power to possess (enslave, exploit) people's lives in league with earthly rulers who impose authoritarian control over their subjects. The term for "castle" (*aulē*) can also mean "palace" or the "courtyard" surrounding a palatial residence. Jesus is later brought under arrest to "the high priest's house" in Jerusalem with its large "courtyard" (*aulē*, 22:54-55), where he is mocked and beaten before being interrogated by

---

17. See Wall, "Finger of God."

the Jewish council and handed over to Pontius Pilate for the final verdict of crucifixion (22:63–23:25). Pilate had likely taken over one of Herod the Great's Jerusalem palaces for his military headquarters and tribunal (Praetorium).[18] Jesus has no place to lay his head (9:58), let alone a palace.[19] Palatial power is arrayed against him, and he storms no actual castle to seize control.

But Jesus will not let Satan's "deep state" domain stand intact. In the cosmic-spiritual realm—with very real earthly-political effects—Jesus implicitly invokes his "stronger one" role: "But when one stronger than he [the satanic strongman] attacks him and overpowers him, he takes away his armor in which he trusted and divides his plunder" (11:22).

Does Jesus, then, ultimately claim the Strongest Man championship and succumb to "might makes right" ideology? Yes—but emphatically on *his own terms*, which is to say *God's terms* in Luke's view, not the rules of the strongman game, which ban cross-bearing from the start. As Jesus treads the seemingly weak, defeatist way of serving, sacrificing, and shouldering the cross, he blazes a new trail of *holy-spiritual* strength; that is, he fulfills his calling, affirmed by John the Baptizer at the start of Jesus's mission, as the "stronger one" (*ischyroteros*) who baptizes "with the *Holy Spirit* and fire" (3:16). "Strongman" Jesus uses his strength to liberate those possessed by powerful, predatory *unholy spirits* under Satan's command.

Moreover, Jesus uses his supreme force to divest strongman Satan of "his armor" and to divide "his plunder" (11:22)—not to pad Jesus's personal protection and prosperity. Jesus aspires to no castle, no hilltop or beachside mansion, no stockpile of weaponry or wealth. Remember—no place to lay his head, no extra suit of clothes, no penny to his name. His "strong" campaign goals—which he not merely shouts as empty promises but shows in his everyday life—promote *disarmament* and *distribution*, securing holistic peace and spreading resources for the common good.

THE COST CALCULATED

Thus far we've seen the division that Jesus's campaign sparks in the cosmic-spiritual realm interlinked with religious-political forces. Jesus's dynamic ministry of driving out evil spirits drives a battering ram through the walls of Satan's metaphorical "castle" and related "houses" of worldly

---

18. Riesner, "Praetorium," 577.
19. Cf. 7:25; Spencer, *What Did Jesus Do?*, 59, 131–36.

power. Jesus divides good from evil, drives out evil oppressors of good people in order to make the world whole. He divides and conquers in order to reconcile the world to its Creator and Redeemer.

That's the panoramic vision of Jesus's polarizing mission. But the divisive effects of his campaign also penetrate nitty-gritty personal, social, and economic dimensions of life, with serious political consequences. We've already seen some fallout in familial and financial matters: Jesus's Nazareth family wants nothing to do with him, and his bare-bones lifestyle scarcely endears him to the business community. This is no way to run a successful campaign. Family values and financial interests are always paramount in voters' minds. Dividing families and divesting funds is a recipe for political disaster. Doesn't Jesus know this?

Yes, and he doesn't seem to care. In fact, he seems quite intentional about dividing people *against* him, deliberately turning away good would-be followers. Notice this shocking sequence on the campaign trail with three prospective supporters: the first says to Jesus, "I will follow you wherever you go"; the second answers Jesus's call with, "Lord, first let me go and bury my father"; the third proclaims, "I will follow you, Lord, but let me first say farewell to those at my home" (9:57–61). One could hardly ask for more commitment than the first one expresses, and the other two make reasonable, even admirable, requests to tend to urgent family business before hitting the road with Jesus.

Yet Jesus puts off all three, setting a staggeringly steep price tag for following him. They must eschew residential comforts (9:58) and ignore normal family obligations, like burying fathers and bidding folk goodbye. "Let the dead bury their own dead" (9:60) sounds as callous as it is absurd. Jesus's political opponents will have a field day with this mal mot. Obviously, Jesus is using hyperbolic rhetoric to encourage top priority support for his movement.[20] But this seems over the top. This "Jesus First" campaign—"Leave Everything to Follow Me"—seems guaranteed to doom him to last place.

Does Jesus mellow a little later in the campaign? Not really. Toward the end of Jesus's final journey to Jerusalem, a "very rich" man approaches him asking for guidance about "eternal life" in God's kingdom (18:18). Unlike other wealthy persons Jesus denounces for their self-aggrandizing conduct (6:24; 12:13–21; 16:19–31; 20:45–21:4), this rich man is a good, Torah-keeping person with a sincere interest in Jesus's mission

---

20. See Spencer, "'Follow Me.'"

(18:20–21). Yet that's not good enough for Jesus: "There is still one thing lacking," Jesus tells the man. "Sell all that you own and distribute the money to the poor, and you will have treasure in heaven; then come, follow me" (18:22). All or nothing. That's more than the rich man can handle, not because he's miserly (one gets the impression he has given alms to the poor and would consider upping his contribution) and not because he is mad at Jesus's audacity. Rather, Luke says that upon hearing Jesus's demand, the rich man "bec[omes] *sad*" (the intensive term *perilypos* suggests "very sad") because, though he truly wants to follow Jesus, he's not ready to part with all his resources (18:23). Who among us not named Saint Francis is?

Jesus candidly acknowledges "how hard" his mission policy is, how "impossibly" high is the cost of following him: "Indeed," he memorably adds, "it is easier for a camel to go through the eye of a needle that for someone who is rich to enter the kingdom of God" (18:24–25). It would also be easier for that camel to be elected Messiah than for Jesus in this extremist mode.

While Jesus does not compromise his "hard" policies for the sake of popularity, he does mitigate them for the sake of solidarity with the needy and potential salvation for all, poor and rich. When Jesus's wider audience (including disciples), stunned over his treatment of this good wealthy religious seeker, asks, "Then who can be saved?" he answers, "What is impossible for mortals is possible for God" (18:26). Jesus is first and foremost an agent of God's magnanimous grace and power. That's good news but still floats in the realm of the "possible," whereas politics deals in hard pragmatic reality. What have you done for me lately? What can you do for me now?

Luke's Jesus offers some other offsetting benefits to the cost of his divisive politics, though one may still fairly question whether the *dividends* are worth it.

Fire and Water

In the middle of his campaign, Jesus suddenly makes a gob-smacking announcement: "I have come to cast fire upon the earth, and how I wish it were already ablaze! I have a baptism with which to be baptized, and what constraint I am under until it is completed!" (12:49–50). Such an odd statement for two reasons: one, at the beginning of his long Jerusalem trek, Jesus *repudiates* James and John's proposal to cast fire on an inhospitable Samaritan village (9:54–55); two, Jesus has already been baptized (3:21–22). Of course, politicians abruptly reverse course and change strategy all the time, especially if they're losing ground.

But Jesus's new course, if that's what it is, doesn't appear designed to bring more people into the fold. Quite the contrary, he seems fixed on creating more division, especially within families: "Do you think that I have come to bring peace to the earth? No, I tell you, but rather division! From now on five in one household will be divided, three against two and two against three; they will be divided father against son and son against father, mother against daughter and daughter against mother, mother-in-law against her daughter-in-law, and daughter-in-law against her mother-in-law" (12:51–53). That's about as partisan as you can get: splitting into household factions across age, gender, and extended family lines—the worst possible recipe for happy holiday dinners. Don't invite Jesus to the party. He'll wreck it for sure.

We indeed "thought" that Luke's Jesus came to pacify rather than polarize a conflicted world, to snuff rather than stoke the fires of enmity. Is he now just venting his frustration over his mixed reception, admitting he's in a hotly contested race with 40 to 60 percent of the population bitterly opposed to his mission? Or worse, is he promising payback for those who resist him, especially his own traitorous family and friends? You tried to throw me over the town cliff in Nazareth! (4:29). It's time for firebrand retribution.

Luke simply lays out this short, raw passage with no apology or explanation. A smart editor—or campaign communications director—might have recommended he leave this part out. But there it is. Politics is a hard-edged, rough-and-tumble business. Deal with it—but perhaps in a diluted form.

I take some refuge in Jesus's baptismal reference. Water beats fire or at least soothes the burn—unless it's the *baptism with fire* (and the Holy Spirit) John announces that Jesus would bring (3:16). But I'm trying to find some grace here, and in the present text Jesus refers neither to his past baptism in the Jordan nor to a future baptism of fiery judgment he will administer. Rather, in this context of division he speaks of another kind of baptism, a constraining, compressing, distressing baptism *he himself will experience*, not execute.[21] Most likely, he's alluding to the chaotic

---

21. The verb *synechō* (lit. "hold together") in 12:50 connotes "constraint," "distress" (Carroll, *Luke*, 273), "experienc[ing] great psychological pressure and anxiety" (Louw

waters of death he feels fast closing around him (cf. Mark 10:38–39), imaging baptism as immersion in death and burial before breaking through to resurrection (cf. Rom 6:1–11). Accordingly, Jesus resists exuding full-blown antagonistic superiority over those divided against him in favor of experiencing wholehearted *sympathetic solidarity* with distressed strugglers in and through the stormy depths (and fiery blasts) of a tumultuous world woefully out of synch with God's righteous realm.

Hate and Love

Still, later on the campaign trail, Jesus appears to undermine sympathetic solidarity with public "hate" speech: "Now large crowds were traveling with him, and he turned and said to them, 'Whoever comes to me and does not *hate* [*misei*] father and mother, wife and children, brothers and sisters, yes, and even life itself, cannot be my disciple. Whoever does not carry the cross and follow me cannot be my disciple'" (Luke 14:25–27). On its face, this may be the worst campaign speech of all time. Jesus seems to try running an option from the strongman's playbook, only to bungle it badly.

Strongmen specialize in the politics of hate, ginning up crowds of beleaguered people against imagined loathsome enemies blamed for all of society's ills. In turn the strongman claims to be the poor people's only true savior, the only one who truly "loves" them and stands up for them. It's a massive ruse, of course. The strongman only cares about his own power, but hate can anesthetize enough of the disaffected masses to believe his lies, embrace him as their champion, and renounce all other loyalties to acclaim his almighty highness.[22] In other words, hate can work politically, sometimes spectacularly.

But that's not what Jesus is doing. When he turns to address the crowd dogging his heels (14:25), he turns more against them than toward them, accentuating the high cost of following his way they must calculate,

---

and Nida, eds., *Greek-English Lexicon*, 315).

22. See Hoffer's classic work on mass movements, *True Believer* (see 36–37 for application to the Jesus movement); cf. Reich, *Common Good*: "Demagogues can use the anger and fear accompanying disruptive change to turn people against one another rather than address the traumas that made them angry in the first place" (28). Further, "Many Americans who for decades have been on a downward economic escalator have become easy prey for demagogues peddling the politics of hate" (92)—an ironic image, in light of Trump's infamous ride down Trump Tower's escalator to launch his first presidential campaign.

just as a tower builder or royal warrior calculates costs of construction or conquest (14:28–32). Towers don't build themselves, and wars don't win themselves: they come at a steep price—but ultimately pay off with great benefit. You can put your name on the tower and throw a big victory party or parade.

But, of course, these prizes go to the head contractor or commander-in-chief, *not* to the bricklayers who break their backs or foot soldiers who lose their lives.[23] You wouldn't catch a strongman dead with a trowel or sword in his hand, though he loves to strut about with a fancy uniform and shiny sword or gun strapped to his belt. He's happy to command the masses to die *for him*, but don't expect him to lead the charge.

Again, if Jesus is suddenly reversing course and trying out a strongman strategy, he's doing a terrible job of it. His choice of images is not pretentious as much as it is preposterous. He's building no physical structures great or small, and he's leading no armies and storming no cities or fortresses. Herod the Great was a master builder and Caesar Augustus a mighty conqueror. Jesus of Nazareth was nowhere near so great or august. And he calls no one to die *for him*. His call to deny self, carry the cross, and follow him (14:26–27) is a call to follow *his cross-bearing lead*, to carry the cross as he does *before* and *for them*, for the people, into the teeth of the oppressive powers that be (cf. 9:21–23, 44; 18:31–33).

We start to sense a sarcastic edge to Jesus's rhetoric about the cost of discipleship to shake gullible people out of their infatuation with tyrants who exploit their volatility and vulnerability. So you're mad at the big bad world and ready to put all your chips on the line for madmen—mad angry and mad crazy narcissists—who claim to be your champion. Don't you recognize the raw deal they offer? You want raw—how about my call for you to hate everyone you love and die on a cross—*with me*. We'll go down together in a blaze of shame! Bombastic hyperbole, bitter irony, biting sarcasm: that's the tone I pick up here, which comes with its own political problems but by no means serves strongman interests.

Back to the hate speech. Authoritarian strongmen are notoriously bitter to the bone. They hate everyone, themselves most of all, though they can't bear to admit it. Hence, they project hatred onto everyone else in a pathetic attempt to garner the love they so desperately need. That's decidedly not Jesus's psychology in Luke or any other Gospel. He's not

---

23. The Trump application is almost too obvious here, with his Trump Tower branding and pining for inauguration and Independence Day military parades in his honor (see Gessen, *Surviving Autocracy*, 29, 155–61).

a seasoned hatemonger. He has strong feelings, even righteous indignation, we might say, for righteous causes, but outright *hatred* doesn't fit his emotional profile.[24] Again, we can't rule out that he loses his cool at an unguarded moment; perhaps his frustration with fickle and foolish crowds temporarily boils over into misanthropic invective. But his call to hate family and self in Luke 14:26 must be evaluated and tempered by his use of "hate" language elsewhere in the narrative, both before and after this text.

In his Sermon on the Plain, Jesus plainly tells his followers that people will "*hate you* . . . exclude you, revile you, and defame you on [his] account" (6:22). The context implies that they will be hated along with Jesus because he sides with the poor and hungry over the rich and satisfied, because he seeks a kingdom that favors the weak over the strong (6:20–26). Remarkably, however, Jesus does not urge his followers to bemoan this "hated" status or retaliate against their haters. Rather, they should consider themselves "blessed" to be part of God's right-making mission opposed by wrongdoers and agents of injustice. This puts them in good company with Israel's venerable prophets who dared to speak truth to abusive power and act with justice and mercy as God's humble servants (6:20–23; cf. Mic 6:8).

Moreover, far from lashing back at their hateful persecutors, Jesus implores his followers, as we've previously noted, "Love your enemies; do good *to those who hate you*; bless those who curse you; pray for those who mistreat you" (Luke 6:27–28)—precisely what Luke's Jesus does from the cross, praying for God to forgive his executioners, "for they do not know what they are doing" (23:34, see strategy 11). Given Jesus's consistent non-retributive disposition—from early in his campaign all the way to the cross—it's hard to take Jesus's hate requirement for discipleship in Luke 14:26 other than in some hyperbolic, ironic, sarcastic sense, as suggested above.

On the financial front, Jesus effectively extends his "hate" rhetoric to money and possessions via his illustration of tower-building costs (14:28) and concluding declaration, "So therefore, none of you can become my disciples if you do not give up all your possessions" (14:33). This fits with other calls to "sell all" for the sake of God's kingdom, including the one issued to a wealthy would-be follower (12:30–33; 18:22). It also fits with one other "hate" statement Jesus makes: "No slave can serve two masters,

---

24. See Spencer, *Passions*, 43–70.

for a slave will either *hate* the one and love the other or be devoted to the one and *despise* the other. You cannot serve God and wealth" (16:13).

American preachers do cartwheels over this verse to protect capitalist interests: Jesus doesn't say you shouldn't make money, a lot of money if you can; just don't love it as much as you love God. That's a nice sentiment but not one Jesus endorses in this text. He sets up a sharp dichotomy between master-powers: God v. Wealth, or God v. Mammon (*Mamōnas*, from Semitic terms for "money/wealth"). Sounds a bit like God v. Beelzebul—a titanic battle between colossal forces of good and evil. Thus personified, "Wealth/Mammon" is no neutral entity but rather a diabolical tyrant hellbent on *possessing* your life and bleeding you dry. It demands all-consuming worship and love and leaves no room for loving God or anyone else. To save your life from Mammon's deathly clutches, you have to resist it, have nothing to do with it, in a word—*hate* it.

Not—note well—hate wealthy *people*, though some "lovers of money" in the audience naturally take offense at Jesus's pronouncement (16:14). But Jesus does not despise these wealth-obsessed persons any more than he denigrates demon-possessed persons. They need to be set free from Master Mammon who has captured their "hearts" (16:15)—that is, their affections, cognitions (mind), and volitions (will). Even so, "You cannot serve God and Wealth" cuts to the bone. No American politician, even the most liberal, would dare say such a thing. Share the wealth, spread the wealth, sure. But by all means, keep growing the economy, increasing wealth and prosperity. Keep serving the interests of wealth (and earning "interest"): the more you make, the more you can share.

To be sure, Jesus's ultimatum about serving God *or* Mammon caps his commentary on the parable in 16:1–8 about a manager fired for dishonest dealing who then uses his financial smarts to "make friends" who welcome him into their homes. Accordingly, Jesus first advises, "And I tell you, make friends [*philous*] for yourselves by means of dishonest wealth [*mamōna*] so that when it is gone they may welcome you into the eternal homes [lit. tents, *skēnas*]" (16:9). It might have been better if Jesus had stopped here instead of proceeding to drop his anti-Mammon bomb. Or maybe not. The parable of the dishonest manager is notoriously difficult to interpret and is scarcely made easier by Jesus's proposition of making friends through dishonest wealth to set yourself up on easy street, whether in earth or heaven. Again, Jesus seems to be trading in irony and sarcasm.[25] "Eternal tents" seem more like a glitzy house of cards ready to fold than a safe house of constant care and comfort.

Loss and Gain

Yet amid Jesus's penchant for parody and paradox that keeps everyone on edge, he manages elsewhere to put a positive spin on his divisive and costly family and financial policies. Following Jesus's stunning dismissal of the rich inquirer who could not divest himself of all his assets, Peter implicitly seeks assurance of the apostles' standing in Jesus's movement: "Look, we have left our homes and followed you" (18:28). Subscript: "We've met your high standards, Jesus. Leaving loved ones and livelihoods has cost us everything. Forgive us for wondering if we made a smart choice. We expect a gigantic (messianic) return on our investment. How's that working out?"

With his disciples teetering on the dizzying hard edge of Jesus's demands, he now speaks positively and practically: "Truly I tell you, there is no one who has left house or wife or brothers or parents or children for the sake of the kingdom of God who will not get back very much more in this age and in the age to come to eternal life" (18:29–30). Though he holds out the promise of future "eternal" reward for all their sacrifice (cf. 6:23; 12:32–33), he's not just offering pie in the sky. He's speaking of a blessed life *in this age*, too, here and now, and applying a calculus of community—a big net gain ("very much more") of loving, caring family members in the household of God.

If natural kin resist God's gracious domain mediated by Christ, they must be left behind, though not permanently. The way remains open for them, as for the rich man Jesus turns away, to come on board. Jesus is not anti-family. Quite the opposite, he welcomes an extended family of mothers and brothers (and sisters) who "hear the word of God and do it" (8:21). Theological affinity transcends biological lineage.

The political philosopher Hannah Arendt concludes her treatise on *The Origins of Totalitarianism* with a nuanced discussion of how authoritarian tyrants and totalitarian regimes prey on "isolated," "lonely," "uprooted" masses: "Totalitarian government, like all tyrannies . . . bases itself on loneliness, on the experience of not belonging to the world at

---

25. See Spencer, *Gospel of Luke*, 174; Porter, "Parable"; Trudinger, "Ire or Irony?"

all, which is one of the most radical and desperate experiences of man."[26] Strongmen are master-traders in exploiting and exacerbating nihilist despair. More recent writers, both right and left of the political center, have decried the "weaponization of loneliness" by authoritarian strongmen and states—a loneliness increasingly jet-fueled by disinformation and hate speech disseminated in cyberspace.[27]

Luke's Jesus is a community builder. It takes a village[28]—actually, villages—and peoples and nations and networks, a worldwide web of sisters and brothers coming together in a mutually supportive constellation. The digital technology is way beyond Luke's Jesus, but the practical theology is there: love God, love your neighbor as yourself (10:27-28)—and love your enemies, too (6:27-36). It's all in the family.

---

26. Arendt, *Origins*, 475 (cf. 474–79).

27. Berkowitz, "Double Weaponization"; cf. Clinton, "Weaponization"; Morabito, *Weaponization*.

28. Clinton, *It Takes a Village*.

Taking a Poll

> **Strategy 9**
> *Gauge the opinion of your most ardent supporters and the wider public concerning your identity and mission ("Who do you say that I am?") and respond accordingly—not to boost your poll numbers by pandering to public opinion—but to clarify your position, correct misperceptions, and make sober predictions about probable outcomes.*

IN THE HOTLY CONTESTED postwar presidential race of 1948, the pollster George Gallup announced a week before the election, "We have never claimed infallibility, but next Tuesday the whole world will be able to see down to the last percentage point how good we are."[1] Or not. Gallup predicted that Republican Thomas Dewey would defeat the Democrat incumbent Harry Truman. Following suit, an early edition of the *Chicago Daily Tribune* on the day after the election brandished the blooper of all blooper headlines: DEWEY DEFEATS TRUMAN. This delighted the actual winning President Truman to no end, as he was photographed "holding up the paper and wearing a grin as wide as the Mississippi River," as the historian Jill Lepore quips.[2] Lesson: Don't count your presidents before all the votes are hatched.

Everyone was determined not to make the same blunder in reporting the next quadrennial election, the 1952 race between General Dwight Eisenhower and Illinois Governor Adlai Stevenson. Enter UNIVAC, the

---

1. Lepore, *These Truths*, 542.
2. Lepore, *These Truths*, 542.

first major electronic computer for business applications in the US.³ Surely it would efficiently process polling and voting data—including comparing early return numbers from the 1944 and 1948 elections—and make solid predictions in the 1952 contest. CBS television and radio coverage on election night, anchored by a young Walter Cronkite with expert analysis from the venerable journalist Edward R. Murrow, included regular check-ins with a reporter who was monitoring UNIVAC. The brainiac machine, however, was sluggish and waffling, which could be interpreted as either cautious or clumsy. Late into the evening, Murrow felt confident enough to declare Eisenhower the victor, while UNIVAC continued to equivocate. But it eventually got on the Ike bandwagon with Murrow and a majority of the country. The famously forthright, no-nonsense Cronkite couldn't resist a little dig at UNIVAC, which "a moment ago still thought there was a 7 to 8 for Governor Stevenson, [but] now says that the chances are 100 to 1 in favor of General Eisenhower. I might note that UNIVAC is running a few moments behind Ed Murrow." (Gallup also made the right call this time, though still off by 4 percent. Ike's margin of victory was large enough to cover this error.)

Murrow himself was more admonitory than amused by the election-reporting drama. In his next-day radio commentary, he preached, "Yesterday the people surprised the pollsters, the prophets, and many politicians. They demonstrated, as they did in 1948, that they are mysterious and their motives are not to be measured by mechanical means." When free people are involved, political outcomes are not "predictable." He further concluded, "We are in a measure released from the petty tyranny of those who assert they can tell us what we think, what we believe, what we will do, what we hope and what we fear, without consulting us—all of us."

I wonder what Murrow would have said about the 2000 (Bush v. Gore), 2016 (Trump v. Clinton), and 2020 (Biden v. Trump) elections. The Supreme Court ultimately decided the will of the people in 2000. Polls and pundits were so sure that Trump couldn't possibly win in 2016 that enough Clinton supporters elected not to vote to help put Trump over the top. (Clinton still received three million more popular votes but not enough in key states to win the electoral college.) And heading into the 2024 election, Trump still denies the results of the 2020 race because, of course, everything—the polls, the press, the political

---

3. For the background information and citations in this paragraph and the next, I'm indebted to Lepore, *These Truths*, 563–65.

establishment—is rigged against him. Democracy is a messy business, and strongmen love messiness.

So forget the polls, except maybe as a parlor game for fun. Put a little money down, even, but don't bet the farm. If you're a serious politician, don't play the game at all. Just hunker down, present your best case to the people, lay out your cards face up on the table, and let the chips fall where they may. Take your cue from Truman, who scoffed at those who predicted a Dewey win long before election night: "I wonder how far Moses would have gone if he'd taken a poll in Egypt. What would Jesus Christ have preached if he'd taken a poll in Israel?"[4] Nice religious touch, Harry (he was a good Baptist, after all), invoking "What Would Jesus Do?" long before WWJD bracelets came into vogue.

What indeed did Jesus care about polls and predictions? He cared deeply about meeting people's critical needs but nothing about entertaining their whimsical opinions, still less pandering to them. His mission was guided from the start by his Divine Father and the Holy Spirit (3:21–22; see strategy 1) and headed, as he increasingly realized, toward the cross, which fit no popular profile for a messianic candidate. If the cross option had been on a polling questionnaire, it would have been unanimously crossed out with a bold X!

Yet just before embarking on his final campaign trek to Jerusalem—which will culminate in his death—Luke's Jesus takes an informal poll, asking his disciples, "Who do the crowds say that I am?" He floats this question at a time when he's "praying alone, with only the disciples near him" (9:18). Thus, as Jesus seeks God's guidance in prayer—maintaining his priority commitment to God's will—he also wants to know what the people are saying about him. On some level, public opinion does matter. As the adolescent "Jesus increased in wisdom . . . and in divine and human favor" (2:52), the mature Jesus appears to court some measure of "human favor," to take some account of popular perspectives along with God's plans.

Why? Luke doesn't say. But I think we can safely assume Jesus's natural interest in knowing how his message and mission are coming across. Further, human identity is inevitably shaped in a social context. Though especially true in more collectivist cultures like eastern Mediterranean societies, even in "rugged individualist" America,[5] we pretentiously self-

---

4. Lepore, *These Truths*, 542.
5. In one of his closing campaign speeches before winning the 1928 presidential election, the successful businessman and mining engineer Herbert Hoover sharply

making men and women remain heavily influenced by our interactions with others. From cradle to grave, we discover who we are through our dealings with other human beings. To some extent, we're who others say we are and see us to be. While Luke's Jesus has a secure sense of self as God's Beloved Son, he is keenly aware of other human beings' influence on his life and wise and humble enough to incorporate that knowledge into his growing self-understanding (2:40, 52). Not shape-shifting to please the crowds, but processing the images the crowds reflect back to him.

In addition to aiding his personal and social formation, assessing crowd perceptions allows Jesus to sharpen his communication. Again, not to cater to public whim or to compromise his challenging word, but to clarify and punctuate his message so that people may grasp what he's truly saying, who he truly is, and where he's really heading—not some fantasy version they might conjure. He hopes to correct people's misperceptions—not least those of his closest disciples. He will not trade in false promises and projections.

In Luke 9, a strategically important chapter, Jesus reorients himself, resets "his face" (9:51, 53) for his long march to Jerusalem (9:51–19:44), both *reviewing the options* indicated by the "polls" (9:18–20) and *previewing the outcomes* he anticipates (9:21–36, 43–45), rooted in his prescient knowledge of human behavior and divine intention.

REVIEWING THE OPTIONS

In our imagined messianic campaign, Jesus does not directly run against any other messianic candidates, though various "false messiahs and false prophets" arise now and again (Matt 24:23–25; Mark 13:21–23; cf. Luke 17:21–23). In any case, Jesus definitely does not run unopposed. As we've seen, Luke's Jesus manages to provoke plenty of opposition from anxious family and neighbors and jealous teachers and officials.

But he also faces other kinds of opponents or, rather, options *imaged* for him by ostensible supporters. These are friendly avatars people construct to fit who they think Jesus is or wish him to be, but they are *false* models all the same, misrepresenting Jesus's identity and mission. Jesus's informal poll turns up four main options, three from the crowds—"John

---

contrasted "the American system of rugged individualism and a European philosophy of diametrically opposed doctrines—doctrines of paternalism and state socialism." (Hoover, "October 22, 1928.")

the Baptist," "Elijah," or "one of the ancient prophets"—and one from Peter (speaking for the disciples): "The Messiah of God" (9:19–20).

The Ascetic Option: John the Baptizer

John the Baptizer never claims to be the Messiah. As we saw in strategy 1, he is content to "prepare the way" for Jesus as the "more powerful one" destined to mediate God's restorative kingdom. Yet this does stop supporters of John's baptismal mission from wondering whether he is the long-awaited anointed one (3:15). The fact that Jesus submits to John's baptism complicates the picture.

But soon John is imprisoned and ultimately beheaded by Herod Antipas for criticizing "all the evil things Herod had done" (3:19–20; 9:9). That would seem to have ended John's "candidacy" for good. But wannabe "king" Herod Antipas (as "tetrarch," he only ruled a quarter-kingdom) is paranoid about potential rivals, actual or paranormal. Many first-century people believed that good or bad spirits could rise from the dead in some physical form, including inhabiting the bodies of living people. Luke reports that "it was said by some that John had been raised from the dead" and was now occupying *Jesus's body*. Herod worries they might be right. Maybe John has come back in Jesus's body to haunt Herod (9:7–9)! Strongman politics meets stranger-things occultism not for the first or last time.[6]

Now, closely following this note about Herod's anxiety, is Jesus's confirmation from his disciples that people are linking his identity with John's, not just in spirit, as we say, to reflect basic agreement, but in bodily essence. "John the Baptizer" is the top polling answer to the question of who people think Jesus is or least hope he is (9:18). Good to know.

What will Jesus do about this? Consider the options. He could use this "Baptist" association to his advantage—maybe not the whole reincarnation bit but at least the John connection—and co-opt John's popularity with the common people who don't much care for Herod themselves. If anything, John's reputation gets a boost after his execution; martyrdom can do that.

Alternatively, instead of riding John's coattails, Jesus could go on full strongman attack: "John went and got himself killed by the penny-ante

---

6. Israel's first monarch, Saul, was reportedly haunted by evil spirits (1 Sam 16:14–23); he also enlisted a medium to conjure Samuel's ghost (28:3–25). On the Nazis' obsession with occultism and the "supernatural imaginary," see Kurlander, *Hitler's Monsters*.

tetrarch Herod. What good is he to you now? I'm bigger, smarter, stronger than John could ever dream of being—he himself said as much, you know. That Baptist guy may have had a lot of followers for a while, but he really was a loser, stupid enough to get himself captured and killed. I like winners."[7]

Yet when Jesus hears about John's top "poll" position, he launches no direct response, positive or negative. He won't speak about John again until late in his campaign when he debates priestly officials who question his authority (20:1–8). We will unpack this exchange in strategy 10 but suffice it for now to say that Jesus invokes John's prophetic authority in a supportive way, without, however, intimating that Jesus is John's avatar or successor.

Jesus certainly never attacks John or feathers his own nest at John's expense. In an earlier scene (discussed in strategy 3), Jesus responds to messengers sent by the imprisoned John to Jesus to confirm whether he really is God's promised Messiah. Jesus's answer—"Go and tell John what you have seen and heard: the blind receive their sight; the lame walk, those with a skin disease are cleansed; the deaf hear; the dead are raised; the poor have good news brought to them" (7:22)—provides a nice summary of Jesus's liberative mission, with a strong accent on Jesus's miraculous restorative works.

Of course, this could be taken as a jibe against John who, though a powerful preacher and baptizer, is no healer or liberator and is now languishing in prison. But that is not at all Jesus's intention, as he makes clear in his ensuing remarks "to the crowds" (7:24), touting John as a great prophet and then some ("Yes, I tell you, more than a prophet"), indeed the greatest person ever "born of women . . . yet the least in the kingdom of God is greater than he" (7:28). This is the first time Jesus presents his upside-down hierarchy, honoring the "least" as the "greatest." By placing John on the lowest rung of the kingdom ladder, Jesus effectively gives him top billing.

Besides his healing work, Jesus's mission differs from John's in other ways. John, the son of Zechariah the priest (1:5, 13), bases his ministry in wilderness of Judea bordering the Jordan River, where he "proclaim[s] a baptism of repentance" in advance of God's climactic coming in salvation

---

7. A not-so-subtle parody of Trump's dig at rival Republican presidential candidate John McCain, a decorated veteran and survivor of brutal torture as a POW in North Vietnam. Trump's taunt: "He's a war hero because he was captured. I like people who weren't captured"; see Neuman, "Trump Doubles Down."

and judgment (3:1–17). He reminds us of the self-exiled priests who established a strict sect on the desert shore of the Dead Sea, purifying themselves through a regimen of washings for God's imminent apocalypse. We have no historical evidence that John ever joined this community, but Luke's portrait suggests an overlapping worldview and agenda.[8]

Jesus has his own ascetic and apocalyptic perspectives but in somewhat less extreme forms—more suitable for mass consumption—even with his radical "sell all" message. (John never goes that far, though he calls for people to share their food and clothing with the needy and for tax collectors and soldiers not to engage in extortionary practices [3:10–14].) Whatever Jesus's shortcomings as a politician, he's better than John at meeting and mingling with common folk where they are (see strategy 7). While Jesus routinely eats and drinks with people, John is a strict teetotaler (1:15)[9] and proponent of fasting (5:33–35).

Still, despite their differences, John and Jesus are both branded as dangerous deviants by some religious teachers: "For John the Baptist has come eating no bread and drinking no wine, and you say, 'He has a demon'; the Son of Man has come eating and drinking, and you say, 'Look, a glutton and a drunkard, a friend of tax collectors and sinners!'" (7:33–34). Typical political exaggeration and defamation of opponents: turn John's desert asceticism into demon possession and Jesus's table fellowship into debauched consumption. Remember that Jesus's rivals also try to demonize him as Beelzebul's agent (11:14–19). Here they add Bacchus to Jesus's alleged role models. Ridiculous on all counts. But mud has a way of sticking if you keep slinging it.

In any case, Jesus accepts the affinity with John as a fellow slandered proclaimer of "the justice of God" (7:29) and faithful brother in God's household on their "mother's" side, the side of Woman Wisdom: "Nevertheless, wisdom is vindicated by all her children" (7:35).[10] To stretch the point into the American political context, a candidate might claim to be a son (or daughter) of Lady Liberty. The "vindicating" proof, however, is in advocacy and action that truly promotes liberty and justice for all.

---

8. See J. Taylor, *Immerser*, 15–48; VanderKam, *Dead Sea Scrolls*, 168–70.

9. He had probably taken a lifelong Nazirite vow of consecration to God (not to be confused with being a Nazarene or person from Nazareth); see Num 6:1–21; Judg 13:2–14.

10. On Woman Wisdom as a personification of the Creator and Redeemer God, see Prov 8:1–9:6; Sirach 24; Wisdom 6–12.

The Prophetic Option: Elijah and Others

Though John qualifies in Jesus's book as "a prophet, yes, and more than a prophet" (7:26), John lacks the venerable history of classic prophets like Elijah and others featured in the Hebrew Bible. These ancient prophets thus offer another model for people's perceptions of Jesus, according to the "polls" taken by Herod (9:8) and Jesus (9:19). Again, Jesus does not directly address his prophetic identity in Luke 9, and nowhere does he claim to (re)embody any particular prophet. But overall, Luke's Jesus embraces his role as God's consummate prophet in line with the Jewish Scriptures' prototypes and predictions.[11]

Though not mentioned by name with John and Elijah as a prophet-model for Jesus, *Moses* would doubtless have garnered some early poll numbers (stay tuned for a surprise joint appearance by Moses and Elijah). Jesus's initial rejection by his own people (4:16–30), subsequent conveyance of his associates across a stormy sea (8:22–25), and claim to wield the "finger of God" against malevolent forces (11:20) recall key events in Moses's career (Exod 2:11–14; 6:9; 8:16–19; Deut 9:10). It's not surprising, then, that early witnesses to the risen Jesus Christ in Acts (Luke's sequel) allude to him as the "prophet like Moses" whom Moses predicted God would "raise up" to succeed Moses and complete his restorative work (Acts 3:22–23; 7:36–37; cf. vv. 23–35; Deut 18:15–22). Note the focus, however, on "a prophet *like* Moses"—not Moses himself resurrected or otherwise metamorphosed into Jesus—though popular expectation that Moses or a Moses-style figure would emerge as an end-time prophet of redemption was "very much in the air in first-century Palestine."[12]

We've also seen the key role that *Isaiah* plays in shaping Jesus's mission from the start (strategy 3). But Isaiah is not the individual model; rather, he provides the script that Jesus would fulfill as God's Spirit-anointed agent of liberation (Luke 4:16–21; Isa 58:6; 61:1–2). The early Jewish-Christian legend (first/second century CE) known as *The Ascension of Isaiah*—recounting Isaiah's brutal martyrdom during King Manasseh's wicked reign (he had the prophet sawn in half) and subsequent resurrection and ascension to heaven where he saw the living Christ—finds no echo in Luke's story. And in any case, the extrabiblical tale makes no claim that Isaiah transmogrified into Jesus and returned to earth.

---

11. See Johnson, *Prophetic Jesus*.
12. Allison Jr., *New Moses*, 83; cited in Poirier, "Endtime Return," 239.

Identifying Jesus with *Elijah* tracks better because of the longstanding biblical tradition that Elijah was directly translated to heaven via whirlwind and fiery chariot (2 Kgs 2:1–12; Sir 48:12) and thus, presumably, could easily transfer back to earth in Jesus's time.[13] But *as* Jesus? That's a different matter. Again, Jesus could have responded in two opposite ways: positively, "Yes, you got me! I'm Elijah returned, more fiery and powerful than ever"; or negatively, "Are you kidding me? Have you seen me riding chariots or staging fire-on-the-mountain showdowns with the prophets of Greco-Roman gods?" (see 1 Kgs 18:20–40).

Overall, Luke presents a complex, nuanced affiliation between Jesus and Elijah. From the outset *John* bears the stronger Elijah stamp, as he prepares the way for Jesus Messiah "in the spirit and power of Elijah" (1:16) (Of course, John's ignominious death by beheading is a far cry from Elijah's chariot transfer to heaven.) For Jesus's part, although he's the chosen one heralded by the Elijah-like John the Baptizer, Jesus also reprises major acts of Elijah's miraculous prophetic ministry (remember that John performs no miracles) involving feeding the hungry, raising the dead, and helping widows (see 4:25–26; 7:11–17, 22; 9:10–17; 1 Kgs 17:17–24). But he's more ambivalent, as we've seen, about Elijah-type fireworks: on the one hand, rebuking his disciples for wanting to call down fire from heaven on an unwelcoming Samaritan village (9:54–55); on the other hand, still mysteriously announcing that he has "come to cast fire upon the earth, and how I wish it were already ablaze!" (Luke 12:49; see strategy 8).

The point is that while Luke's Jesus takes up Elijah's prophetic mantle to good effect, he does not treat it as a straitjacket constraining his entire mission. Above all he is uniquely God's Spirit-suffused Son and Messiah. Let Jesus be Jesus.

The Messianic Option: Davidic and Others

Although there's no reason to doubt Jesus's sincere interest in what the crowds are saying about him, his main aim is to gauge his disciples' opinion: "But who do *you* say that I am?" (9:20). Recently, in the wake of Jesus's dramatic storm-stilling, the "terrified and amazed [disciples] . . . said to one another, 'Who then is this?'" (8:25). They're still not sure about this one they've left everything to follow. Have they made any progress in

---

13. See Mal 4:1–5; Xeravits, *King*, 184: "Elijah appears as the only figure whose personal eschatological return was expected in the Old Testament."

grasping Jesus's true identity? "Who do you say that I am" now? Peter promptly and succinctly registers his vote: "The Messiah [or Christ] of God" (9:18–19). Not John, not Elijah, not any other prophet redivivus: You are the Messiah. Period.

Peter seems to have found his feet, delivering a "rock" solid confession of faith worthy of the nickname Jesus gave him. Finally, someone other than the Lord's angel (2:10–11), a pair of geriatric prophets (2:25–38), and some demons (4:41) explicitly acknowledge Jesus as Messiah. Remember that even John remains uncertain about Jesus's precise status (7:18–20). Jesus has not made it easy. Though alluding to his "anointed" vocation via Isaiah in his Nazareth campaign launch speech (4:18–21), he has not said outright at any point, "I am the Messiah. I'm the One. Vote for me!" From the view of his politically ambitious supporters, Jesus is maddeningly self-effacing, non-egoist. He seems averse to saying, "I am," and promoting "I" interests.[14] How can you persuade people to "Vote Jesus Messiah" if you never call yourself "Messiah" and ask for their vote? Well, Peter tries to correct course. They can come down from the mountain and get back into the fray with a fresh, fervent messianic campaign!

Or not. As it happens, the candidate himself is not so impressed with Peter. Whereas Jesus took in the reports of his identifications with John, Elijah, and other prophets with no comment, he jumps on Peter and company, "sternly" commanding them *not to tell anyone* that he is the Messiah (9:21). He doesn't deny his messiahship, but he wants to keep it under wraps or at least doesn't want his surrogates broadcasting it.

Why not? Is Jesus suddenly having second thoughts, getting cold feet, wondering whether he's up to the messianic challenge or whether he wants the hassle? A quiet, magisterial contemplative life on a mountain has its appeal. As we've seen, the crowds dog him everywhere else he goes, including the desert (4:42) or a city he tries to "slip quietly into" (9:10–11). But they leave him alone on the mountain. Yet while Luke's Jesus exhibits some "growing pains" in his messianic vocation (2:40–52;

---

14. Contrast Jesus's magisterial "I am" statements in John's Gospel, such as "I am the bread of life" (John 6:35) and "I am the light of the world" (8:12), though he does not say them to boast or boost his status; he also humbly confesses, "I do nothing on my own, but I speak these things as the Father instructed me" (8:28; cf. 5:19). Nothing like Caesar Augustus's self-tribute, *Res Gestae*, which he composed for engraving on two bronze pillars outside his mausoleum in Rome. "*What I Did*," as Mary Beard renders *Res Gestae*, "is a relentlessly egocentric first-person narrative, 'I did this . . .', 'I did that . . .'; first-person pronouns, 'I', 'me', 'mine', are repeated almost a hundred times in the short modern text" (Beard, *Emperor*, 41).

4:16–30; 8:42–48) and natural desires for privacy, he is not paralyzed by self-doubt or agoraphobia. Jesus may not be a self-promoting narcissist, but he has a strong sense of self as God's beloved Son and chosen servant; and though he turns away would-be disciples who don't meet his stringent demands (9:57–62; 18:18–25), he does not turn away desperate masses in need of healing, feeding, and teaching (6:17–19; 9:10–17; see strategy 8).

So, again, if Jesus does the restorative work of God's Messiah, why is he uneasy about accepting the title? Why not flood the zone with banners, billboards, buttons, and other Messiah merch to get the good word out to the whole country? On some level, Jesus is concerned about his deputies' perceptions of what the title "Messiah" or "Christ" *means* and how they expect Jesus to fit the *mold* they've constructed for him. Jesus is *God's* Messiah: Peter gets that right confessionally, but Jesus is worried that he and fellow apostles are still way off conceptually, stuck in conjured dreams of *their* ideal Messiah.

We don't know the precise Messiah specifications the disciples have in mind, and as we've noted before, the matter is complicated by the fluidity of early Jewish expectations. To expand the picture, we should appreciate that first-century politics in Roman Judea and Galilee was fueled by explosive messianic fervor. The imperial-colonial environment was ripe for rebel movements led by various figures following various models. Theudas and a figure known as "the Egyptian" were two ringleaders mentioned by Luke and Josephus.[15] Though not purporting to be the Messiah per se, they claimed divine authorization for their liberative campaigns.[16]

Both Theudas and the Egyptian fancied themselves as prophet-generals in the mold of Joshua, Moses's immediate successor: Theudas assembled four hundred men at the Jordan River, promising to part its waters and launch a reconquest of the promised land (cf. Josh 3); the Egyptian "false prophet" (*pseudoprophētēs*), as Josephus calls him, aimed to retake Jerusalem from Roman control by marching on Jerusalem and miraculously crumbling its walls, like Jericho of old (cf. Josh 6). Both campaigns ended in disaster, including death for Theudas. The Egyptian managed to escape Roman counterforces, but hundreds of his men were slaughtered.

While messianic hopes may have been tethered to some degree to various prophetic, martial, priestly, and sapiential (wisdom-teaching) models,[17] the dominant Messiah profile entailed a *royal Davidic* figure

15. Acts 5:36; 21:38; Josephus, *Ant.* 20.97–99, 167–72; *J.W.* 2.258–63.
16. See Gray, *Prophetic Figures*, 114–20; Horsley and Hanson, *Bandits*, 160–72.
17. On the complex messianism of the Dead Sea Scrolls, including expectations of a

destined to restore Israel's theocratic kingdom of righteousness and justice by some powerful means. Two key texts, one from Psalms, the other from Isaiah, set the stage for this coming royal Messiah:

> The kings of the earth set themselves,
>   and the rulers take counsel together,
>   against the Lord and against his anointed, saying,
> "Let us burst their bonds apart
>   and cast their cords from us."
> .... the Lord ... will speak to them in his fury, saying,
> "I will set my king on Zion, my holy hill."
> I will tell of the decree of the Lord:
> He said to me, "You are my son;
>   today I have begotten you.
> Ask of me, and I will make the nations your heritage
>   and the ends of the earth your possession.
> You shall break them with a rod of iron
> and dash them with a potter's vessel." (Ps 2:2–9)
>
> ~
>
> For a child has been born to us,
>   a son given to us;
> authority rests upon his shoulders,
>   and he is named
> Wonderful Counselor, Mighty God,
>   Everlasting Father, Prince of Peace.
> Great will be his authority,
>   and there shall be endless peace
> for the throne of David and his kingdom.
>   He will establish and uphold it
> with justice and with righteousness
>   from this time onward and forevermore. (Isa 9:6–7)[18]

In the final throes of the Jewish War against Rome (66–73 CE), one Simon, son of Gioras, tried to take on this royal, enemy-conquering Messiah persona. Josephus lumps him among various "bandits" and "tyrants" seeking to seize Israel's throne (*J.W.* 2.652–63). Simon got further than most, such that "not a few of the populace obeyed him as a king" (*J.W.*

---

prophetic-priestly-royal trio ("the Prophet and the Messiahs of Aaron and Israel," 1 QS 9.10), culminating in an apocalyptic war between the "sons of Light" and the "sons of Darkness," see Vermes, *Introduction*, 163–67.

18. See also Pss. Sol. 17:21–23 (first century BCE): "Raise up for them their king, the son of David, to rule over our servant Israel in the time known to you, O God. Undergird him with strength to destroy the unrighteous rulers . . . to shatter all their substance with an iron rod" (R. B. Wright, "Psalms," 667).

4.510). Nevertheless, though finally wrangling chief command and control of a motley crew of Jewish resistance fighters in Jerusalem, he ultimately surrendered to Roman captors on the devastated temple grounds while wrapped in a purple cloak over white undergarments—a pathetic last-ditch display of royal bravado. Not long thereafter "King" Simon was ignominiously executed in Rome (*J.W.* 7.154–55).[19]

Though historically Simon ben Giora came on the political scene thirty-five to forty years after Jesus, Luke writes after the Roman-Jewish War, knowing full well how Rome dispatched with rebels and rabble-rousers, would-be monarchs and messiahs—including Jesus. Yet from the start Luke maintains that Jesus came into the world as "the Son of the Most High, and the Lord God will give to him the throne of his ancestor David" (Luke 1:31–32). Embodying the "good news of great joy for all the people," Jesus "is born in the city of David [as] a Savior, who is the Messiah, the Lord" (2:10–11). Luke remains convinced that Jesus is the real Messiah—*despite* Jesus's reticence to promote his messiahship, to say nothing of Jesus's death on a Roman cross, which he *fully anticipates* (see below). How then is Jesus Messiah any different than John the Baptizer, Theudas, the Egyptian, Simon ben Giora, and other failed agents of change? He seeks a more *peaceful* revolution than most first-century rebels—he calls nobody to take up arms for him and his people—but that just makes him easier to kill!

By any account, Luke's Jesus has some serious explaining to do after these initial "poll" results in advance of his final "march" to Jerusalem. Pollsters typically not only track current voting preferences but also forecast final outcomes. Where are things heading? If Jesus is not the kind of Messiah that Peter and company expect, what kind is he, and what will come of him and his movement? Jesus does not need a poll to answer these questions. He knows what lies ahead, and his followers do not get a vote on the matter. But Jesus and God (along with a couple of surprise visitors) give them a stunning preview of coming events, which turns out to be a lot more than they bargained for.

PREVIEWING THE OUTCOME

The post-poll forecast in Luke 9 comes in two forms: verbal and visual, declarative and illustrative. What others say about Jesus is not

---

19. Horsley and Hanson, *Bandits*, 118–27; Novenson, *Grammar*, 142–45.

determinative. The disciples must carefully pay attention to what Jesus and God have to say and show (cf. 8:8–9, 18).

Transcriptions

In chapter 9 Luke twice quotes Jesus's predictions of his messianic destiny: first, on the mountain, immediately after Peter identifies Jesus as God's Messiah; then, near the foot of the mountain several days later.

> The Son of Man must undergo great suffering and be rejected by the elders, chief priests, and scribes and be killed and on the third day be raised. (9:22)

~

> Let these words sink into your ears: The Son of Man is going to be betrayed into human hands. (9:44)

That is grim: suffering, rejection, betrayal, execution. Not the recipe for a successful messianic campaign. While there are biblical precedents for righteous, suffering servants of God assured of God's vindication—including later examples involving hope of resurrection to heavenly life for the Maccabean martyrs (Dan 12:2–3; 2 Macc 7:11–14)—the notion of a brutally executed *Messiah* scarcely squared with expectations of deliverance, salvation, and victory. Even if God raised him up to new life in heaven, what good would that do his suffering people on earth?

In the first text, Jesus predicts his resurrection "on the third day," but almost as a tack on. It's hard to get past the parts about suffering, being rejected, and being killed. In the second text, the focus is all on Jesus's betrayal, with no repeat of resurrection. The disciples, we're told, "did not understand this saying . . . and were afraid to ask him about this saying" (9:45). Can't say that I blame them. Their misunderstanding is understandable: Jesus is making no sense. At least for now he keeps all this disaster talk in house. His polling numbers will plummet if he goes around broadcasting this defeatist outcome, with or without the resurrection add-on. How about fighting first with all your might before conceding defeat? Isn't that the Messiah way?

Notice again Jesus's avoidance of Messiah language. After Peter calls him God's Messiah, Jesus directly shifts to his preferred self-designation as *the Son of Man* or *Son of Humankind* (*anthrōpos*, the generic term for "human"). Jesus's reference to himself in the third person (*not* "I am the Son of Humankind") might be taken variously as pretentious, off-putting, self-distancing, or just banal. All humans are children of other human beings. But that may be part of Jesus's point, the point of *solidarity* we've stressed before. Jesus is "Son of Everyone" who has ever lived, extending back to "son of Adam, son of God" (3:38), representatively restoring the full image of God in every human being as the model Son of Humankind.

But there is also a strong link in Luke's story between Jesus's identity as Son of Humankind and his exercise of *divine authority*, for example, authority to (1) forgive sins (5:24), (2) govern Sabbath activity, including the right to heal the sick (6:5), and (3) eat, drink, and sleep where he pleases (7:34; 9:58). Jesus is his own man, which is to say, *God's man*. Moreover, though it doesn't register on the "poll" reported by Jesus's apostles, Son of Humankind was another popular designation in some early Jewish circles for God's chief royal agent of salvation for God's people suffering under oppressive foreign domination.[20] Such a figure was expected by the prophet-seer known as Daniel in the heat of Antiochene tyranny over Judea in the second century BCE.

> I was watching the night visions,
>   and lo as it were a *son of man*
>   was coming upon the clouds of heaven.
> And he came as far as the ancient of days [God],
>   and the attendants were present with him.
> And royal authority was given to him,
>   and all the nations of the earth according to posterity,
>   and all honor was serving him.
> And his authority is an everlasting authority,
>   which shall never be removed—
>   and his kingship, which shall never perish. (Dan 7:13–14 NETS)

This "son of man" ("like a human being," NRSVue) will judge and crush the "beastly" tyrant Antiochus IV and inaugurate an "everlasting kingdom" "given to the people of the holy ones of the Most High [God]" (7:27; see vv. 15–27).

While Judas Maccabeus and fellow freedom fighters in God's name partially fulfilled this kingdom vision by breaking the yoke of Antiochene oppression, within a century independence gave way to Roman domination. Maccabean rule—which merged royal and priestly authority—was scarcely "everlasting," prompting people to keep their eyes peeled for the

---

20. See full discussions of the Son of Man figure in Bauckham, *"Son of Man"*; Collins and Collins, *King*, 149–203; Wink, *Human Being*.

consummate "Son of Humankind" to come riding on the clouds and take care of business once for all.[21]

In addition to his present role as sin-forgiving, Sabbath-healing, and table-fellowshipping Son of Humankind, Luke's Jesus also envisions himself in a *future* role as the climactic, cloud-riding Danielic agent of God's eschatological judgment and salvation.

> For as the lightning flashes and lights up the sky from one side to the other, so will the Son of Man be in his day. But first he must endure much suffering be rejected by this generation. Just as it was in the days [of] Noah, so, too, it will be in the days of the Son of Man. . . . [In] the day of Noah . . . the flood came and destroyed all of them. Likewise, just as it was in the days of Lot . . . it rained fire and sulfur from heaven and destroyed all of them; it will be like that on the day when the Son of Man is revealed. (Luke 17:24–30)

> People will faint from fear and foreboding of what is coming upon the world, for the powers of the heavens will be shaken. Then they will see "the Son of Man coming in a cloud" with power and great glory. Now when these things begin to take place, stand up and raise your heads, because your redemption is drawing near. (21:26–28; cf. 12:8–9; 22:66–70)

Note again, however, that this power version of the Son of Humankind—is set in the *future*: "*But first, [the Son of Humankind] must endure great suffering and be rejected* by this [present] generation." Right, right— but then he will be raised from the dead after three days and taken into heaven to prepare for a quick turnaround back to earth via a chariot of clouds (with or without fire)—right? Not that quick, as it happens. Luke is the only New Testament writer to specify that the risen Jesus stays on earth another *forty days* before ascending into heaven, pending his return at an *unknown time* (only God knows, and he's not telling anyone, even Jesus) (Acts 1:1–11). By the time Luke writes his Gospel and Acts, fifty years or so have passed with no return. That's a whole extra generation (and today we're still counting).

Back to Jesus's campaign within Luke's story, Jesus partly defines his messiahship in authoritative Son of Man terms. He's the one destined to manifest supreme power to redeem God's beleaguered people, vanquish their enemies, and execute God's rightful rule over the world—*someday*.

---

21. See 1 En 46:1–8; 48:1–9; 62:6–16; 69:26–29; 4 Ezra 13:3–4.

But not right now and not before he suffers and dies at the hands of present evil rulers. He assures his followers that God will raise him from the dead in three days, but what happens then? He never forecasts his ascension or sets any clear dates for his return. The signs of the end times include "wars and insurrections" and natural disasters, but that pretty much defines all times, not least in Israel's history (21:7–11). Rome's devastating assault on Jerusalem and the temple should stir God to send the Son of Humankind and all the hosts of heaven to the rescue (21:20–28). But that catastrophe does not happen until 70 CE, forty years after Jesus's death—and still, to belabor the point—no return by the time Luke writes his Gospel (or since).

Perhaps, then, we can forgive the disciples—and the wider population, when they get wind of it—for wondering about Jesus's ominous messianic outlook. And if it's not perplexing enough to hear Jesus predict his own demise, he proceeds to call his disciples to "deny themselves, take up *their cross daily* and follow me" (9:23). As we saw in strategy 8, Jesus also goes public with this cross-bearing call (14:25–27)—the worst campaign pitch ever, I suggested. Remember, the Roman world of Jesus's day traded in real crosses and crucifixions, not in cross-shaped jewelry or talismans dangling from people's necks or rearview mirrors.

To be sure, Jesus promises his fellow cross-bearers that they will "save their life" by *losing it* and that, if they remain committed to the Son of Humankind, they can count on being resurrected when he "comes [again] in his glory." Moreover, some of them, he says rather cryptically, "will not taste death before they see the kingdom of God" (9:23–27). But any contact with *crosses*, certainly on a "daily" basis, remains terrifying, even with the prospect that Jesus will not leave his followers hanging there forever. That's a risky proposition. How do we know you'll come through for us, Jesus—after *your own death*, no less? Again, politics plays to pressing present problems. What can you deliver here and now to make our lives better?

Politics also deals in the concrete and practical, not the abstract and paradoxical. Leave that head-scratching stuff to the philosophers. "Lose Your Life (on a *Cross*) to Save It!" Again, the worst bumper sticker ever! Bring in the biologists along with the philosophers to discuss the paradoxical cycle of life and death, even life *out* of death. Talk about Spring stuff like seeds buried in the ground and sprouting (cf. John 12:24–25). Fine, but I'd rather stay above ground and avoid dangerous *cross*walks as long as possible. And in the meantime, I'd rather put off thinking about death and dying and "taste" as much of the good life as I can (cf. Luke 12:16–19). Jesus has room to improve his communication skills as an agent of hope and change.

Transfigurations

But the picture brightens with two transcendent events that Luke splices between Jesus's two gloomier predictive statements. The first event, set eight days after Jesus's first forecast of his death and resurrection, places Jesus back on the mountain to pray, now accompanied only by Peter, James, and John (9:28–36). This trio of confidants, however, is not up to supporting Jesus's prayer vigil; instead, they become "weighed down with sleep" (9:32), perhaps still under the heavy weight of Jesus's dismal cross talk. In such a state of stupor, they miss most of the dazzling show that breaks out on the mountain. Make-up, costume, lights, action: "While Jesus was praying, the appearance of his face was changed, and his clothes became as bright as a flash of lightning." And voila! Two additional figures "appeared in glory" with Jesus—Moses and Elijah (9:29–30). Yes, those two towering ancient prophets set for major roles in God's kingdom finale. Jesus is clearly not Moses or Elijah reincarnate, but their appearance with him on the mountain enhances his messianic status and promise of victory. This is more what the disciples are looking for. This feels more like a glorious coronation overwhelming all that dour crucifixion talk.

Indeed, this luminous transfiguration marks the most dramatic *preview* of Jesus's royal destiny in God's kingdom Peter, James, and John could have hoped to "see" (9:27). Pity they missed most of it (8:33). But even if they'd stayed awake, the dialogue between Jesus, Moses, and Elijah would have disturbed them, because the main topic of conversation in this minidrama is Jesus's "exodus" (*exodos*, 9:31): his exit or departure from this world—his *death*! Of course, the presence of Moses evokes the historic exodus of God's enslaved people. But the talk here focuses not primarily on the people's exodus led by Jesus (with or without Moses)—certainly not on Caesar's forces drowning in the Mediterranean Sea (to update the demise of Pharaoh's pursuing army in the Red Sea)—but on *Jesus's personal exodus* that *he* must experience. Under the flashes of lightning on the mountaintop, the shadows of death still lurk, projecting Jesus's death and resurrection in a different light. Transfiguration does not bypass trauma; it presses through it, uses it, redeems it. There's no other way for Jesus Messiah. "*But first*, he must endure much suffering and be rejected by this generation" (17:25).

When Peter and company finally awake, they get a groggy glimpse of the dazzling portrait of Jesus with Moses and Elijah but don't seem to catch a word they're saying about Jesus's "exodus." The three disciples stay in the dark about the true course of Jesus's messianic mission. Still, Peter likes what he sees—or rather, what he thinks he sees—and is anxious to capture this moment before Moses and Elijah scoot away. So "just as [this prophetic pair] were leaving him, Peter said to Jesus, 'Master, it is good for us to be here [now that we're awake!]; let us set up three tents: one for you, one for Moses, and one for Elijah'" (9:33). Let's keep this scene rolling. Let's camp here for a while. Bask in the banner moment and enshrine it forever.

Or shifting to our imagined campaign mode: "We can lead people on guided tours up here, stage big rallies at the foot of the mountain and around the country, run eye-popping video ads of the transfigured Jesus talking with Moses and Elijah!" Luke adds the parenthetic commentary that Peter has no clue "what he is saying" (9:33). Well, obviously, but it sure feels better than all that recent downer-talk about suffering, cross-carrying, and dying.

But God wants no more of Peter's nonsense. While Peter was nattering on about his silly tent-building project, "a cloud came and overshadowed them, and they were terrified as they entered the cloud. Then from the cloud came a voice that said, 'This is my Son, my Chosen, listen to him!" (9:34–35; cf. 3:21–22). God and God's Son merit the last authoritative word—the integrative word of crucifixion and resurrection, exodus and transfiguration—that promptly shuts up Peter and cohorts again.

After the divine voice speaks from the cloud, Jesus is "found alone (*monos*)" (9:36). Moses and Elijah are gone. But the effect of isolation seems more pervasive: the company of Jesus's closest disciples offers him cold comfort in light of their cluelessness. The stunning transfiguration scene ends in eerie silence and absence, which lingers over the coming days: "And they kept silent and in those days told no one any of the things they had seen" (9:36).

Which is not to say that a tender hush comes over the world around Jesus and his followers. Far from it. When they descend the mountain, they are met by a "great crowd" buzzing over the disturbing case of a boy afflicted by terrible demon-induced shrieks and seizures. The boy's desperate father shouts at Jesus, "Teacher, I beg you to look at my son;

he is my only child. . . . I begged your disciples to cast it out, but they could not" (9:37–40). Turns out that while Jesus was on the mountain with three somnolent disciples, the other nine were proving incompetent to help this demon-possessed child.

Predictably, Jesus heals the boy, but not before the scene becomes more boisterous and chaotic—partly because of *Jesus's* explosive first response: "You faithless and perverse generation, how much longer must I be with you [all] and put up with you [all]. Bring your son here" (9:41). Not the bedside manner we might wish. The afterglow of the transfiguration is gone in a flash of frustration with the whole lot Jesus has to deal with: dunderhead disciples, clamoring crowds, panicked parents, depraved demons. As a last-ditch demonstration, "the demon dashed [the boy] to the ground in convulsions" while he was being brought to Jesus. Then "Jesus rebuked the unclean spirit, healed the boy, and gave him back to his father" (9:42).

But what a convulsive path to transformation: physically convulsive for the evil-spirit-seized boy, emotionally convulsive for the Holy-Spirit-seized Son of God.[22] The "greatness of God" is manifest through it all (9:43)—*through* all the tumultuous frustration God's Messiah experiences *with* his beleaguered people. It's probably best not to videotape and advertise this volatile scene—except that Luke lets it leak for all the world to see!

Who will people say that Jesus is now?

---

22. See Spencer, "Faith on Edge,"; Spencer, *Passions*, 197–203.

Making the Last Push

Strategy 10
Press your case to the end. Don't let up. Close out your campaign with maximal dramatic flourish, designed to make the greatest impact on the public. Make your final arguments as persuasive as possible with rhetorical force and flair.

IN THE LAST STRATEGY, we discussed various opinions people hold about Jesus as he prepares to "set his face" for Jerusalem (9:51). These views cast Jesus into various prophetic and messianic molds, none of which fit perfectly. As Jesus seeks to clarify his identity and mission to his disciples, he only confuses them more. They scarcely fathom his announcement that he is the Son of Humankind destined to be betrayed, executed, and raised from the dead (9:22, 44), to say nothing of his call that they "take up their cross daily and follow" him on his death march (9:23).

This distressing news is somewhat alleviated when Jesus's top three apostles catch a glimpse of Jesus's brilliant change of face on the mountain with Moses and Elijah. But this transfiguration is temporary and mixed with troubling talk of Jesus's "exodus" from the world (9:28–36). After descending the mountain, they find themselves back in the swirl of conflict with destructive demonic forces overwhelming desperate people and inept disciples—a situation Jesus manages but not without considerable frustration (9:37–43).

All political campaigns have their rough spots, but they generally avoid projecting their candidate's deadly defeat! And they usually take pains to conceal their candidate's negative outbursts. Tensions continue to mount on the winding road from Galilee to Samaria to Judea and its holy city Jerusalem (9:51–19:44). We've noted various volatile incidents along this journey. We now add two dire pronouncements of Jesus's fate that reinforce his predictions in Luke 9, both introduced with the imperative *Idou*, which primarily means "Look!" but also implies "Listen!"

> Listen (*Idou*), I am casting out demons and performing cures today and tomorrow, and on the third day I finish my work. Yet today, tomorrow, and the next day I must be on my way, because it is impossible for a prophet to be killed outside of Jerusalem. Jerusalem, Jerusalem, the city that kills the prophets and stones those who are sent to it! (13:32–34)
>
> ~
>
> Look (*Idou*), we are going to Jerusalem, and everything that is written about the Son of Man by the prophets will be accomplished. For he will be handed over to the gentiles, and he will be mocked and insulted and spat upon. After they have flogged him, they will kill him, and on the third day he will rise again. (18:31–33)

Jesus will persevere day after day advancing the liberative and curative work of God's kingdom (cf. 11:20). But he remains convinced that this mission will culminate in his arrest and execution in Jerusalem. Established authorities—Jewish and gentile—regard him as a threat to their power that must be eliminated. Strongmen don't play well with others. Cooperation and compromise are not in their playbook. Why talk with your critics and rivals when you can kill them? A much faster and more final solution.

But what kind of serious threat does Jesus pose to the political powers that be? He mounts no military march on Jerusalem, like some rebel prophetic-messianic pretenders (see strategy 9). Remember his reluctance to tout himself publicly as Israel's King or Messiah. He never openly denounces Caesars Augustus or Tiberius or High Priests Annas or Caiaphas. He takes a general swipe against fancy-dressing, palace-dwelling elites (7:25) and a more pointed jab at "that fox" Herod Antipas (13:32). But Herod's been called worse names, including a shameless adulterer by John the Baptizer. While Jesus supports John, he never directly condemns Herod's marriage to his brother's wife or any other misdeeds. Jesus is not aiming to displace any ruler or dispossess any regime other than Satan's. He's not running to be king (or president) of anything. He's not that kind of politician, which amounts to saying he's no politician at all. Recall that he resolutely turns down Satan's deal to make him King of the World because, as Jesus insists, only the Lord God is worthy of worship and service (4:5–8). Jesus promotes *God's kingdom*, not his personal domain.

Still, Jesus is far from politically neutral or socially congenial in the conventional sense. He's eccentric and edgy in his lifestyle and teachings. He stirs things up as he tries to make things right for the disadvantaged and neglected, the last and least. His use of restorative power for the common good makes him a popular figure, in spite of his efforts to tamp down public enthusiasm. And a popular figure is a threatening figure to both establishment elites and authoritarian aspirants. Best to keep him on the watch list and be ready to strike if his numbers spike and his ambitions swell, which is exactly what happens—or at least seems to happen—when Jesus approaches and enters Jerusalem. At last, he appears to shed his shyness, pull out all the stops, make a final splash. He will not go down without a fight, pushing for every last "vote" he can get.

MAKING A GRAND ENTRANCE

Jesus knows how to command attention if he wants. He knows how to make a grand entrance—sort of. Though commonly called the Triumphal Entry, it's nothing like the colossal parade that would attend Caesar's or any conquering war hero's visit. No chariots, no soldiers, no trumpets, no banners, no welcoming city dignitaries, no supercilious strutting or preening or Jesus's part. It's more parody than copy of a triumphal entry—more non-triumphal, even anti-triumphal.[1] But it has its moments.

Though no extensive planning goes into Jesus's final entry into Jerusalem, he does make one transportation arrangement. At the Mount of Olives on the city's eastern edge, near the suburbs of Bethphage and Bethany, Jesus sends two disciples into one of these villages to "find there a colt that has never been ridden, untie it and bring it here." Somehow Jesus knows this or has made some private pre-arrangement. It's all a bit mysterious. Jesus adds that if anyone asks why they're commandeering the animal, they should simply say, "The Lord needs it" (19:28–34). This is the only time Jesus plays the "Lord" card to gain something for himself. He is staging some kind of eventful entry with *royal* special effects, apparently following a well-known script from the prophet Zechariah:

---

1. See Spencer, *Luke*, 491–96.

> Rejoice greatly, O daughter Zion!
> > Shout aloud, O daughter Jerusalem!
> See, your king comes to you;
> > triumphant and victorious is he,
> humble and riding on a donkey,
> > on a colt, the foal of a donkey. (Zech 9:9)[2]

The postexilic prophet-priest Zechariah expected God to ride into Jerusalem as a king in a grand apocalyptic finale to restore God's people. He would come in "humble" mode on a donkey—not a warhorse or chariot—but still come "triumphant and victorious," defeating his people's enemies once for all and taking a final stand from his command post on the Mount of Olives over the entire world: "And the Lord will become king over all the earth; on that day the Lord will be one and his name one" (14:9; see vv. 1–8).

Is Jesus finally breaking out of his shell and staking full-on public claim to being Israel's Messiah King? Is he about to hype his Davidic lineage and announce himself as David's ultimate royal successor? Solomon's inaugural procession as his father David's first successor featured his riding a mule into Jerusalem (1 Kgs 1:33, 38, 44). Is Jesus evoking that historic scene from Israel's golden era? A crowd that notices Jesus's entry into Jerusalem believes that something royal and revolutionary is afoot. They shed their cloaks and spread them on the road in front of Jesus like a red carpet while bursting forth with a Psalm version of "All Hail the King": "Blessed is the king who comes in the name of the Lord! Peace in heaven, and glory in the highest heaven!" (Luke 19:36–38).[3] While Jesus does not overtly encourage the excited crowd, he does not discourage them either. When some Pharisees plead with Teacher Jesus to shush his supporters—perhaps trying to spare him from being charged with disturbing the peace—he responds, "I tell you, if these [people] were silent, the stones would shout out" (19:39–40).

But just when hopes for Jesus Messiah swell to their highest pitch in Luke's story, Jesus bursts the bubble. He stops on the edge of the city limits and breaks down in tears, sobbing over its terrible fate, as he envisions it. In a far cry from liberating Jerusalem from Roman control and reinstituting the glorious kingdom of David and Solomon, Jesus blubbers over the city in tortured grammar, "If you had known on this day, even you, the things of peace but now . . ." (19:42, my translation following

---

2. Quoted in Matt 21:5; John 12:15.
3. Adapted from Ps 118:26, part of a standard Hallel hymn sung at Passover.

the Greek order).[4] He then proceeds to forecast the terrible devastation Jerusalem will suffer at the hands of its (Roman) enemies, "because you did not recognize the time of your visitation from God" (19:43–44). Strategically staged weeping—say, at funerals for national heroes or tragic victims of terrorist attacks or natural disasters—can be a boon to a political candidate. But best not to overdo it—and certainly don't do it while the crowds are lauding you as the coming king. Talk about raining on your own parade! Breaking down weeping, lamenting Jerusalem's cataclysmic defeat, bemoaning the citizens' spiritual obtuseness. What kind of Messiah is that?

In any case, Jesus definitely does not enter Jerusalem unobtrusively. He makes a scene, causes a stir. And he's just getting started. Upon entering the city, he first heads to the temple. Nothing unusual about that. Visiting dignitaries and commoners alike typically paid first respects to local deities in temples and shrines. In Caesar's case, Greco-Roman temples were often dedicated to gods *he* was thought to personify. Of course, the Jerusalem temple was believed to house the one God of Israel. Foreign officials must tread very lightly and respectfully lest they provoke a riot. Jews of all classes must pay homage, not least during high holy seasons, such as the annual Passover commemorating Israel's historic exodus from enslavement—which is precisely the time that Jesus comes into Jerusalem (see Luke 22:1, 7–8).

But on this occasion, Jesus comes to the temple not so reverently to worship God as rudely to denounce the deficient worship taking place there. The crier over Jerusalem becomes a decrier of current temple practice, staging a dramatic demonstration of expelling temple sellers (of required sacrifices) under the auspices of ancient prophet-critics Isaiah and Jeremiah: "It is written, 'My house shall be a house of prayer' [Isa 56:7], but you have made it a den of robbers [Jer 7:11]" (Luke 19:45–46). How exactly Jesus "began to drive out" the temple clerks is not specified. He couldn't do that much damage by himself (he upends no tables and chairs, as in Matt 21:12//Mark 11:15, and wields no whip, as in John 2:15), but he pushes and shoves enough to make a point. It's nothing personal. Jesus is not bucking to be high priest. This is no takeover, no coup. And Jesus is not mounting an anti-temple campaign. Quite the opposite, he's effectively calling for a thorough housecleaning to restore the sacred

---

4. Jesus speaks here in "short, choppy sentences" (Tannehill, *Luke*, 285) and "fractured syntax" (Tiede, *Prophecy*, 79, 86) that "throbs with the agitation of his heart" (Danker, *Jesus*, 314); see Spencer, *Luke*, 496.

temple institution that he believes the present priestly officials have defiled. Again, he's doing it out in the open; no subtlety here.

Moreover, he keeps returning to the temple "every day" of Passover week (Luke 19:47), though not to keep protesting with boisterous demonstrations. Rather, he turns to a calmer, more deliberate campaign of teaching large audiences in the temple commons. He's a big hit: "All the people were spellbound by what they heard." All the people, that is, except the chief priests and their associates "who kept looking for a way to kill him!" (19:47–48). Luke does not specify their motives, but we can easily imagine their consternation over Jesus's disrupting the peace on their home temple turf and exciting the masses with his provocative prophetic actions and statements.

They can't very well publicly seize Jesus, however, with his popularity peaking, and they have to tread carefully about inciting the Roman authorities against Jesus as an insurrectionist and rival king. They need more direct evidence from Jesus's lips about his royal-messianic aims, preferably expressing violent intent against Caesar. So they resort to planting spies in Jesus's audience who pretend to ask him sincere questions "in order to trap him by what he said and then to hand him over to the jurisdiction and authority of the governor [Pontius Pilate]" (20:20). Wise to their schemes, Jesus nonetheless plays along and answers their loaded questions, using this occasion to make his final arguments.

MAKING FINAL ARGUMENTS

For all our modern preoccupation with influencing people's beliefs and behaviors through carefully curated images, captions, and videos, we have nothing on the ancients for putting on a rhetorical show. Indeed, our punchy sound bites and flashy photo ops, for all their technological enhancements, come across as cheap and crass in comparison with the sophisticated performances of persuasive argumentation by master statesmen orators like Cicero in the Roman Republic or by American politicians in a bygone era.

The televised debates that have become a staple of modern presidential campaigns typically limit candidates to short responses (two minutes or less) to complex issues, thus accommodating people's limited attention spans and accentuating one-line zingers, if speakers are quick enough to drop one in at the right moment to ensure endless replay in ads and news reports. Alternatively, one "oops" moment can doom a candidate's chances, as with Rick Perry's brain freeze on identifying the third bloated federal agency he proposed to eliminate (after fumbling to recall the name, he literally said, "Sorry, oops," on the debate stage).[5] In any case, one can scarcely imagine today a politician's ability to engage in (much less the public's appetite for) rigorous debate, like that in 1858 between Stephen A. Douglas and Abraham Lincoln in a series of seven three-hour head-to-head confrontations over a single issue (slavery) across the state of Illinois.[6]

Though Jesus comes from backwater Nazareth with no formal rhetorical training, he more than holds his own answering the leading questions posed by temple authorities and their agents. More accurately, Luke—a sophisticated Greek writer steeped in ancient rhetoric—casts Jesus as an astute orator and debater (in Greek) in his final public teaching.

Following Aristotle's *On Rhetoric* were various handbooks in the Hellenistic period providing a set of "preliminary exercises" (*progymnasmata*) in rhetoric and composition for students.[7] Cicero was an expert teacher as well as consummate political campaigner and statesman in the Aristotelian rhetorical tradition, focused around three main lines of argumentation: *logos*, *ethos*, and *pathos*; that is, (1) rational induction and deduction, (2) moral authority and example, and (3) emotional appeal and aversion.[8] Jesus employs these to good effect in addressing his critics in the temple, though he does not share Cicero's goal of becoming part of the political establishment.[9] For his part, Luke's Jesus (1) raises provocative questions of evidence and logic (*logos*, 20:3-7, 41-44), (2) appeals to authoritative moral exemplars like John the Baptizer, Moses, Abraham, David (*ethos*, 20:4, 37, 41-44), and even Caesar (tongue in cheek,

---

5. This was during the Republican presidential primary debate on November 11, 2011. At the time, Perry was the popular governor of Texas. In a weird ironic twist, Perry later became Secretary of the US Department of Energy in the Trump administration. This was the very government department Perry forgot in the debate.

6. Each expounded their views for a full hour, followed by half-hour rebuttals. These debates were the highlight of the 1858 US Senate race in Illinois. Both men ran for president in 1860; see Meacham, *There Was Light*, 161-70; Lepore, *These Truths*, 275-79.

7. See Kennedy, *Progymnasmata*; Parsons, *Luke*, 15-39.

8. See M. Cicero, *How to Win an Argument*, 15-40.

9. M. Cicero was an outsider to Rome's elite circle but very much wanted in; see Q. Cicero, *How to Win an Election*, 4, 9.

20:24–25), and (3) rouses emotions of anger, fear, amazement, and admiration (*pathos*, 20:19, 26, 39).

Luke 20:1–21:4 marks a rhetorical tour de force for Jesus, though it does not keep him from being arrested, tried, and killed by week's end. Indeed, it only propels those events as Jesus publicly outstrips his powerful critics, thus stoking their desire to end his surging campaign by eliminating him. But again, Jesus does not go down without a trenchant rhetorical fight, scoring vital points in five rounds of debate on a range of key issues about God's eternal rule that will endure beyond the death of Jesus, the destruction of Jerusalem and its temple, and all other diabolical plots to maintain worldly power.

Prophets and Authority (20:1–8)

Luke provides no syllabus or transcript of Jesus's daily teaching sessions in the temple, only the general description that he was "proclaiming the good news," that is "evangelizing" (*euangelizomai*) or "gospelizing" (20:1).[10] At this stage in Luke's story, we know the basic contours of this message. In the Jerusalem temple, Jesus continues promoting the same "evangelical" issues he raised when he launched his campaign in the Nazareth synagogue (4:16–30). Unlike then, however, when his hometown took offense at his gospel mission, now the people appear to welcome it.

But a coalition of religious leaders, identified as "the chief priests and the scribes . . . with the elders," 20:1) are more suspicious, posing a first question to Jesus that reflects their core concern: "Tell us, by what authority are you doing these things? Who is it who gave you this authority?" (20:2). There it is in a word: *authority*. That's what obsesses authoritarians, what keeps them up at night and drives their every move during the day: how to bolster authority and fend off any challenge to it. Again, authoritarian strongmen and oligarchies are inherently paranoid; their hold on authority is inevitably weak and wobbly.

The religious officials particularly want to know the *source* of Jesus's disruptive authoritative demonstrations in the city and temple. Who's really backing you, Jesus? Hint: Is it Satan or some other nefarious terrorist force? (Remember the "Beelzebul" charge [11:15–20].) Or who do *you claim* is backing you, Jesus? Hint: will you come right out and claim to be God's Son or God himself right here in God's house? That would

---

10. See M. Bird, *Evangelical Theology*, 30–31.

be blasphemy. (Remember the blasphemy charge against Jesus when he pardoned a man's sins [5:17–24].)

Jesus doesn't take the bait but rounds on his interrogators with a shrewd counter query: "I will also ask you a question, and you tell me: Did the baptism of John come from heaven, or was it of human origin?" (20:3). On one level, Jesus uses a classic deflective technique: shift the focus to another controversial figure, in this case John the Baptizer. The strategy is not without risk. Recall that the fiery ascetic, apocalyptic prophet John was not exactly the darling of elite society, religious or political. Some religious teachers charged that John "has a demon" (that old calumny again), and Herod Antipas imprisoned and beheaded John for meddling in his royal family business (7:29, 33; 9:7–9). But many *common people* love John, all the more no doubt since his unjust execution by an unpopular ruler, and the temple leaders know this. Jesus plays on this public sentiment to address the question of his authority indirectly through John's career.

Here's the conundrum facing Jesus's questioners. On the one hand, if they say John's mission was authorized "from heaven"—that is, by God—then they indict themselves for not believing his message and receiving his baptism. On the other hand, if they minimize John's work as purely "of human origin"—that is, flawed and fallible—they invite the ire of the crowds who revere John as a great prophet (20:5–6). Jesus has them between a rock and a hard place, and they decide that pleading ignorance in the matter—"We don't know where John's authority came from"—is preferable to a straight answer. In turn, Jesus declines to admit flat out where *his* authority comes from (20:7–8).

But the implied point is patent. As surely as John was a true prophet of God, so is Jesus and then some (as God's Son and Messiah). The proof is precisely in what Jesus has been *doing* and *saying* all along—his whole resumé of redemptive deeds and words bearing the unmistakable mark of God's goodness and greatness (cf. 7:16; 9:43). His is the consummate authority derived from acting and speaking as the *greatest servant* of God and all God's people (9:46–48; 22:24–27). Such authentic authority is what ambitious authoritarians fear most.

Sonship and Management (20:9–19)

Jesus now delivers his last parable in Luke. Though still teaching the wider temple audience, he primarily targets the priestly leaders, though they've posed no further questions and don't realize until the end of the parable that he's dressing them down. As usual with Jesus's short stories, this one packs more punch than first expected. When the temple officials finally feel the sting, they become intensely hostile to Jesus—"want[ing] to lay hands on him at that very hour"—but still fearing public outcry if they seize Jesus (20:19).

This provocative parable broadly extends the discussion about exercising authority but shifts it to the arena of vineyard estate management involving an owner-landlord, his son, a corps of clerk slaves, and a labor force of tenant farmers. As we noted in strategy 8, Jesus simply assumes in his stories the pervasive system of slavery in the ancient Roman world, neither denouncing nor applauding the institution as such. Yet he certainly has no vested interest in any system that inequitably benefits large estate owners at the expense of indentured workers.

Admittedly, however, the present story stands out from Jesus's other agricultural-economic parables by casting God in the slave-master and landowner role and Jesus as his partner-son in the family business. Jesus does not typically insert himself into his parables (they are not autobiographical tales) and only once gives God a credited cameo role—in that case calling a self-centered wealthy landowner to account, not representing one! (12:16–21). Yet while naming neither God nor himself in this final parable, their respective master and son parts are obvious—but *not* as role models for estate management or agents of economic policy.

The story is about working out God's ways in the world/land God has created (see Ps 24:1), with particular focus on Israel, the people God planted as a beloved vineyard to bear fruit for God's glory and humanity's good (Isa 5:1–7; Luke 13:6–9). From the beginning, the Bible has envisioned world management as a collaborative stewardship between God and humanity, the latter being mostly responsible for day-to-day operations (Gen 1:26–31). No micromanager, God entrusts the world's care and development to God's steward-people. Unfortunately, the story has too often turned tragic, failing to fulfill its good potential. Jesus now brings the tragedy up to the present moment, with pointed application to the priestly leaders who have egregiously betrayed their special calling as guides and caretakers.

Jesus dares to cast these current leaders as *tenant farmers* charged by the Master/Creator God with cultivating God's estate/realm. Though welcoming this presumption of their status as God's appointees, they would bristle at this tenant-farmer image. Temple officials were typically part of the landed aristocracy, owning villas and estates maintained by *their* subordinate staff. It gets worse as Jesus characterizes them as workers who stage a coup in the master's absence. First, they beat up three separate slave-accountants the master dispatches to audit the farmers' production. These three opportunities the master gives his laborers may recall the repeated witness God has borne to appointed leaders through legal, prophetic, and liturgic agents (cf. the tripartite Hebrew Bible: "the law of Moses, the prophets, and the psalms," Luke 24:44), only to have their exhortations fall on deaf ears and hardened hearts.[11]

But despite these workers' obstinacy, the vineyard owner still wants his venture to succeed. So he takes a big risk, some would say a foolish one given the farmers' reckless behavior, on sending not a fourth slave-auditor but his own *"beloved son"* instead. "Perhaps," the master says, with an eerie mix of angst and hope, "they will respect him" (20:13). The estate lord is so willing to give his stubborn stewards another chance that he sends them an extension of himself, his very son, whose life he puts on the line—whose life the tenant farmers in fact violently take! This is their big chance to seize the estate by eliminating the inheritor: "So they threw [the son] out of the vineyard and killed him" (20:14–15)—just as temple leaders are now plotting to kill Jesus, God's Beloved Son (3:22; cf. 9:35) sent to redeem the world.

"What then will the owner of the vineyard do to them" now (20:15)? The tenant farmers' devious plan is set to blow up in their faces, when the absentee landlord "will come"—personally, in due time—"and destroy those tenants and give the vineyard to others" (20:16). Just so, Jesus suggests, the current temple establishment can expect to crumble for rejecting God's Son (20:17–18). He says this with no glee, however. His tears are barely dry from bewailing the devastation of Jerusalem he anticipates because its leaders do "not recognize the time of your visitation from God" (19:41–44). *Perhaps*—hoping against hope—there's still a chance to turn things around. Unfortunately, by the time Luke writes, that window seems shattered, as hopes shift to the Son of Humankind's expected (but still not realized) return.

---

11. See Spencer, *Luke*, 517.

Taxes and Advertising (20:20–26)

Having been knocked back on their heels by Jesus's counterquestioning and storytelling against them, the temple authorities take a different tack to undermine Jesus. They recede to the background by a double shift of focus: first, to some "spies" they plant in the audience as "honest" questioners (20:20); second, to Caesar, the object of the leading question, "Is it lawful for us to pay tribute to Caesar or not?" (20:22). Taxes are always a loaded political issue, all the more when imposed by a foreign tyrant. The people would listen very closely to Jesus's answer, and he could easily land himself in hot water. Republican President George H. W. Bush all but guaranteed he would not win a second term in 1992 when he avowed in his 1988 convention speech, "Read my lips: no new taxes"—a promise he could not sustain with a Democrat-controlled Congress.

The planted agents play their role to the hilt by prefacing their tax question with a flattering comment: "Teacher, we know that you are right in what you say and teach, and you show deference to no one but teach the way of God in accordance with the truth" (20:21). Well, isn't that nice? They don't believe a word of it, but it sounds good and maybe it will set Jesus at ease and off his guard enough that he says something to offend the Roman authorities or the Jewish people or both. Flattery is a well-known tactic to curry political favor. Cicero's brother Marcus advised him "to learn the art of flattery [*blanditia*, blandishment]—a disgraceful thing in normal life but essential when you are running for office. If you use flattery to corrupt a man there is no excuse for it, but if you apply ingratiation as a way to make political friends, it is acceptable."[12] Flattery is not Jesus's way, however, whether on the giving or receiving end. He sees right through his questioners' game of "craftiness"—*panourgia* (20:23)—a Greek term literally meaning, "readiness to do anything,"[13] or as we might say, "working all the angles" to achieve one's aims.

Still, though he's no flatterer—the scheming interlocutors ironically get it right when they announce that Jesus "show[s] deference to no one but teach[es] the way of God in accordance with the truth"—Jesus cleverly works his own rhetorical angle on the hot button tax issue. He first puts the onus back on his questioners (again), insisting that they "show [him] a denarius" (20:24), a common coin of the Roman realm, a typical day's wage for a menial laborer. Some have suggested that one denarius was the

---

12. Cicero, *How to Win an Election*, 42.
13. BDAG, 754.

annual poll tax Rome imposed on the population, but precise tax data for first-century Judea is hard to come by.[14] In any case, a Roman denarius represents an apt visual aid for Jesus's response about taxes. Further, Jesus shrewdly involves his interrogators in the demonstration by having them show Roman coins *they* possess that *he* has nothing to do with.

Jesus doesn't carry any money, remember, not because he has accountants who handle his business affairs, but because he doesn't seek to acquire any money or purchase any possessions, even as he summons people to sell everything they own and give alms to the poor (12:33; 18:22). Jesus has no property to be taxed, and we have no idea if or how he pays Rome's head tax. He fellowships with tax collectors but as a means of calling them "to repentance" regarding their extortionary practices (5:32; cf. 3:12-13). Levi leaves his tax booth altogether (5:27-28), and chief tax officer Zacchaeus donates half of his wealth and restores fourfold to anyone he's overcharged (19:8-9). Jesus is not good for Rome's tax revenue operation, but he's not anti-tax so much as apathetic about the whole matter. He's absorbed in other business—the work of God's kingdom, not Caesar's. What does he care about Caesar's realm, and more to the present point: why do his questioners seem to care so much about Caesar's business, with Caesar's denarius ready to hand?

That's just the cost of doing business in an imperfect world, right? You have to buy stuff to get by, and it's preferable to pay taxes than go to jail or worse.[15] It has been common—and convenient—to interpret Jesus's crisp response, "Give to Caesar the things that are Caesar's and to God the things that are God's" (20:25), as a rational, practical via media in an imperfect world. Don't unduly rock the ship of state. Be a good citizen, do your civic duty, pay your taxes. But, of course, don't worship the state. Give God, not the government, the highest glory, render your spiritual service to God, pay your tithes to support God's work. Keep "church and state" as separate as possible, but honor both realms as much as you can. "We must obey God rather than any human authority" (Acts 5:29), but that mostly applies in extreme situations when human authorities ban the free exercise of religion and demand exclusive loyalty to a fascist or

---

14. See Udoh, *To Caesar*, 207-43.

15. An early first-century Galilean teacher named Judas (not Iscariot) spearheaded a nonviolent protest movement against Roman taxation on grounds that only God merited tribute payments. According to Josephus, Judas was willing to suffer death for his convictions, and his sons, James and Simon, were in fact crucified by the Roman governor of Judea, Tiberius Alexander (46-48 CE; *Ant.* 18.3-9, 23-25; 20.100-102; *J. W.* 2.118; Horsley, *Jesus*, 77-89).

communist state. So runs a common, genteel modern interpretation of Jesus's politics. But the situation proves more complicated in Jesus's world.

For all its tyrannical tendencies, the Roman Empire did not prohibit practicing other religions as long as they did not promote outright rebellion against the regime, which sometimes encouraged worshipping Caesar as divine. But again, provided that you did not directly curse Caesar as a false god and otherwise tolerated imperial rule (including paying taxes), you could generally worship any god(s) you pleased. Rome especially respected the Jews' tenacity for worshiping their One God unless such devotion led to blatant revolt against Rome—which it did often enough, as we saw in strategy 9. This was an era rife with political tension.

Though allowing for a degree of multiculturalism, including what we might call religious ecumenism, Caesar was not exactly subtle about promoting his preeminent interests. As the ultimate social media icon, he literally stamped his image everywhere he could, including on every denarius with accompanying message. This is the linchpin of Jesus's argument: "Whose head [icon, *eikona*] and whose title [epigraph, *epigraphēn*] does it bear?" "Caesar's" (*Kaisaros*), they tersely admit. They don't bother to recite the engraved inscription circling Caesar's head like a wreath, but they all know it: "Tiberius Caesar Augustus, son of the Divine Augustus."[16] On their face (!), these are blasphemous words in the Jerusalem temple.

The Jews were adamantly opposed to graven images of their God (Exod 20:4-6; Deut 5:8-10), much less to those advertising foreign dignitaries and deities—especially in Jerusalem. Josephus reports that Pontius Pilate came close to inciting a major riot at the outset of his governorship in Judea by allowing Roman soldiers to parade into Jerusalem with images of Caesar on their shields and banners (*J.W.* 2.169-74; *Ant.* 18.55-59). They might as well have lit these images on fire and launched them at the people. So why, in the name of all that is holy, are Jesus's questioners carrying around these incendiary Caesar coins in their pockets—in God's house![17]

Jesus does not go so far as to charge his interrogators with blasphemy, and he's not aiming to stir the people to rebel against Rome via tax revolt or any other means. But he skates close to the insurrectionist line and does not pull back as much as commonly thought with his rejoinder about giving Caesar and God their respective dues. Jesus is not brokering

---

16. See Herzog, "Dissembling," 346-47; Oster, "Show Me"; Spencer, *Luke*, 521-23.

17. See W. Carter, *Matthew*, 440: "Imperial coins were portable billboards, instruments of propaganda which reminded users of the emperor's political power and Rome's status as the favored of the gods" (referenced in Schiess, *Bible and the Ballot*, 150).

a deal or negotiating a settlement between Caesar and God, like a judge might do in a divorce case. And he's not engaging in territorial diplomacy, demarcating "two kingdoms" (Caesar's and God's) for peaceful coexistence.[18] In one sense, Jesus is a theological absolutist: All things are God's! That's what being the Creator and Redeemer means, which makes Caesar a usurper. Caesar merits none of God's business. Giving Caesar his due may well suggest giving him what he deserves—which amounts to nothing. Or a softer implication, though not by much: give Caesar's worthless coins *back to him* once for all and never pick one up again. Wash your hands of everything having to do with Caesar.

Of course, Jesus is too savvy to voice this protest out loud (he's not ready to die just yet). And we cannot be certain of all the nuances underlying his response. But we can be fairly certain he's making no banal "Honor the emperor" (cf. 1 Pet 2:17) pledge to satisfy local authorities. His interlocutors know that something hotter simmers behind Jesus's response. His answer leaves them "amazed" and "silent" (Luke 20:26), which is to say, astounded and confounded. They're not quite sure what Jesus means, but they know it's best not to pursue this line of inquiry any further.

Marriage and Afterlife (22:27–40)

Enter a new group of questioners: the Sadducees, a priestly party "drawn mainly from the governing class and aristocrats in Jerusalem," distinct from the Pharisees, an influential corps of scholar-teachers.[19] The Sadducees dominated temple administration and the Jewish Council (Supreme Court). The Sadducees claimed ancestral ties to Levi, Moses, Aaron, and Zadok, the latter referring to the high priest during the reigns of David and Solomon. Their name may derive from "Zadokites," descendants of Zadok (cf. Ezek 43:15), but this remains disputed.[20]

In any case, unlike Jesus, the Pharisees, and most other Jewish teachers and leaders, who embraced a wide scriptural canon of Law (Torah), Prophets (Nevi'im), and Writings (Ketuvim), and expected a general resurrection of the dead, the Sadducees were strict Torah-only adherents who denied bodily resurrection and afterlife, issues with scant support

---

18. See Schiess, *Bible and the Ballot*, 139-54, for a careful, nuanced critique of a "Two Kingdoms" approach to this text in the history of interpretation.

19. Saldarini, *Pharisees*, 105–23, 225–27, 231–34, 298–308 (the quotation is from 302); cf. Josephus, *Ant*. 13.298

20. See Babota, "In Search," 28–29.

in the five Torah books of Moses, Genesis–Deuteronomy.[21] Accordingly, certain Sadducees now try to expose Jesus's erroneous belief in resurrected heavenly life for God's people. Fine, fervent religionists never tire of scoring doctrinal points against heretical opponents, as they perceive them. But what does that have to do with politics? The Roman authorities have little interest in the tangled weeds of Jewish theological disputes (see Acts 18:12–17). Let the Jews choke themselves on these esoterica if they choose, but we couldn't care less about them unless, of course, they spark anti-imperial rebellion.

Yet religion and politics are never that neatly divided, certainly not in ancient Israel where royal and priestly authorities were expected to work together to advance and administer God's kingdom on earth. Given Israel's long-standing vulnerability, however, to conquest by foreign empires, questions persisted about when and where God's kingdom would be fully realized: Now and/or then? Now and/or always? Here and/or there? On earth and/or in heaven? The Sadducees put their eggs in the basket of *this world*, which happened to be working out pretty well for them, even under Roman rule. For them it paid to serve God here and now. Who needs heaven? Conversely, Jesus and other Jewish teachers sought to establish God's heavenly realm on earth as much as possible, anticipating the eternal consummation of God's restored universe with resurrected bodies. Either way "kingdom" ideals remained politically charged.

As do marriage and family matters. Those never fail to stir the political pot, whether with John the Baptist's critique of Herod Antipas's illicit marriage to brother Philip's wife, or with modern disputes over gay marriage and a host of other divisive "family values" issues. Or with the Sadducees' weird case that they present Jesus concerning the heavenly marital life of a *seven-time childless widow* (20:28–33). Actually, though having seven dead husbands would have been rare, it was not unusual in the ancient world for young women to be multiply widowed, since they were typically married in their early teens to older men (late twenties) who rarely lived to fifty.[22] But the question the Sadducees pose to Jesus—"In the resurrection [to heaven], whose wife will the woman be [which of her seven former husbands would be the lucky guy]?"—was absurd, intentionally so from the Sadducees perspective. They thought this riddle

---

21. See Acts 4:1–2; 23:6–10; Josephus, *Ant.* 13.203, 297–98; 18.16–17; *J.W.* 2.164–65.
22. Garnsey and Saller, *Roman Empire*, 161, 233.

would stump Jesus and discredit his pro-resurrection, pie-in-the-sky position, in turn bolstering their present political power.

But Jesus spoils their "gotcha" moment with a thoughtful answer rooted in Scripture—the Torah, in fact—which the Sadducees claim to accept as authoritative. He first argues that heavenly life, while not denigrating earthly life, is qualitatively different, lived out in a new body no longer subject to disease and death in a new complete, restored family of God's children with no further need for marriage or childbearing. But then he delivers his main point—"the fact that the dead are raised"—based on Moses's testimony in Exodus 3:13–15 about his famous burning bush encounter with "the Lord" he identifies as "the God of Abraham, the God of Isaac, and the God of Jacob" (Luke 20:37). Jesus takes Moses to mean that God must have raised these three founding fathers of Israel from death to eternal life, since the Lord "is not God of the dead but of the living, for to him all of them are alive" (20:38).

God is manifestly *pro-life*—pro-living, pro-aliveness, pro-present-and-future-life for all living beings. Neither here nor anywhere else does Jesus directly address critical life-and-death issues concerning abortion, women's rights and life choices, health care across the life span, or capital punishment that fuel hot debate in today's politics. But his teachings and actions certainly carry weighty implications for such complex issues, worthy of serious debate (not knee-jerk prooftexting and pontificating) by Christians today.

In any case, Luke's Jesus stakes his claim to be more authentically and comprehensively pro-life than the Sadducean temple officials, who appear to be more pro-*their*-lives in this world at the expense of the people they've been appointed to serve—by the living God! For his part, remember that Jesus expects to die soon, abetted by chief priestly authorities jealous to protect their power. But he also expects God to raise him back to life (9:21; 18:31–33). He expects God's kingdom to prevail forever in heaven and earth. And remarkably, "some of the scribes" (legal associates of the chief priests and elders) agree with him at this stage of the debate. Not that they necessarily buy into Jesus's role as God's Messiah, but they do commend his overall response to the Sadducees: "Teacher, you have spoken well," they say with genuine admiration, it seems, as they "no longer dared to ask him another question" (20:41).

Sonship and Messiahship (20:41–44)

So: game, set, and match to Jesus in the great Passover temple debate. For a while, his hostile investigators are forced to concede the high temple ground to Jesus. But that doesn't mean he's off the hook. Jesus's public embarrassment of the temple authorities only ramps up their desires to eliminate him. It would seem smart for Jesus to quit poking the bear while he's ahead, with arguably his most favorable poll numbers, including some scribal support. Yet he plows ahead.

As his interrogators go silent, Jesus turns the tables to ask them a question. But he no longer shows them the courtesy, to say nothing of respect, of addressing them directly. Instead, he poses his question about the temple hierarchs to the audience: "How can *they* say . . . ?" Say what? What's the topic Jesus raises? It's the *Messiah*! (20:41). So finally, Jesus tackles this core issue concerning his identity and mission; the house of God in the city of David seems like the perfect spot for a grand announcement. Finally, he drops all those gloomy premonitions of death, rallies the people, and claims his glorious messianic victory. *Or not*. We've been disappointed before in Jesus's political acumen.

This time Jesus does not disappoint as much as he discombobulates. Taking his cue perhaps from the Sadducees' preceding riddle about the seven-time widow, Jesus offers his own brainteaser, a messianic mystery:

> How can they say that the Messiah is David's son? For David himself says in the book of Psalms,
> "The Lord said to my Lord,
> 'Sit at my right hand
> until I make your enemies a footstool for your feet.'"
> David thus calls him Lord, so how can he be his son? (20:41–44)

That's an interesting puzzle to ponder. "Word games," as one scholar dubs Jesus's question here,[23] are fun to play (and good for mental agility). So is Jesus just providing a little divertissement from the tense debate? Doubtful, since he's dealing with serious matters of Scripture and messiahship. Yet he doesn't seem to be dealing with them that seriously. What's Jesus's purpose behind this riddle *he never answers*?

Hard to say given Jesus's (and Luke's) lack of commentary. But it's worth probing. As Jesus appealed to Moses's Torah teaching in the previous scene, he now quotes from David's Psalms. Quoting Scripture is

---

23. Novenson, *Grammar*, 16; cf. 85–86.

usually a good move for a candidate but not when you suggest a *contradiction* between two texts, as Jesus does between Psalms 2 and 110.

In Psalm 2, the LORD God ascribes divine sonship status to "his anointed" Davidic king destined to rule from Zion (Jerusalem): "I will tell of the decree of the LORD: He said to me, 'You are my son; today I have begotten you'" (2:2–7). As we've noted before, this and other texts stoked expectations that the Messiah would come from David's divinely appointed royal line, effectively making the Messiah both son of David and son of God. But then in Psalm 110, the text Jesus leads with, "David himself" (as Jesus emphasizes) introduces another royal "lordly" figure addressed by *the* LORD, a figure distinct from David and dominant over him ("The LORD said to *my lord*"). Jesus teases out the possibility that this other mighty "lord" whom "the LORD sends out [to rule] from Zion" (110:2) is another way of referring to God's Messiah in the Davidic line. But how can that be since the Messiah would then be *both David's son and lord*?

To complicate matters further, Psalm 110 was not widely interpreted in messianic terms in early Jewish thought, not least because it identifies the LORD's ruling agent as "a *priest* forever according to the order of *Melchizedek*" (Ps 110:4). The notion of a priest-king was not entirely alien to Israel's history (the early Maccabean rulers assumed this dual identity), but speculation about an eschatological figure representing the eternal "order of Melchizedek"—the shadowy ancient "King of Salem" who once blessed Abraham and received tithes from Israel's founding father (Gen 14:17–20)—was rare and rarefied. Luke has no interest in Melchizedek or a priestly messiah.[24]

If your head is spinning over Jesus's little messianic Psalm puzzle, welcome to the club. This is definitely *not* straight talk (strategy 6). We seem no closer to understanding Jesus's point. But maybe that is part of the point: that interpreting scriptural tenets and messianic politics is complicated stuff, full of tension and nuance, not reducible to simple slogans and talking points. Quoting a Bible verse here or there, in or out of context, might draw a quick round of Amens, but it won't get you very far

---

24. In the New Testament, only the writer of Hebrews claims that Jesus fulfilled Melchizedek's high priestly role (Heb 5:5–10; 7:1–22.) Melchizedek also appears in a collections of fragments among the Dead Sea Scrolls (11QMelichizedek) as an exalted heavenly being destined to play a leading role in the final deliverance (including atonement) of God's people and defeat of Beliar/Satan; see Vermes, *Complete Dead Sea Scrolls*, 532–34; Xeravits, *King*, 68–75;

in understanding the truth, the whole and often hard truth about critical matters of life and death.

Speaking of life and death—specifically, Jesus's life and death, very much on his mind now—the reference in Psalm 110:1 to placing "my lord" at the Lord's "right hand" may subtly confirm Jesus's hope of resurrection and exaltation by God. To be sure, this psalm says nothing about "my lord's" postmortem life. But another psalm does: Psalm 16 links David's status as God's "right-hand" man with hopes of escaping the grave and enjoying full life "forevermore" (16:8–11). And notably, Luke's second volume applies this very text—in tandem with Psalm 110:1—to the risen-exalted Jesus:

> But God raised [Jesus] up, having released him from the agony of death, because it was impossible for him to be held in its power. For David says concerning him,
> "I saw the Lord always before me,
>   for he is at my right hand so that I will not be shaken;
> therefore my heart was glad, and my tongue rejoiced.
>   moreover, my flesh will live in hope.
> For you will not abandon my soul to Hades.
>   or let your Holy One see corruption.
> You have made known to me the ways of life;
>   you will make me full of gladness with your presence"
> [Ps 16:8–11]....
> For David did not ascend into the heavens, but he himself says,
>   "The Lord said to my Lord,
>   'Sit at my right hand,
>   Until I make your enemies your footstool.'" [Ps 110:1]
> Therefore let the entire house of Israel know with certainty that God has made him both Lord and Messiah, this Jesus whom you crucified. (Acts 2:24–36)

We should not necessarily project this complex post-resurrection reasoning back to Jesus in the last tumultuous days of his earthly life. Still less should we expect any of this to make sense to Jesus's temple audience during Passover season. As we've repeatedly stressed, politics does not typically trade in subtleties, complexities, and inferences. Successful politicians, certainly of the strongman type, wield battering rams and blunderbusses rather than surgical instruments and intricate strategies. But isn't that part of the problem? Couldn't we all do with a heavier dose of high-minded, interconnected thought and feeling to meet the needs of an increasingly diverse and complex world?

Facing Defeat

> **Strategy 11**
> *Struggle with every last ounce of energy to keep yourself and your campaign alive. But in the throes of crushing defeat, accept the outcome, and do not succumb to bitter invective and vengeful threats. Instead, persist to the end in acts of loving service and hopes of new beginnings.*

IN THE PREVIOUS STRATEGY, we observed Jesus's robust messianic campaigning for God's kingdom during the opening days of Holy Week (as Christians call it) in Jerusalem. Though working no miracles and striking no conquering strongman pose, Jesus shows considerable strength of character, voice, and action in challenging the unjust temple authorities seeking his demise. He more than holds his own on their temple turf. By all accounts, he wins his public debates with these authorities and emerges stronger than ever with the people.

Yet Jesus is under no illusion that messianic victory is finally in his grasp. He weeps over Jerusalem's failure to "recognize the time of your visitation from God" (Luke 19:44) and tells a final parable exposing the authorities' murderous intent to kill him—God's "beloved son" (20:9–19)—which Jesus expects to be realized, as he has predicted multiple times (9:22, 44; 13:33–35; 18:31–33). After his scintillating debate performances, he doesn't talk or act like a vindicated victor. Despite some scribes' approval of his rebuttal to the Sadducees (20:27–40), he proceeds to lambast wealthy scribes who "devour widows' houses" (presumably through predatory legal maneuvers) even as they make a big show of their prominence and piety in marketplaces and synagogues (20:45–47). Jesus then launches into more doomsday talk about expected Roman assaults on Jerusalem and persecutions of Jesus's followers, alleviated only by Jesus's climactic return to earth at least a generation *after* his death, resurrection, and exaltation to heaven (21:5–37). Help is delayed, hope deferred.

Meanwhile, "the chief priests and the scribes [kept] looking for a way to put Jesus to death, for they were afraid of the people" (22:2). (Of course, crowd support can quickly fizzle or turn sour [see 23:18–23].) The religious authorities align with Satan (in Luke's view) to recruit a traitor among Jesus's apostles, one Judas called Iscariot, to deliver Jesus into their hands (22:3–6). Again, none of this is lost on Jesus. He knows what is going down and lets it happen. In his final gathering with his twelve confidants (including Judas)—in a rented Jerusalem apartment to celebrate the Passover meal—Jesus announces that one of them will betray him (he doesn't expose Judas by name) and that Simon Peter will deny him, despite Peter's protest that he is "ready to go with [Jesus] to prison and to death!" (22:21–34). (He isn't. At Jesus's trial later that night, Peter thrice disavows all knowledge of Jesus [22:54–62].)

Further, during the Passover meal, Jesus shockingly identifies the elements of bread and wine with *his broken body and shed blood*, respectively, in other words with his impending violent death (22:14–20). This would be his *Last Supper*, the last meal on death row, as it were, before his execution. He would not share such food and drink again with disciples "until the kingdom of God comes" (22:18) in some new, climactic form, presumably when Jesus returns in glory at some unspecified time. All of this *is* lost on the twelve disciples, however, as they proceed to squabble once again concerning "which of *them* was to be regarded as *the greatest*" in Jesus's realm (22:24). While Jesus talks about his mission of suffering service, his followers continue to play strongman politics (22:14, 25–27). Again, Jesus envisions his apostles eating and drinking with him at his royal table in a *final, future* instantiation of God's kingdom (22:28–30). But betrayal and denial, defeat and death come first, fast, and hard on the historical agenda.

Luke's Jesus finds no joy in this fate, including no "joy" in the prospect of resurrection and exaltation "set before him," beyond the cross, as one New Testament writer claims (Heb 12:2). Luke's Jesus is no happy martyr. In a terrible sweat of anguish, he soon implores his Divine Father to "remove this cup" of suffering and death from him at the eleventh hour. But once he senses God's denial of his impassioned plea, Jesus accepts that he must drink the lethal cup to the full and carry the cross to its bitter dead end. That's the way it goes, the way Jesus ultimately accepts as God's will without virulent recrimination against either his fickle followers or his malicious opponents (22:39–46). Moreover, he doesn't simply succumb to his bad fortune with passive resignation and displacement of hope onto a postmortem, paradisiacal future but instead persists in active, compassionate ministry to friends and foes alike until his last breath. Luke's narrative is much concerned with showcasing *how* Jesus faces death and defeat.

A bedrock principle of democracy demands free and fair elections in which, after hard-fought campaigns, losers promptly concede and pledge to accept the new administration (until the next election!), and winners do not gloat unduly over their defeated rivals and certainly do not lock them up (or worse). Rigging landslide elections in their favor, squawking about unfair elections if results don't go their way, and jailing or killing opponents: that's the playbook of strongmen demagogues, not gentlemen democrats.

For the most part, American political history has exemplified peaceful transitions of power, even after acrimonious election campaigns. Once the razor-close 2000 Bush v. Gore election was settled by a narrow 5–4 Supreme Court decision five weeks after the election, the losing candidate, Al Gore, publicly conceded:

> Just moments ago, I spoke with George W. Bush and congratulated him on becoming the 43rd president of the United States. . . . I offered to meet with him as soon as possible so that we can start to heal the divisions of the campaign and the contest through which we've just passed. . . . I call on all Americans—I particularly urge all who stood with us—to unite behind our next president. This is America. Just as we fight hard when the stakes are high, we close ranks and come together when the contest is done. And while there will be time enough to debate our continuing differences, now is the time to recognize that that which unites us is greater than that which divides us. . . . Now the political struggle is over and we turn again to the unending struggle for the common good of all Americans and for those multitudes around the world who look to us for leadership in the cause of freedom.[1]

Bush's victory speech was equally gracious and conciliatory:

---

1. Gore, "2000."

> Vice President Gore and I put our hearts and hopes into our campaigns. We both gave it our all. We shared similar emotions, so I understand how difficult this moment must be for Vice President Gore and his family. He has a distinguished record of service to our country as a congressman, a senator and a vice president. . . . This evening I received a gracious call from the vice president. We agreed to meet early next week in Washington, and we agreed to do our best to heal our country after this hard-fought contest. . . . Our nation must rise above a house divided. Americans share hopes and goals and values far more important than any political disagreements. Republicans want the best for our nation, and so do Democrats. Our votes may differ, but not our hopes. I know America wants reconciliation and unity. I know Americans want progress. And we must seize this moment and deliver.[2]

Two major exceptions, however, mar America's democratic history. When Abraham Lincoln won the presidency in 1860, a block of Southern states opted to secede from the Union, sparking a bitter four years of Civil War (and Lincoln's assassination soon after he won a second term). One hundred sixty years later, in 2020, Donald Trump refused to concede the presidency to Joe Biden, denying in the face of patent counterevidence that Biden had decisively won both the popular vote and the Electoral College. Trump finally vacated the Oval Office but only after lodging a bevy of lawsuits, hatching every conspiracy theory in the book, and instigating an insurrection on the US Capitol on January 6, 2021. Even after multiple federal and state indictments against him and his cronies for voter fraud, election tampering, and inciting insurrection, he keeps insisting that he won the 2020 race as he campaigns for 2024, claiming "I AM BEING ARRESTED FOR YOU" (all caps original in the tweet, August 3, 2023) and pledging, "For those who have been wronged and betrayed, I am your retribution" (June 26, 2023) against the current illegitimate administration, whose leaders he would surely lock up after retaking the White House.

Trump's sense of victimization knows no bounds ("No one has ever been treated so unfairly"), extending to outrageous, to say nothing of sacrilegious, claims by his surrogates and supporters, which Trump happily reshares through the media, of his close affinity *with Jesus Christ*. One egregious example occurred during the first week in April 2023, which happened to coincide with Holy Week. When the Manhattan district

---

2. Bush, "2000"; cf. Reich, *Common Good*, 123–25.

attorney brought charges against Trump on thirty-four felony counts of falsifying business records (including hush money payments to a porn star) to influence his political campaign, Trump defenders couldn't resist making the Jesus connection. "Seems there was someone else who was tortured and crucified this week," a popular Trumpist website posted. One of Trump's most loyal and powerful allies, Congresswoman Marjorie Taylor Greene, trekked from her home state of Georgia to Manhattan on the day of the indictment to preach, "Jesus was arrested and murdered by the Roman government. There have been many people throughout history that have been arrested and persecuted by radical corrupt governments, and it's beginning today in New York City."[3]

Just like Jesus during the first Holy Week? How does that fact check against Luke's canonical account of Jesus's arrest, trials, and death?

ARREST IN GETHSEMANE

After the Passover meal, Jesus leads his disciples to the Mount of Olives just outside Jerusalem for the late-night prayer vigil where he pours out his anguished soul to God and urges his followers to pray for relief from the looming "time of trial" (22:39–46). They're scarcely up to the challenge, however, opting for sleep over prayer—actually, overcome with sleep "because of grief [or pain, *lypēs*]" (22:45). Luke doesn't specify the source of their grief, but we may assume a swirl of despair over Jesus's continuing talk about his death, recently laced with perplexing predictions of *their* betrayal and denial. The reality of a failed Messiah finally sinks in. Cognitive dissonance and emotional upheaval knock them out. But not for long, as they experience a rude awakening.

Kiss Off

No sooner does Jesus tell them, "Get up and pray you may not come into the time of trial" (22:46), than they "suddenly" find themselves invaded by a large arrest party of temple police (22:56) led by "Judas, one of the twelve"—one of their own—as Jesus predicted. The authorities only want to seize Jesus, however (not his disciples), whom Judas aims to identify with a *kiss* (22:47). Judas thus turns a common gesture of affection among friends and loved ones, even a sign of forgiveness (cf. 7:36–47; 15:18–24),

---

3. Klepper, "Trump arrest."

into a signal of utter disaffection with Jesus and intent to eliminate him. We don't know Judas's full motivation for betraying Jesus. Luke simply says that "Satan entered into Judas" and he was offered money by the temple officials to deliver Jesus (22:3–6). At any rate, Judas was no long-term planted spy in Jesus's apostolic circle; he had been chosen by Jesus (6:16) and evidently signed on in good faith, pinning his hopes on Jesus's mission. But now that Jesus seems doomed to defeat, we may assume that Judas aims to cut his losses as he moves in for the traitorous kiss.

But Luke's Jesus will have none of this charade. Unlike other Gospel accounts where Judas applies the kiss (Matt 26:48–49; Mark 14:44–45), in Luke, Jesus halts Judas with a sarcastic rebuke as he leans in for the kiss: "Judas, is it with a kiss that you are betraying the Son of Man?" (22:48)—calling out Judas by name for the mockery he dares to make of the friendship, loyalty, and trust they once enjoyed. To put it in American slang, Jesus effectively tells Judas to "kiss off" (or "kiss my ass"). While Jesus makes no countermove to zap Judas or resist arrest, he does not simply play along as if nothing nefarious is afoot. Make no mistake: the priestly authorities, their police force, and the apostle they bribed to lead them to Jesus are all enacting a travesty of justice.

Sword Play

Though Jesus has no plans to fight his way out of arrest, his snarky response to Judas may have emboldened other disciples to suggest, "Lord, should we strike with the sword?" (22:49). They are no doubt itching for a fight, especially since just before heading out to the Mount of Olives, Jesus urges them to procure a sword (if they don't have one) and be prepared to use it in the impending period of peril (22:35–38). In this passage (unique to Luke), Jesus appears to shift abruptly from his pacifist campaign to a last-ditch call to arms. But is that his intent, or is he up to something else with his disciples, who, remember, are struggling to grasp the deadly fate that Jesus expects?

Jesus first reminds his confidants of their *past* carefree missions of advancing God's kingdom by healing the sick and freeing the bound in Jesus's name. In those campaigns, "when I sent you out with a purse, bag, or sandals," Jesus now asks, "did you lack anything?" To which they respond, "No, not a thing" (22:35; cf. 9:1–6; 10:1–9, 17–20). They might also recall Jesus's *peace* policy explicitly laid out in the second mission,

"Whatever house you enter, first say, 'Peace to this house! And if a person of peace is there, your peace will rest on that person'" (10:5–6).[4] (If they are not received peacefully, they should simply move on, shaking the dust from their feet as an act of nonviolent protest and leaving final judgment to God [10:10–16].) The core of Jesus's mission remains curative not destructive, restorative not vindictive. And he never repeals his radical call to "love your enemies; do good to those who hate you; bless those who curse you; and pray for those who mistreat you" (6:27–28).

"But *now*," Jesus says en route to the Mount of Olives, "the one who has a purse must take it, and likewise a bag. And the one who has no sword must sell his cloak and buy one"—a desperate measure for a "lawless" time (22:36–37) that he subsequently pinpoints, addressing his arresters, as "your hour and the power of darkness" (22:53). That nice, trustful, peaceful, helpful strategy of the past won't work at this dire hour. It's do or die time now in the Wild West, time to stock up and arm up.

Is Jesus being serious here? Deadly serious, but probably not literal, though the disciples might wish he were (they would rather take this sword talk literally than his cross talk). Jesus knows there will be no opportunity to get a sword before his rapid-fire arrest, trial, and execution. But he knows his disciples all too well and may sense that some are already carrying concealed weapons. In any event, his comment prompts them to say, right on cue, "Lord, look, here are two swords" (22:38). As if to say, beaming with pride, "We're way ahead of you, Lord, we've got your back!"

To which Jesus replies in thinly veiled sarcasm, "It is enough" (22:38), which is to say, "Enough already!" with this martial talk. Two swords are not close to "enough" to match the armaments of the temple police, to say nothing of the Roman garrison. Two swords are laughable and antithetical to Jesus's cross-bearing, enemy-loving mission.

---

4. "This [Lukan] saying . . . makes peace central to Jesus's kingdom imagination" (McKnight, *Bible*, 71). We dealt above (strategy 8) with Jesus's puzzling rhetorical counterquestion and answer, "Do you think that I've come to bring peace on earth? No, I tell you, but rather division!" (12:50). We should also note another zinger Jesus delivers midway in his journey to Jerusalem: "The good news of the kingdom of God is being proclaimed, and everyone tries to enter it *by force*" (16:16). By force, not peace? Or worse, *be forced* into God's realm (the verb form can be taken either way). I agree with McKnight that Jesus's forceful language is for emotional effect, not to incite militant action. It signals that people are passionately "willing to go all-in for Jesus's kingdom imagination" (63). In my commentary, I suggested that people are "desperately beating the door down" to enter and embrace Jesus' gracious, peaceful community (*Luke*, 409–10).

Yet when the arrest party approaches, the disciples look for Jesus to give the sword-strike command. Actually, one impetuous disciple acts on his own and slices the right ear of the high priest's slave (a member of the officials' posse) (22:50). The term for "ear" in the next verse is the diminutive *ōtion* (22:51), which can refer to an outer ear part or earlobe. Not exactly a lethal blow. One gets the impression of a flailing sword swipe that just happens to nick an enemy ear. Jesus then responds, first, with a cutting rebuke of his swashbuckling follower, "No more of this!" (22:50)—"Cut this business out, stop it!"[5]—and second, with a remarkable therapeutic gesture toward the injured slave, "He touched his [wounded] ear and healed it" (22:51). This act dramatically embodies Jesus's principle of *doing good to those enemies who hate you*. Jesus sticks with that principle to the end, even in the face of crushing defeat.

Again, however, this is not to say that Jesus lets his enemies off the hook. His last words delivered to the whole arrest party—whom Luke fully identifies here as "the chief priests, the officers of the temple police, and the elders"—cut home in their own way: "Have you come out with swords and clubs as though I were a rebel? When I was with you day after day in the temple, you did not lay hands on me. But this is your hour and the power of darkness!" (22:52–53).

Though peacefully surrendering, Jesus pointedly indicts his captors as bullies and cowards, coming at him with a "crowd" (22:47) of heavily armed law enforcers on a remote hillside in the dead of night, too afraid to confront him publicly in the light of day. Such strongmen, slinking around in the darkness to seize the "rebel" Jesus as a supposed menace to society. Some menace, this one who reaches out and heals one their associates. Jesus is in fact a threat to their unlawful use of authority, to their "power of darkness" on which he dares to shine the light of truth and justice. So who are the real criminals here?

TRIALS IN JERUSALEM

The arrest squad takes Jesus straightaway to the high priest's "house" (22:54), his official palatial residence containing an area for suspects awaiting trial, where Jesus is held the rest of the night. The next morning,

---

5. The phrase *eate heōs toutou* literally means "leave or allow this until." But its idiomatic thrust pushes deeper than simply "let it be." Rather, it carries "the implication of strong admonition—'stop, quit, cease'" (Louw and Nida, eds., *Greek-English Lexicon*, 659).

he is whisked through three sham trials before the Jewish Supreme Court (22:66–71), the Roman Governor Pontius Pilate (23:1–5), and the Galilean tetrarch Herod Antipas (23:6–12), respectively. Pilate then renders the final verdict against Jesus: death by crucifixion (23:24–25). No appeal, no reconsideration. Jesus is dead by three o'clock that afternoon (23:44–46). We readers barely have time to catch our breaths before Jesus takes his last breath.

As fast as the so-called trials proceed in Luke's account, they nonetheless provide significant glimpses into how Jesus faces his political defeat and personal death. He engages in no martyrial grandstanding (Socratic or Stoic) or strongman bravado. Many might call his a "weak" end, a pathetic death (cf. 1 Cor 1:18–2:4). Yet he maintains a quiet dignity throughout the terrible proceedings and makes some significant statements to his accusers about his vocation as Messiah, Son of God, and Son of Humankind (Luke 22:66–23:3).

Held in the High Priest's Residence

Wherever Jesus is being detained in the high priest's compound, he's in ear- and eyeshot of the courtyard where household servants and security personnel are warming themselves in the chilly night around a fire. Surprisingly, Peter slips into this group (he had been tracking the arrest party "at a distance," 22:54–55). What's Peter up to here? I doubt he knows. Perhaps he's seeing if there is some way to spring Jesus from custody. Perhaps he wants to make good on his pledge to "go with [Jesus] to prison and to death!" (22:33). In any case, he has a hard time mustering the courage to do anything but warm himself and hang out with Jesus's arrestors. It gets worse when three individuals in the courtyard—first a female servant and then two unidentified men—expose Peter in the firelight as one of Jesus's followers, triggering his vehement triple denials that he knows anything about Jesus (22:55–60).

Remember, this is just what Jesus predicts Peter would do (22:34). But Peter only remembers when the cock crows during his third denial and "the Lord turn[s] and look[s] at him" (22:60–61). This is the sixth of seven significant "turnings" (*strephō*) of Jesus in Luke's Gospel.[6] Here Jesus turns and *looks intently at* (*emblepō*) the fickle Peter, much as the servant woman had "stared at" (*atenizō*) at him before exposing him as

---

6. Luke 7:9, 44; 9:55; 10:23; 14:25; 22:61; 23:28; see Spencer, *Luke*, 374–75.

Jesus's disciple (22:56–57). In each case, Peter melts in the firelight under laser glares: first, flatly denying the woman's testimony against him, then fleeing the scene and bitterly weeping after meeting Jesus's gaze and recalling his forecast of Peter's disloyalty (22:61–62). Jesus says nothing to Peter now. He doesn't need to. His look says it all.

Absent a fuller description, we might surmise a range of emotions in Jesus's eyes from derision and disappointment to compassion and forgiveness. In any event, Jesus has no intention of bringing Peter down with him. And it's hard to imagine him thinking, "See, I told you so, you spineless coward and ingrate," especially since earlier in the evening just prior to predicting Peter's denials, Jesus addresses Peter by his given name, pleading, "Simon, Simon, listen! Satan has demanded to sift you like wheat, but I have prayed for you that your own faith may not fail, and you, when once you have turned back, strengthen your brothers" (22:31–32).

Jesus does not turn against his beloved followers even when they fail to support him in his direst hour. During his ordeal of devastating defeat, he continues to pray for and work for the restorations of both friends and foes (Judas eerily excepted).[7] Jesus may prompt Peter to "weep bitterly" over his denials of Christ (22:62), but he himself will not succumb to bitter recriminations against those who abandon or attack him.

Tried before the Jewish Council

As daylight comes, prisoner Jesus is brought before the Jewish council or Supreme Court, "the assembly of the elders of the people, both chief priests and scribes" (22:66), presided over by the high priest. He's not brought to trial in good shape, however. The guards overseeing Jesus harass him through the night at the high priest's residence with a cruel game of blind man's bluff. After blindfolding Jesus, they repeatedly beat him and mock his prophetic vocation with the taunt, "Prophesy! Who is it that struck you?" (22:63–65). Luke consistently shows Jesus to be a true "prophet mighty in deed and word before God and all the people" (24:19). But Jesus does not stoop to his opponents' base level and use his

---

7. A troubling aspect of Luke's story swirls around the question of why Peter the denier gets a second chance while it is denied, it seems, to Judas the betrayer. It becomes even more troubling at the outset of Luke's second volume when the restored Peter presides over the business of replacing Judas as an apostle after Judas's grisly demise (Acts 1:15–20).

prophetic gifts for their amusement or to spare himself from their brutish assaults. And neither does he waste his breath uttering some prophetic counterblast against them. He refuses to play their bullyish game.

When the council gets their crack to examine Jesus, they flatly demand, "If you are the Messiah, tell us" (22:67). They want his outrageous (as they judge it) claim to messiahship on the record, clear and plain. No more insecurity or humility or whatever has driven Jesus's reticence thus far about his messianic candidacy. Do you think you're the Messiah, or not? While Jesus still shies away from giving a definitive answer, he does not hesitate to assert in various ways—implicit and explicit, sardonic and straightforward—his present and future authority to judge his inquisitors.

First, he snaps back, "If I tell you [I'm the Messiah], you will not believe, and if I question you, you will not answer [implication: so why should I answer you?]" (22:67–68). Jesus audaciously assumes the right to question these chief justices, but why bother?

Second, he utters his boldest rejoinder about his destiny as God's supreme agent or "right hand" man: "But from now on the Son of Man will be seated at the right hand of the power of God" (22:69). Though again, Jesus does not say outright, "I am the Son of Humankind," as Daniel envisioned—the one God's heavenly court will vindicate and grant full "kingship and dominion" over an "everlasting kingdom" in heaven-and-earth (Dan 7:13–14, 26–27; cf. Luke 21:27)—he more than hints at his consummate eschatological power.

Third, when the council picks up this signal of Jesus's affiliation with the "power of God" and asks point blank, "Are you then, the Son of God?," Jesus quips back, "You say that I am" (22:69–70). Yet another cheeky response and not as oblique as it might seem. Jesus's use of the emphatic verbal expression, "I [myself] am" (*egō eimi*) carries a strong resonance, which the priestly judges would not miss, with God's revelation of the Divine Name (LORD, I AM WHO I AM) to Moses (Exod 3:13–15). That does it. Case closed: "What further testimony do we need? We have heard it from his own lips!" (Luke 22:70). Well, not exactly in so many words. But they've already made up their minds Jesus is guilty of blasphemy and false claims to being the royal Messiah, which would make him a rebel against the Roman Empire. Time to hand him over to Pilate for the final verdict, the capital sentence.

Prophet, Messiah, Son of Humankind, Son of God: a cluster of loaded titles the judicial authorities try to get Jesus to claim—fraudulently, profanely, dangerously in their view—in order to protect their political power. Jesus accepts these roles but does not advertise them or argue for them at length with these close-minded leaders. Yet he stands his ground without cowering or caving into official pressure. And he leaves a few sharp, stinging statements lingering in the air.

Tried before the Roman Governor

In the tense decades preceding the Roman-Jewish War (66–73 CE), an uneasy alliance characterized relations between the Jewish council in Jerusalem and the Roman provincial government based in Caesarea. No love was lost between priestly hierarchs and Roman prefects like Pontius Pilate, but they depended on each other to keep the public peace and their personal power—no small task in the supercharged political environment of Passover (celebrating ancient Israel's liberation from Egyptian enslavement).

The Jewish priestly prosecutors play to Pilate's prime interests by charging Jesus with insurrection against Rome on three counts: "We found this man [1] inciting our nation [*ethnos*, the Jewish people], [2] forbidding us to pay taxes to Caesar and [3] saying that he himself is the Messiah, a king" (23:2). Well, they get one out of three right, sort of. Jesus has accepted others' acclamations of his royal messiahship and did not explicitly deny he was the Messiah before the council, but he personally spearheads no rabid "crusade for Christ," no unabashed, no-holds-barred messianic campaign. And he certainly incites no military or tax revolt against Rome. Whatever critique may underlie his advice, "Give to Caesar the things that are Caesar's" (20:25, see strategy 10), only by devious misinformation can it be twisted to mean, "Give Caesar nothing but hell." The present cadre of priestly officials appear to have no qualms about misinformation to maintain their power.

But what about Pilate? He asks Jesus directly, "Are you the king of the Jews?" (23:3)—emphasizing in Greek, "*You* [*Su*]?" Pilate may have gotten wind that Jesus caused a little stir when he first entered the city and the temple, but he hardly looks like a rival king and commands no troops or rebel gangs. "*You*—a king? Seriously?" To which Jesus replies in his now familiar curt manner: "You say so"—again emphasizing "You [yourself, *Su*] say so" (23:3). Not quite a brusque "if you say so" but close. Jesus is weary of these kangaroo courts.[8] More to the point, Jesus shifts the onus

---

8. Skinner's description of the Jewish council's interrogation of Jesus, which is also

to Pilate. This is *your* show, *your* call to make, *your* earthly kingdom that *you're* protecting. So what are *you* going to do?

Pilate may seem to take the high ground by announcing "to the chief priests and the crowds, 'I find no basis for accusation against this man'" (23:4). But don't be deceived. Pilate is deftly walking a political tightrope between the priestly leaders hostile to Jesus and a segment of the crowd hyping him. Pilate is trying to ensure this Jesus of Nazareth business doesn't blow up in his face. He's happy to tweak the noses of the Jewish council to keep them in line (they can't just waltz into my court and expect me to accede to their demands) and throw the people a bone, especially one with little meat on it (as Pilate judges Jesus). But amped up festival crowds can change on a whim and/or easily provoke counterprotests (see below).

When the prosecutors keep contending that Jesus "stirs up the people by teaching throughout all Judea, from Galilee where he began even to this place" (23:5), it's doubtful that Pilate buys this exaggeration of Jesus's influence. But the mention of Galilee sparks his interest because Rome's client-ruler of Galilee, Herod Antipas, happens to be in town for Passover. Pilate and Herod are far from bosom buddies. In fact, Luke says they have been "enemies" (23:12). That may be overstating it, but they are neighboring rival administrators of Caesar's realm. Pilate sees a low-cost opportunity to forge a political alliance with Herod (keep your enemy close kind of thing) by sending the Galilean Jesus to Herod for a second judicial opinion. Far from playing the king, Jesus serves as a pawn in the power battles in Roman Judea and Galilee. Before day's end, Pilate and Herod come together over this Jesus affair and even become "friends" (23:12). Strongmen love to pile on against (perceived) weaklings. Bonding through bully-hood.[9]

---

apt for Pilate's examination: "a show trial without the show, a judicial farce" (*Trial*, 75).

9. As evidenced in Trump's infatuation with and cozying up to A-list modern autocrats like Putin (Russia), Erdoğan (Turkey), Orbán (Hungary). Duterte (Philippines), Kim (North Korea), and Bolsonaro (Brazil). See Gessen, *Surviving Autocracy*, 49–56; Richardson, *Democracy*, 101–9; for a critique of "authoritarian reactionary Christianity" promoted by Putin, Orbán, Bolsonaro, and Trump, see Gushee, *Defending Democracy*, 96–103, 114–43.

Tried before the Galilean Tetrarch

Luke reports that "when Herod saw Jesus, he was very glad," even giddy, "for he had been wanting to see [Jesus] for a long time because he had heard about him and was hoping to see him perform some sign" (23:8). This is odd since Herod earlier feared that Jesus might be John the Baptizer returned from the dead to haunt him for beheading John (9:7–9). Moreover, some Pharisees warned Jesus to flee from Galilee because Herod sought to kill him, to which Jesus retorted, "Go tell that fox for me, 'Listen, I am casting out demons and performing cures today and tomorrow, and on the third day I will finish my work'" (13:31–33)—as if to say, "Tell that conniving Herod I will do my miraculous restorative work in his backyard, if I please. He can't scare me off." But now in Jerusalem, the vulpine Herod has become Jesus's fanboy.

It's hard to account for the volatile whims and tastes of tyrannical rulers. Of course, Herod now has little to fear from Jesus, under Pilate's (not Herod's) custody. Herod can afford to interrogate Jesus safely and satisfy his curiosity about this quirky Galilean teacher and wonder-worker, perhaps even prod him to perform a trick or two. In turn, Herod might boost his standing a little with Pilate and the chief priests.

Jesus has no intention, however, of performing for Herod's amusement, even if doing so might enhance his chances of release. Jesus responds to Herod's lengthy pleading and questioning with stone-cold silence: he gives him "no answer" (23:9). Thus shamed by Jesus's insolence and egged on by continuing accusations from the priestly scribal bloc, Herod has his soldiers humiliate Jesus with a dress-up hazing act, outfitting him in "an elegant robe"—fit for a king (hah!)—and sending him back to Pilate (23:10–11), who no doubt has a good laugh upon seeing Jesus in his new regalia.

Returned to the Roman Governor for the Final Verdict

For all his willingness to mock Jesus as a would-be king, Herod is no more convinced than Pilate that Jesus poses any actionable threat worthy of execution. Or maybe Herod opts not to buck Pilate's jurisdiction in Judea. For his part, Pilate keeps trying to talk down the priestly leaders from their demands for Jesus's crucifixion, which they've now ramped up by enlisting "the people" (*laos*) in their cause, not all the Jewish people by any means but rather a rabble-rousing mob Pilate can ill afford to ignore.

As a compromise, Pilate proposes giving Jesus a good flogging before releasing him (23:13–15).

But the whipped-up gang has no interest in defusing the situation. They want violent action, a bloody spectacle to spice up the Passover holiday: "Away with this fellow! Crucify him! Crucify him!" (23:18, 21). For some revolutionaries among them, a certain method lurks behind their madness as they try to strike a deal with Pilate to release the murderous rebel Barabbas instead of Jesus—a twisted prisoner swap. It's a preposterous proposal—trading the pacifist Jesus for the insurrectionist Barabbas—but it's worth a shot (23:18–21). And it is a telling indicator of their political opinion of Jesus. As Matthew Skinner comments,

> The sharp contrast sustained between Jesus' apparent harmlessness and Barabbas's clear participation in violence suggests that Pilate's audience not only renounces Jesus but also opts for a very different alternative. In rejecting Jesus, the people thus reject the kind of leadership he would exercise. . . . Jesus stands before them now, looking silly in his radiant robe, by all appearances utterly powerless while the governor presumes to dictate his fate. At least Barabbas the insurrectionist tried to make tangible changes in the social order; Jesus, the political commodity being passed around by political officials who see nothing royal about him, appears not to be the kind of effective king some people had previously hoped he would be.[10]

Silly-looking, soft-speaking, passive, and pacifist Jesus. Who needs that? We'll take our chances with Barabbas. Away with Jesus!

This is a terrible deal for Pilate. He scarcely wants to put a convicted killer and insurgent back into play, but the mob has him over a barrel.[11] As Pilate keeps pressing his plan to beat and release Jesus, the crowd screams louder and louder, "and their voices prevail" (23:23). To prevent a full-scale riot, Pilate caves in and satisfies the outcry for Jesus's crucifixion—and Barabbas's release (23:24–25). A myopic decision by Pilate and not a little ironic: the Judean slice of Rome's kingdom threatens to unravel over Jesus without Jesus lifting a finger and barely raising his voice.

Many interpreters have suggested that Luke aims to mitigate Pilate and the Romans' responsibility for Jesus's death and lay the heaviest

---

10. Skinner, *Trial*, 81–82.

11. Luke knows nothing about the supposed custom mentioned in Matt 27:15–18 and Mark 15:6–9 of releasing a prisoner at Passover. In Luke, the mob hatches the scheme to free Barabbas impromptu.

blame on the Jewish authorities and their henchmen. I'm not sure about that: Luke did not hesitate earlier to introduce Pilate as tyrannical Judean governor known for slaughtering a group of Galilean worshippers in Jerusalem (13:1).[12] Pilate is no sweetheart, no champion of jurisprudence, and no friend of Galileans. Though he has no special axe to grind against the Galilean Jesus, Pilate has no bleeding heart for Jesus either. He couldn't care less whether Jesus lives or dies.

If Jesus's blood has to be spilt to maintain a modicum of public order, so be it. Pilate projects no profile in courage, justice, or diplomacy. He's just another scared strongman desperate to cling to power by any means necessary, including ceding power for the moment to a maniacal mob. Yet make no mistake: Pilate has the final "say so," as Jesus reminds him (23:3). He alone has the authority to pronounce the death verdict. He must take responsibility for it. Jesus's blood will forever be on Pilate's hands, however much he might try to scrub them clean (cf. Matt 27:24).

CRUCIFIXION AT GOLGOTHA

In the fraught hours since his nighttime arrest, Jesus has been maligned and mistreated by multiple judicial and law enforcement agents and summarily sentenced to death—no legal representation, no right to appeal, no deliberative process—a total mockery of the right to a "speedy trial" by equating "speedy" with "slipshod" or "shotgun." Though Jesus maintains his dignity and makes a few trenchant comments in his defense, he has little control over the feverish events swirling around him. But en route to the site of crucifixion, aptly named Golgotha or "Skull Place," and during the hours he hangs on the cross, has some vital things to say. Though mustering no tour de force martyrial address or apologetic oration (*pace* Stephen in Acts 7:2–53), the condemned and dying Jesus makes several pithy statements to great redemptive effect.

Though Luke propounds no theory of atonement in his account of Jesus's death, the narrative portrays Jesus as Savior to end of his life on the cross, ironically signaled in a three-part chorus of taunts:

---

12. Whatever Luke's intended political angle, Christian history has been blighted by a flood of anti-Jewish (mis)interpretation of the Gospel Passion narratives, laying the lion's share of blame for Jesus's death on "the Jews" indiscriminately. For critical assessments, see Farmer, ed., *Anti-Judaism*; Fredriksen and Reinhartz, eds., *Jesus*.

Jewish leaders and bystanders: He saved others; let him save himself if he is the Messiah of God, his chosen one! (23:35)

Roman soldiers: If you are the King of the Jews, save yourself! (23:36)

A criminal crucified beside Jesus: Are you not the Messiah? Save yourself and us! (23:39)

Some Messiah, some King, some Savior you are! Indeed, but not in the way these mockers imagine. Saving others as he surrenders his life. Seeding grace and blessing—not bile and recrimination—as he goes down in defeat. That's how non-strongman Jesus Messiah dies.

Dead Man Walking

Catholic Sister Helen Prejean, CSJ, a leading advocate of abolishing the death penalty in the US, wrote a moving account of her ministry to two death row inmates up to their executions. The influential work, entitled *Dead Man Walking* (1993), has spawned poignant adaptations in film (1995), opera (2000), and theater (2002).[13] Portrayals of the condemned man's final walk from holding cell to death chamber are especially chilling.

Christian tradition developed various stagings of Jesus's passion tracked along his final Via Dolorosa or "Way of Suffering," more or less based on the New Testament Gospels. Pilgrims annually flock to Jerusalem during Holy Week to retrace Jesus's final steps in Jerusalem and environs along fourteen so-called "Stations of the Cross." We focus here on two "stations" Luke features in Jesus's terminal cross-walk from Pilate's tribunal to Skull Place.

First, the Roman soldiers leading Jesus away to his execution dragoon one Simon of Cyrene to walk "behind Jesus" carrying his cross (beam) (23:26). Normally, the condemned criminal would carry his own cross, the instrument of his own torturous death. Luke does not specify why the soldiers commandeer another carrier, but we can be sure it's not out of compassion for Jesus as a human being, still less out of respect for him as a "king." Likely, in his bruised and beaten state, Jesus is simply too weak to bear this heavy beam.

Simon, a Jew from the north African province of Cyrenaica (modern Libya) in town for Passover, just happens to be in the vicinity of the

---

13. Caponegro, "Sister Helen."

crucifixion procession. Perhaps he has some curiosity about Jesus or desire to witness the death march spectacle, but there's no indication that he's a closet disciple of Jesus or, conversely, one of the rabble clamoring for his crucifixion. He's just an innocent bystander but one still subject to imperial authority. The scene is all about flexing Roman muscle, forcing all subjects, innocent or not, to comply. Yet in Luke's deft portrayal, the scene also reflects, unwittingly to the soldiers or Simon, the ideal way of discipleship prescribed by Luke's Jesus: *taking up the cross and following Jesus* (9:23). And it also reinforces Jesus's *weak* campaign strategy: strength through weakness, salvation through sacrifice (9:24–25)—through *shared* sacrifice, carrying the cross *together*, bearing one another's burdens. God's salvation is mediated through the anti-strongman, the weak king, the weakling Jesus.

Second, among the larger throng who accompany his terrible death walk, Jesus focuses on a group of women mourners, "beating their breasts and wailing for him" (23:27)—a clear indication, by the way, that the mob clamoring for his crucifixion do *not* represent the majority of "the people." In the last of his significant "turning" points (see above), Luke's Jesus "turns" and addresses the wailing women: "Daughters of Jerusalem, do not weep for me, but weep for yourselves and for your children" (23:28). Yet with this "Don't Cry for Me" plea, Jesus is not making some muscular, self-sufficient claim that he doesn't need the weak women's pitiful tears.[14]

Remember, Jesus came into Jerusalem weeping over its tragic resistance to God's "visitation" (19:41–44). He's not suddenly turning coolly stoic and stolid (no more tears) but rather continuing to show warmhearted sympathy and solidarity with fellow sufferers—especially with women and children (see strategy 3)—those most innocent casualties of masculine-militant power. He continues by addressing these "daughters of Jerusalem," "For the days are surely coming when they will say, 'Blessed are the barren, and the wombs that never bore, and the breasts that never nursed'" (23:29). Jesus is not calling for strict apocalyptic asceticism (celibacy and childlessness) but is acknowledging the common opinion "*they will say*" concerning the hard times that will come down especially hard on vulnerable mothers and children. He anticipates that Rome's hammer blow against him and God's realm in the present crisis hour will escalate

---

14. Contrast the hit song, "Don't Cry for Me, Argentina," composed by Webber and Rice for the album and musical *Evita*. Its bravura signature line—"The truth is I never left you, all through my wild days, my mad existence, I kept my promise"—is sung in the role of Eve Perón, a strong *woman* figure, as it happens.

into rapacious all-out war against God's people, callously *not* excepting women and children.[15] It's a wrenching time to weep, a time to mourn (cf. Eccl 3:4).

Dying Man Witnessing

The English word "martyr" derives from the wide-ranging Greek term for "witness" (*martys/martyreō*). English usage has narrowed the application to the singular event of bearing witness *unto death* and *through death* for a righteous cause. But with or without "martyr" connotations, how one faces death—the fine art of dying (*ars moriendi*)—has long been viewed as prime authentic evidence of one's character and what one values most *in life*.

Though lacking the surfeit of gory details and glorious declamations of early Jewish (Maccabean) and Christian martyrologies, Luke's comparatively modest account of Jesus's crucifixion bears profound witness to the remarkable witness that Jesus gives concerning himself and his Divine Father in his dying hours. Amid the devastating "spectacle" (23:48) of Roman power casting its dark shadow "over the whole land" (23:44),[16] God's gracious, redemptive realm in Jesus Messiah continues to emit light, life, and love.

Again, Jesus makes no soaring martyrial speeches, but his three dying statements—two of them prayers—speak volumes and have a notable impact on "the people [who] stood by watching," ordinary people (*laos*) distinguished from the Jewish "leaders" (*archontes*) who continued to "scoff" at Jesus (23:35). No more raucous crying out, "Crucify him!" by a rabid segment of the populace. After witnessing this terrible ordeal, "when all the crowds [*ochloi*] who had gathered there for this spectacle saw"—and heard—"what had taken place, they returned home, beating their breasts" in horror and, we can hope, some degree of remorse (23:48–49). How Jesus dies hits them hard.

---

15. Jesus's cryptic closing comment to the weeping women about green versus dry wood (23:31) may reflect different flammable degrees. Green wood burns less easily than dry. Perhaps, then, Jesus intimates that his death on a "green wood" cross, searing as it is, is but a prelude to the "dry wood" conflagration which Rome's firepower will ignite in Jerusalem; see Spencer, *Luke*, 591.

16. "This spectacle [*theōria*] [that the crowds] saw [*theōrēsantes*]" evokes the Roman theater (*theatron*) or arena, staging vicious attacks by wild beasts against traitors and other expendables; see Wilson, *Unmanly Men*, 170, 233–34; 1 Cor 4:9.

Jesus's *first saying*—"Father, forgive them, for they do not know what they are doing" (23:34)—functions as an epigraph to the whole crucifixion account, a counter-inscription to the derisive "This is the King of the Jews" placard nailed to the crossbeam above his head (23:38). The horrible breath-constricting torture of crucifixion is not conducive to speechifying. Whatever a condemned victim has to say must be said quickly. The initial last words from the cross are inevitably the strongest. By now, however, we should not be surprised that Jesus's strongest final words do not fit the typical strongman register. No going out in a blaze of vitriol and vengeance. No "Damn you all to hell." And no petitioning his Father to send an angelic strike force to rescue him (cf. Matt 27:63). Instead, Luke's Jesus opts for compassion and conciliation, imploring his Father to forgive his persecutors.

Of course, Jesus's prayer may be interpreted in various ways to make it less radical or more palatable to modern sensibilities: "Father, *You* forgive them (if You can)—but *I* can't, not while they're inflicting all this pain on me"; or "Father, forgive (only) those who are *ignorantly* caught up in this mess—but not the leaders who know full well what they're doing"; or wiggling out of the whole thing, as some Christian manuscript copyists did, by scrubbing Luke's text clean of the saying, probably motivated by anti-Jewish sentiment (mustn't let "the Jews" off the hook for killing Jesus).[17]

In any case, on a pastoral-psychological level, the issue of forgiving one's abusers—particularly of using Christ's example as a pressure point—must be handled with great sensitivity. The last thing victims of abuse need is guilt over not being ready or able to forgive as magnanimously as the dying Luke's Jesus does.[18] God bless, truly, those who forgave face-to-face (via teleconference) in Christ's name the white supremacist young man who had gunned down nine of their relatives and friends during a midweek Bible study and prayer meeting at the "Mother Emanuel" AME Church in Charleston, South Carolina, on June 17, 2015.[19] But God bless,

---

17. For thorough analyses of the text-critical issues surrounding this verse, see Strahan, *Limits*, 8–27; Brown, *Death*, 975–81. Both accept its authenticity to Luke, though Brown muses, "It is ironical that perhaps the most beautiful sentence in the PN [passion narrative] should be textually dubious" (*Death*, 980).

18. See Mayo, *Limits*.

19. See Von Drehle, Newton-Small, and Rhodan, "How Do You Forgive?"; Nussbaum, *Anger*, 77–78.

just as truly, those who couldn't grant such forgiveness and would rather God didn't either.

Either way, the dying Jesus suffers in solidarity with victims of physical and political violence, even as he exemplifies love and mercy toward enemy violators. An unfathomable profile in redemptive compassion in the face of vindictive strongman oppression: I am your restoration, your reconciliation—not your retribution.

In Jesus's *second saying*, he turns from addressing his Father on behalf of his persecutors to speaking more intimately with one of the criminals hanging beside him on another cross. In this public, painful, humiliating hour of Jesus's death, individuals still matter to him. In an eerie fulfillment of Jesus's Last Supper disclosure that he would be "counted among the lawless" as forecast by Isaiah (Luke 22:37/Isa 53:12), he is literally crucified between two "criminals, one on his right and one on his left" (Luke 23:32–33).[20] One of these outlaws joins in the "Save yourself" taunts against Jesus Messiah—adding, "and [save] us, too!" while you're at it (23:39). Jesus makes no effort to remonstrate with this sniping convict. The other criminal has plenty to say, however—indeed, Luke gives him the most lines in the crucifixion scene—first, setting the judicial record straight with his fellow criminal (we deserve this sentence, but "this man [Jesus] has done nothing wrong"[21]); second, pleading to "Jesus, remember me when you come in your kingdom" (23:42). Jesus answers, "Truly I tell you, today you will be with me in paradise" (23:43).

The history of religion, Christianity included, has been marred by so-called holy wars, sacred crusades, and glorious suicide missions carried out in the name of "God" and spurred by the promise of postmortem bliss in an eternal "paradise" (with or without seventy thousand virginal attendants). The Greek *paradeisos* transliterates a Persian term representing a

---

20. The term for "criminals" here (*kakourgoi*) literally means "evildoers." Gessen refers to mafia-style autocracies like that of Putin and Trump as "government of the worst—a kakistocracy" (*Surviving Autocracy*, 28; cf. 29–37).

21. Among Trump's most frequently repeated statements, "I've done nothing wrong" ranks close to the top. It began early in the 2015 campaign. When asked at the Family Leadership Summit in Ames, Iowa, whether he ever sought God's forgiveness, Trump stunningly replied, "I am not sure I have. I just go on and try to do a better job from there. I don't think so. I think if I do something wrong . . . I just try and make it right. I don't bring God into that picture. I don't." But to establish his Christian bona fides, he did hasten to give the evangelical audience a little eucharistic crumb: "When I drink my little wine—which is about the only wine I drink—and have my little cracker, I guess that is a form of asking for forgiveness, and I do that as often as possible because I feel cleansed" (reported in E. Scott, "Trump believes"). Well, then, I guess all is forgiven.

lush garden environment. In Jewish apocalyptic tradition, paradise evokes images of the primordial, prelapsarian Garden of Eden revamped after errant Adam and Eve's expulsion into an eternal haven for God's faithful people.[22]

Luke's Jesus only refers to paradise in this brief exchange with the criminal on the cross, and he never uses the promise of afterlife utopia as a bargaining chip to coax people into sacrificing their lives for God's kingdom. Along the way, Jesus assures his followers that their present sufferings and persecutions will accrue to "great reward in heaven" (6:22–23) and that they will ultimately "save their life" by losing it in cross-bearing discipleship (9:23–24). But he doesn't aim to bribe or blackmail anyone in exchange for his or God's "protection"—that's the stuff of venal mob bosses and strongmen—and most importantly, he's truly *leading the way*, himself bearing the brunt of the suffering-dying-rising ordeal to realize God's redemptive realm. Above all, strongmen use anyone and everyone to save their own necks and protect their own power. That is not Jesus's MO.

The petitionary criminal next to Jesus is in no position to do anything whatsoever *for* Jesus. He simply asks to be remembered when Jesus "comes in [his] kingdom." This would be a good cue for Jesus to ramp up his earlier statements about returning as the mighty Son of Humankind (17:22–37; 21:25–27; 22:69) with something like, "Mark my words: I am coming back with all the thundercloud authority of God's kingdom behind me to get my revenge on the whole lot of you." But no. Nothing more about a grand royal return. Just a simple, though stunning, pledge to a fellow dying man that "today *with me [met' emou]* you will be" in God's flourishing garden, following the Greek word order that prioritizes fellowship, partnership, solidarity *with Jesus*, at his side in life after death as in death.

Jesus makes his paradise promise to the pleading criminal "around noon time" (23:44), the hottest, brightest time of day appropriate for maximizing the torture and exposure of crucifixion. This is Rome's high-handed spectacle, endorsed by Jewish priestly hierarchs, set to Rome's imperial tempo and temperature. Or so it thinks. But in Luke's worldview, a higher reality and greater realm breaks into this horror show: the reality and realm of God, Creator of the cosmos and King of Israel. From noon to three o'clock, "the sun's light failed [eclipsed, *eklipontos*], and the curtain of the temple was torn [split, *eschisthē*] in two" (23:44).

---

22. See Charlesworth, "Paradise."

Although the Father will not spare his Son from drinking the "cup" of suffering and death (cf. 22:42; 23:36), no one should think for a second that the Father approves of these heinous proceedings and leaves them unanswered. In Jesus's agonizing last three hours of earthly life, God turns off the stage lights, shuts off the power, brings down the curtain not just on Skull Place but "on the whole land"—the whole vaunted Roman Empire. And not just on Rome's tyrannical system but also on the Jewish authorities' oppressive temple establishment in which the high priest claims privileged access to God via the sacred curtain.[23] God cannot bear for the moment—for three horrific hours of moments that seem like an eternity—to look on God's beloved world and holiest sanctuary that have so egregiously betrayed God's good purposes.

But all is not gloom and doom. Hope of resurrection and restoration is never extinguished in Luke's story, however dark and dim things may appear to be. Though making no last-gasp claim to return in vindicating victory and detailing no beatific vision of his paradisiacal destiny, Jesus does, with his *third saying*, leave this conflict-torn world in a peaceful, trustful, hopeful state: "Then Jesus, crying out with a loud voice, said, 'Father, into your hands I commend my spirit.' Having said this, he breathed his last" (23:46). Echoing Psalm 31:5—part of an extended passionate plea for divine succor in the face of persecution—Jesus entrusts his life and life's work, on the brink of extermination, into God's creative hands. In God's kingdom, expiration anticipates resuscitation, crucifixion augurs resurrection. Though unjustly and unconscionably battered and bruised in death, Jesus does not go down to defeat broken and bitter in spirit.

And it is this indomitable spirit, conveyed in pronouncements of forgiveness, fellowship, and faithful hope, that has such a profound effect on the majority of witnesses—on "all the crowds," presumably including the group that earlier shouted, "Crucify, crucify him!"—prompting them to leave the spectacle in excruciating anguish, not excited glee. They go home "beating their breasts" (23:48), signifying their psychically beaten state. Whatever their opinions about Jesus's messianic credentials, they know in their hearts that they've just witnessed a terrible miscarriage of justice: the brutal execution of an innocent man.

Beyond the crowds' gut-punched reaction, the most shocking response comes from a *centurion*, the Roman officer most likely supervising the crucifixion squad. From his front row seat to Jesus's "performance"

---

23. Once a year on the Day of Atonement to sprinkle a bull's blood on top of the ark of the covenant as a purification offering for the people's sins (Lev 16).

in this grotesque show, when the curtain falls the centurion senses on some level the invisible hand of God at work ("he praises God") in this "certainly . . . innocent" man Jesus (23:47). Too little, too late, we might snap back. You get no credit for hindsight praise of God after carrying out Pilate's death sentence against Jesus. Still, Luke places on record another Roman commander—following the one stationed in Capernaum in Luke 7:1–10 (see strategy 3)—who recognizes Jesus's superior moral authority over the current perverse purveyors of military and religious might.

Keeping Hope Alive—and Active

Strategy 12
Do not let death and defeat have the last word. Keep participating in God's ever-renewing, ever-evolving mission in the world to bring life out of death, joy out of sorrow, hope out of despair. Find the new beginning bursting to sprout from every ending. Rise above (ascend) defeat. Keep the campaign Spirit alive through dynamic memory, witness, vision, and action.

LUKE HAS NOT HESITATED to expose the thickness and fickleness of Jesus's (male) disciples. They have been slow to see, hear, grasp, and accept Jesus's self-expending (even to death), serving-oriented mission—desperately clinging to their visions of grandeur and versions of strongman politics: Which of us is or will be the greatest in the land, Jesus Messiah's right hand man (9:26; 22:24)? As Jesus's failed mission (as they saw it) began to dawn on them, crumbling their lofty dreams, they try to cut their losses through various cowardly means: betrayal, denial, desertion, seclusion. Not a pretty picture.

Yet, though holding the disciples accountable for their misunderstanding and misguided actions, Jesus does not write them off (well, except for Judas) or pile snide opprobrium on them. A degree of sympathy even seeps through reports that the disciples sleep through Jesus's final agonizing prayer session "because of grief" (22:45) and that the arrested Jesus turns and looks at Peter after he repeatedly denies Jesus in the high priest's courtyard (22:61).

And there's no denying the shattering impact that Jesus's death has on all his followers, whatever their personal aspirations and levels of investment in his movement. In strategy 11, we encountered a company of distraught women who beat their breasts and sob over the condemned Jesus en route to Golgotha (23:27). After Jesus expires and most spectators trudge to their homes lamenting his horrific crucifixion (23:48), a cadre of Jesus's "acquaintances" (*gnōstoi* who have some "knowledge" of him), "including the women who had followed him from Galilee, stood at a distance watching these things," hanging back for a while, no doubt frozen in shock (23:49). The eleven apostles may or may not have been among these distant onlookers. They are not identified as such until the next chapter where we find them huddled in an undisclosed Jerusalem locale (24:9, 33), perhaps back in the upper room where they'd shared the Passover meal with Jesus (22:10–13).

While plodding the seven-mile journey from Jerusalem back to their home village of Emmaus, two previously unknown devotees of Jesus, Cleopas and an unnamed companion, tersely encapsulate the despair now engulfing Jesus's supporters: "We had hoped that he was the one to redeem Israel" (24:21). Such hopes among the collective "we" of Jesus's followers no doubt spanned a spectrum of redemptive goals from personal-individual salvation to political-national restoration, but in any case, these hopes were pinned on Jesus as God's Spirit-anointed agent of liberation (4:18–19). But the cross dissolves all such hopes. What good can the defeated, dead Jesus do now? It's not like he can dust himself off, regroup, and run again for "election" in four years. How can God, still less "we," possibly *redeem* the devastating loss of God's beloved Son and Messiah? Will there ever be light in our world again, or will the sun remain forever eclipsed? Cognitive dissonance and emotional upheaval inundate the Jesus movement, threatening to throttle it and condemn it to the detritus of history.[1]

Yet here "we" are over two millennia later with millions across the globe enthusiastically following and serving Jesus, the "Savior who is the Messiah, the Lord" (2:11). And "we" are here today because Luke and other first-century Gospel writers passed down the story from "eyewitness" tradition at "the beginning" (1:1–2) that Jesus was raised from the dead on the third day, as he had predicted, and transported into heaven on the fortieth day, awaiting a glorious return to earth at some future time (24:50–53; Acts 1:1–11). Thus, the apparent ending of the story on

---

1. See Spencer, *Seven Challenges*.

the cross is no ending at all but rather the bridge to a *new beginning*, a transition to new life, a transfiguration (cf. Luke 9:28–36). Simple as that.

Except it was not remotely simple for Jesus's first followers. Luke tells no simple "Voilà" story about Jesus's resurrection. In fact, there's no story *of* the resurrection itself: no hidden cameras inside the tomb capture the moment; no one witnesses Jesus's actual emergence from the grave into the world; there are no sightings of Jesus first walking around in graveclothes. Surely—but slowly—it dawns on Jesus's supporters, starting at "early dawn" on Sunday for a group of women (24:1), that Jesus *might be* alive. In their cognitive-emotional state of despair, it takes time to "see" the living Christ and even longer to process who or what they had "seen." Their post-resurrection encounters with Christ on earth are intermittent. He has an unnerving way of popping in and out on them and then finally departing with the prospect of an open (unscheduled) return flight.

The risen Jesus chides Cleopas and companion for being "slow of heart to believe" that he's alive, walking and talking with them, fulfilling the scriptural prophets' forecasts about the Messiah's suffering and humiliation giving way to enlivening and glorification (24:25–26). But such prophecies are far from obvious, and Jesus does not spell them out or rush to reveal himself when the couple doesn't immediately recognize him. Luke is a committed believer in the saving work of the crucified-risen Lord Jesus Christ, but he's not a naïve believer or brainwashed booster. He honestly relates the first disciples' continuing struggle to wrap their minds and hearts around the whole complex of Christ events—not least his resurrection, ascension, and expected reappearance (*parousia*)—as a means of grappling with the same concerns in Luke's own Christ-centered community forty-plus *years* later.

Consider three thoughtful angles displayed in Luke 24 to keep the hope of Jesus's messianic realm alive—and active: (1) Remembering the Message (24:1–12), (2) Revisioning the Messiah (24:13–35), and (3) Reframing the Mission (24:36–49).

REMEMBERING THE MESSAGE

Jesus's women disciples—led by Mary Magdalene, Joanna, and another Mary (mother of James)—who had followed him from Galilee and witnessed his crucifixion from a safe distance, expect, like everyone else, that Jesus's death has ended his earthly existence. They probably hope, along with many Jews, for a general end-time resurrection, and if so, they doubtless believe Jesus merits a glorious last day resurrection and honored place in God's eternal kingdom. In the meantime, however, they presume his corpse would decompose like any other human body.

At least these women—*unlike* Jesus's other supporters, including the male apostles—do not maintain their safe distance and abandon Jesus's deceased body to the ravages of vultures, curs, and maggots. Crucifixion victims typically hung for days before being cast into shallow graves or pits. Surprisingly, however, a Jewish council member named Joseph from the Judean town of Arimathea, "a good and righteous man . . . [who] had not agreed to [the council's] plan and action" against Jesus, gains Pilate's permission to take Jesus's body, wrap it in a linen burial cloth, and place it in a "rock-hewn tomb" just before the Sabbath begins at sunset on Friday (23:50–54). (Joseph represents a notable *exception* to the Jewish establishment's opposition to Jesus, as the centurion does on the Roman side.) Mary Magdalene and company follow Joseph to the tomb, observe "how [Jesus's] body [is] laid," and make plans to return after the Sabbath to anoint Jesus's corpse with perfumes and spices as a gesture of devotion and preservation, stemming the stench of decay for awhile (23:55–56).

When the grieving women, however, return to the tomb early Sunday morning, they suffer another major shock as they notice the tomb's open entrance and the stark absence of Jesus's body. The tomb is not entirely empty, however, as "two men in dazzling clothes" suddenly appear beside the women, scaring them to death (24:1–4). What a scene! It gets stranger as these two shining messengers (angels? Moses and Elijah again?) inform the women that Jesus "is not here" (obviously) because he "has risen" from the dead (oh really?). But they couch this stunning news in a sideswipe rebuke: "Why do you look for the living among the dead? Remember how he told you, while he was still in Galilee, that the Son of Man must be handed over to the hands of sinners and be crucified and on the third day rise again" (24:5–6).

Though a "told-you-so" argument rarely lands well and, in this case, seems insensitive to the women's bereaved state, it still makes a valid point concerning *remembrance* as a key source of faith and hope in trying circumstances. In response to the messenger's words, Mary Magdalene and friends indeed "remember [Jesus's] words" and report this dramatic experience "to the eleven [apostles] and to the rest" (24:8–10).

Apart from Jesus's two predictions of his third-day resurrection (9:21–22; 18:32–33)—which the women now recall—he more recently exhorted his disciples to continue memorializing his life-giving death in the Lord's Supper: "Do this in *remembrance* of me." In other words, "Eat this broken piece of bread and drink this cup of wine in remembrance of my broken body 'given for you' and shed blood 'poured out for you'" (22:19–20). Such "remembering" is no mere mental exercise of data retrieval but rather a full-bodied representing (re-presenting, re-incarnating) of the whole dynamic complex of Jesus's career from conception to resurrection, from Spirit-filled womb to empty tomb.

In the crucible of twentieth-century totalitarian threats to democracy and terrible holocausts against the Jews and other targeted populations, Hannah Arendt forged the principle of remembered *natality* as the critical antidote to the paralyzing fear of *mortality*: "The decisive fact determining man as a conscious, *remembering* being is birth or 'natality,' that is, the fact that we have entered the world through birth. The decisive fact determining man as a desiring being was death or mortality, the fact that we shall leave the world in death. . . . What ultimately stills the fear of death is not hope and desire but *remembrance* and gratitude."[2] Accordingly, for Arendt, natality is the seminal act underlying constructive politics, with the emphasis on *act/action*: "Since action is the political activity par excellence, natality, and not mortality, may be the central category of political, as distinguished from metaphysical, thought."[3]

Though primarily a secular political philosopher, journalist, and activist, Arendt was deeply influenced by Christian biblical and theological tradition. In *The Human Condition* she writes about natality with almost evangelical passion:

> The miracle that saves the world, the realm of human affairs, from its normal, "natural" ruin is ultimately the fact of natality, in which the faculty of action is ontologically rooted. It is, in other words, the birth of new men and the new beginning, the action they are capable of by virtue of being born. . . . It is this faith in and hope for the world that found perhaps its most glorious and most succinct expression in the few words with which the Gospels announced their "glad tidings": "A child has been born unto us."[4]

---

2. Arendt, *Love*, 51–52 (from her revised doctoral dissertation [emphasis added]); cf. in this volume the interpretive essay by J. Scott and Start, "Thought Trains," 146–48.

3. Arendt, *Human Condition*, 9.

4. Arendt, *Human Condition*, 247.

Though giving no Scripture references, Arendt echoes the KJV of Isaiah and Luke. Christian theology has long regarded Isaiah's prophecy of a coming supreme Davidic savior ruler ("For unto us a child is born, a son is given," Isa 9:6–7) as fulfilled in Jesus Christ, certified by angelic annunciation to the shepherds in Luke on the night of Jesus's birth: "And the angel said unto them, Fear not: for, behold, I bring you *good tidings* of great joy, which shall be to all people. For unto you is born this day in the city of David a Savior, which is Christ the Lord" (Luke 2:10–11; cf. "glad tidings," 1:19). The natality of Christ trumps his mortality with dynamic potentialities of ever renewing "new beginnings."

In the final words of her trenchant and harrowing analysis of *The Origins of Totalitarianism*, Hannah further roots her natalist hope against hope in new beginnings (natalism inoculating against nihilism) in the very fabric of creation and anthropology as expounded by Saint Augustine:

> Forms of government . . . have stayed with mankind regardless of temporary defeats—monarchies, and republics, tyrannies, dictatorships, and despotism.
> But there remains also the truth that every end in history necessarily contains a new beginning; this is the promise, the only "message" which the end can ever produce. Beginning, before it becomes a historical event, is the supreme capacity of man; politically it is identical with man's freedom. *Initium ut esset homo creates est*—"that a beginning be made man was created" said Augustine [*City of God* 12.20]. This beginning is guaranteed by each new birth; it is indeed every man.[5]

REVISIONING THE MESSIAH

To this point in Luke's Gospel, no one has personally *seen* the risen Jesus. The women at Jesus's tomb witness his absence, not his presence. Their vision is of a void, a vacancy filled by alien visitors who report Jesus's resurrection and relocation to some other, as yet undisclosed, place. Have the two dazzling messengers themselves seen the risen Jesus? Has anyone? All the women have to go on at this stage is the word of these two—oh, yes, and the *memory* of Jesus's prophetic word. As we've just

---

5. Arendt, *Origins*, 478–79. I'm indebted in this section on Arendt to Hill, "When Hope Is a Hindrance."

argued, that vital act of remembering carries great potential, but it remains shaky without firsthand encounter with the living crucified Christ. And given the common prejudice of the time against women's testimony (supposedly prone to hysterical conjurations), the odds are not good that the male apostles will believe them. In fact, they don't. The women's "words seemed to [the men] an idle tale (*lēros*)"—utter "nonsense" (CEB, NIV), "humbug"[6]—"and they did not believe them" (24:11). Peter at least dashes to the tomb to check the story for himself and notices "the linen [burial] cloths by themselves"—with *no body* in them—but that just leaves him confused and "amazed," not convinced of the women's story or of Jesus's resurrection (24:12). Apparently, by the time Peter arrives, the two special agents have left the scene to tend to other business.

Though we learn, belatedly and briefly, that Jesus soon appears to Peter (24:34), the first narrated encounter with the risen Jesus is experienced by two devotees, Cleopas and a companion (possibly his wife), on the road from Jerusalem to Emmaus (24:13–35). This meeting, however, is anything but typical, and not just because it involves a resurrected figure walking and talking on earth. This figure—Jesus of Nazareth, crucified three days prior—first appears *incognito*, walking and talking along the Emmaus road with two supporters who *do not recognize him* (24:16), even as they talk about him and their relationship with him!

It frankly makes for a funny, almost farcical, scene, with Jesus pranking the clueless, hopeless couple as they bemoan the loss of their beloved messianic candidate who, unbeknownst to them, is right there with them! It's hard not to burst out laughing when Jesus sidles up to the "sad looking" pair, casually asks them with a straight face, "What are you discussing with each other?," and Cleopas whips back, "Are you the only stranger in Jerusalem who does not know the things that have taken place there in these [recent] days?" To which Jesus replies, continuing his deadpan routine, "What things?," which prompts their summary report of Jesus's powerful prophetic mission tragically cut short by crucifixion and now beset by confusing reports of his missing body (24:17–24). Luke does not specify why Cleopas and his companion's "eyes were kept from recognizing [Jesus]" (24:16). The passive voice may intimate some providential purpose behind the misrecognition (God wants to teach them a lesson [see below]). More practically, we may wonder whether Jesus is wearing some disguise or modifying his familiar voice or whether the

---

6. BDAG, 594.

travelers' perceptual channels have been scrambled by their cognitive dissonance and emotional distress. Whatever the reason, they appear as bumbling fools in a comedy of errors.

Humor and laughter make good medicine to cope with tragedy. Laugh to keep from crying or at least stop crying for a few moments. Laugh it off and keep going. But there seems to be more than comic relief behind this extraordinary post-resurrection narrative that Luke (alone) showcases, something more profound than prankish for those with eyes to see.

First, on the road, the risen Jesus (as yet unrecognized) shifts from inquisitive to instructional mode, teaching Cleopas and companion about the Jewish scriptural-prophetic template for a Messiah who must first "suffer . . . and then enter his glory." No more playful foolery. Now Jesus exposes the couple as perilously "foolish . . . and slow of heart to believe all that the prophets have declared!" (24:25–27). They will later recall how "our hearts [were] burning within us while [Jesus] was talking to us on the road, while he was opening the scriptures to us" (24:32). The encounter with this "stranger" is turning serious, significant even, though in the present moment, they're not sure how. But they want to know more as they reach their Emmaus home at day's end, and though Jesus "walked ahead as if he were going on" his own way, they convince him to stay the night (24:28–29).

Then, sitting at the supper table, Jesus again shifts roles, this time from guest to host, as "he took bread, blessed and broke it, and gave it to them" (24:30). Where have we seen this before? Where might Cleopas and partner have seen this before? Ah yes—when Jesus wondrously took-blessed-broke-gave five loaves of bread (and two fishes) to feed the five thousand in the desert (9:16–17) and later served the Passover loaf to his disciples in the upper room. And remember, in this Last Supper, Jesus identifies the bread with his body about to be "given [in death] for you" and institutes this table act as a central act of perpetuating *remembrance* of him (22:19). Which is precisely how it functions in Cleopas's home in Emmaus on the first Easter supper: "*Then*"—at the moment of Jesus's bread service—"their eyes were opened, and they recognized him" (24:30).

Wonderful! What a moment that must have been, and what conversation must have ensued. Or would have if Jesus had stuck around for it. But capping off this already very strange inaugural post-resurrection appearance, "he vanished from their sight" just after the point of recognition (24:31). It's normally considered rude to "eat and run" from a dinner party. Jesus doesn't even stay to eat. He sits, serves, and runs. Now you see him, now you don't.

While this incident demonstrates that Jesus's risen body has a supernatural capacity for teleportation, that's hardly Luke's main point. As I've repeatedly stressed, Luke is not promoting a strongman campaign or peddling a' superhero graphic novel. Luke presents Jesus Messiah in various roles but none more vital than his *ministerial-nourishing* role as God's benevolent *servant of all*. "I am among you as one who serves (*diakonōn*)," Jesus tells his disciples at the Last Supper (22:27). Whatever changes resurrection brings, retirement from service is not one of them. Jesus's greatest position in God's kingdom continues to be as the sympathetic suffering servant with the least, last, and lowliest—modeled in part after the suffering servant figure in Isaiah's songs (42:1–9; 49:1–7; 50:4–11; 52:13–53:12)—who, though never identified as the Messiah, provides the most likely biblical basis for Jesus's claim that it was "necessary that the Messiah should suffer these things and then enter into his glory" (Luke 24:25–27; cf. vv. 44–46). Thus, the *scriptural-prophetic* and *ministerial-nourishing* templates for Jesus's messianic mission merge in the Emmaus road incident.

In short, word and food, text and table mark the principal means through which Jesus is heard and seen, remembered and recognized. By these means, Jesus lives on through his followers, *if*, to continue the pressing perceptual challenge facing Jesus's disciples, they have "ears to hear and eyes to see," *if* they embrace the dynamic representative potential of these elements. In religious terms, inspired study of the Jewish Scriptures and sharing meals (especially, but not limited to the Lord's Supper [Holy Communion/Eucharist]) become *sacramental* mediators of Jesus's blessed presence.

But these means, however meaningful, are not ends. They do not contain Jesus, like some magic genie lamp, still less control him via some magical wish-formula. As in life, all the more so in death and resurrected life, Jesus exceeds the grasp of his followers. Just when you've got him in your sights, he vanishes; just when he sits down for a nice meal, he vacates his seat. But in Luke's view, this is no cheap parlor trick or child's game of hide-and-seek. This is the way of life with Jesus Messiah, a way traced in holy writ by "Moses and all the prophets" (24:27) and in mealtime fellowship but not etched in cold stone tablets or tables. It is an open way, an elusive way, an expansive way that keeps one alert to new beginnings and fresh encounters with God's grace in all the strange dimensions of life—including in the *stranger* Jesus embodies and embraces (24:18; cf. Matt 25:35–45).

And most importantly, the way of Jesus Messiah is broader than Jesus himself. It is less *about* him than *with* him in seeking and serving God's redemptive realm. As Isaiah's suffering servant and Daniel's Son of Humankind are representative figures of God's people, God's "holy ones" (Dan 7:25–27), so Jesus incarnates God's good purpose for all humanity and, indeed, all creation bearing God's image. The living Jesus does not micromanage this mission. He doesn't crave the spotlight. He doesn't pretend "I alone can fix it" and most certainly does not crow, "I am your retribution" against your perceived enemies and grievances. Jesus Christ lives and thrives in *beloved community*,[7] not in self-absorbed ascendancy.

REFRAMING THE MISSION

In his final post-resurrection appearance, Luke's Jesus clarifies his identity and the mission he's entrusting to his followers. Within the hour of Jesus's disappearing act from their table, Cleopas and companion dash back to Jerusalem to report to the eleven apostles and associates (probably including Mary Magdalene and women friends). The Emmaus couple finds the group abuzz with their own talk of Jesus's resurrection: "He has appeared to Simon [Peter]!" (Luke 24:33–34). While the visiting pair are relating their own amazing story, "Jesus himself" materializes again, announcing to this larger assembly, "Peace be with you" (24:36). Nice thought but bad timing. No advanced warning, no door knocking—just sudden presence and greeting, inducing more panic than peace. "Startled and terrified," the group first thinks they're seeing "a ghost" or "a spirit" (*pneuma*), and not necessarily the "holy" type (24:37). With all that's happened the last few days, they are easily spooked, and the risen Jesus keeps acting rather spookily.

But he now settles down for a while and tries to ease the anxious hearts and minds of his followers. His therapy session, as it were, unfolds in four stages.

---

7. See Martin Luther King Jr., "Facing the Challenge": "We have before us the glorious opportunity to inject a new dimension of love into the veins of our civilization.... The end is reconciliation; the end is redemption; the end is the creation of a beloved community. It is this type of spirit and this type of love that can transform opposers into friends."

Bridging the Gap

The flow of action in the present episode reverses that of the Emmaus incident. The latter has a centrifugal thrust, keeping Jesus at a distance even when he's nearby: he operates incognito on the road, keeps walking when the couple reaches their home, and, finally, after being persuaded to stay for dinner, disappears when he's recognized "in the breaking of the bread" (24:35) but before anyone's taken a bite. But now in Jerusalem, Jesus operates in more centripetal motion, reaching out to his followers and drawing them toward him in closer connection. Specifically, he invites them to *see* and *touch* his *hands* and *feet* (24:39–40)—the parts of his body nailed or tied to the cross. Luke does not mention nail prints (as in John 20:25–27) or rope marks but probably implies them.

While Jesus encourages inspecting his hands and feet as proof of his identity and corporeality—"It is I myself," the crucified one now alive in "flesh and bones," no mere spectral spirit (Luke 24:39)—his gesture provides more than forensic evidence. It also signals intimate fellowship, connection, communion, solidarity, sympathy—seeing and feeling with his followers. Jesus confirms the essence of his "body . . . given for you" (22:19), forever bound with his people in their sorrow and joy, suffering and rejuvenation.

Taking a Break

This remarkable move by the crucified-resurrected Jesus sparks mixed feelings among the assembly. They are thrilled, of course, by Jesus's warm outreach, "yet for all their joy they were still disbelieving and wondering" what to make of this whole eerie experience (23:41). Understandably. This is a lot to take in while in a state of shock. Thankfully, however, this time Jesus doesn't vanish the moment he reveals himself. He sticks around to eat and talk, offering much needed instruction.

But this "sacramental" table fellowship stands on no ceremony or ritual. On this occasion, Jesus does not sit down at a set table or take, bless, and break bread. Incidentally, impulsively even, he blurts out to his befuddled followers, "Have you anything here to eat?" as if all this popping around has worked up an appetite. Promptly, "they gave him a piece of broiled fish [leftovers?], and he took it and ate it in their presence" (24:42–43). Thus fortified, Jesus proceeds to share some vital information.

Before unpacking Jesus's teaching, however, we should consider the import of his impromptu snack break. On one level, it further proves the risen Jesus's human bodily identity. Ghosts, angels, spirits, and other supernatural beings do not need to eat; they have no digestive systems. For all its paranormal shape-shifting capacities, Jesus's resurrected body still needs food—and he will *still* not use his God-given powers to zap up an order of bread (or fish) for personal consumption, as the devil tried to get him to do at the beginning of his mission (4:1–4).

Accordingly, on another level, this eating vignette shows Jesus's continued need for others' help and hospitality. Not that he *demands* service or a big spread. No snapping fingers or barking orders at the wait staff; he just makes a simple request for something to eat. In Luke's narrative, the provision of *fish* recalls two dramatic episodes: first, Jesus's initial revelation to Simon Peter, in which Peter casts his net at Jesus's command and hauls in a huge catch (5:1–11); and second, Jesus's breaking and blessing of two fish (plus five bread loaves) and giving them to the disciples to feed the multitude (9:12–17). Now, however, the tables are turned: Jesus asks for and receives a *piece* of fish (no heaping plate or basketful) *from* his disciples.

The crucified-risen Jesus Messiah continues to experience ordinary, interdependent life with his fragile, fallible followers. He's no spine-tingling extraterrestrial showcasing a magical extravaganza. A piece of fish humbly requested, gratefully received; a material body nourished, mutual fellowship enacted. A truly sacred act, a sacrament.

Charting the Mission

As in the Emmaus incident, Jesus clarifies his person and work through inspired word as well as food. Again, he "opened their minds to understand the scriptures" that adumbrate the suffering-dying-rising trajectory of his messianic career (24:44–46). But now he also discloses the goals and scope of his ongoing mission entrusted to his emissaries: "Repentance and forgiveness of sins is to be proclaimed in his name to all nations, beginning from Jerusalem. You are witnesses of these things" (24:47–48).

Jesus has no need or aim to restore his good name that the authorities had dragged through the mud to Skull Place, to run again, as it were, for Messiah and prove all his detractors wrong and put them in their place beneath his feet. God has vindicated him by raising him from the dead. God's approval is all that matters. Jesus has no lust to take Caesar's imperial throne, Pilate's gubernatorial seat, or the high priest's supreme judicial bench. His seat at God's right hand is sufficient. Yes, the messianic work will continue, but Jesus is happy for his followers to take up his mantle—not as his malicious avengers, however—but as his mission ambassadors to "all nations, beginning in Jerusalem."

This is not to upshift to some maniacal plan of world dominance after being rejected by Israel's leaders but to recommit to God's historical plan for God's "firstborn son" Israel (Exod 4:22; Hos 11:1)—personalized and perfected in God's Messiah-Son Jesus—to be a blessing to "all the families of the earth" (Gen 12:1–3), a beacon of "light to the nations" (Isa 42:6; 49:6; cf. Luke 2:29–32). The plan is for world "repentance and forgiveness of sins." Though such language may evoke modern evangelistic harangues against sinners, insisting that they turn or burn, the thrust is less condemnatory than salutary, less wrong-branding than right-making. Jesus's messianic project is about making the whole world whole, changing embittered hearts and minds (repentance) for the betterment of all creation, bringing alienated people together (forgiveness) for the common good.

I happen to be drafting these words on the day after Jimmy Carter turned ninety-nine years of age. By many accounts, though he had some signature presidential achievements, most notably the Camp David peace accords, Carter was an average-to-mediocre, one-term head of state roundly defeated for reelection. Be that as it may, after losing the 1980 race, Carter did not sulk, cry "Foul!," blame everyone else for his shortcomings, threaten retaliation, and pine to return to public office. Instead, he settled in to do his best humanitarian work locally and globally. Instead of throwing a tantrum and toppling the blocks that didn't stack his way, Carter has built innumerable houses for displaced people through the Jimmy and Rosalynn Carter Work Project arm of Habitat for Humanity. Instead of railing against the world, he has promoted world health and peace, including eliminating the scourge of Guinea worm disease[8] and facilitating fair and peaceful elections in other countries. Jimmy Carter can rightly boast, though that's not his style, of the longest,

---

8. Carter Center, "Guinea Worm": "When The Carter Center began leading the international campaign to eradicate Guinea worm disease in 1986, there were an estimated 3.5 million cases in at least 21 countries in Africa and Asia. Today, that number has been reduced by more than 99.99 percent." Only *six* cases were reported January 1 to August 1, 2023.

most productive, most redemptive (as a devout Christian, he would like this term)[9] postpresidential career in American history.

Taking His Leave

Jesus does not leave his followers high and dry to fend for themselves. Along with appearing to them in his risen body and instructing them about their mission, he promises to equip them soon with the "power from on high" they will need to get the job done (24:49)—that is, the same Holy Spirit that empowered his work (3:16, 21–22; 11:13; Acts 1:4–8; 2:1–4). But Jesus does leave them physically. He leads them from their temporary Jerusalem quarters to a place in nearby Bethany from which he's "carried into heaven" (24:50). And as he's lifting off, he raises his hands to extend a final blessing to his beloved supporters, which buoys their spirits and brings them "with great joy" back to Jerusalem where they commune "continually in the temple blessing God" (24:50–53).

The Lukan Jesus's messianic campaign—for all its challenges to the point of excruciating suffering and death—ends on a resounding note of benediction, not malediction. *Blessing*: not cursing, complaining, condemning like self-absorbed, so-called strongmen. *Blessing*: that's what real men (and women) of God do from start to finish.

---

9. Balmer aptly titles his biography of Carter *Redeemer*.

Postscript
Resolutions of a Concerned Citizen

FEW AMERICAN CHRISTIANS ACROSS the religious and political spectrum doubt that we stand at a critical crossroad in our nation's history, with the very survival of democracy and the republic, as we've known it, at stake. The system has been fragile from the start, requiring vigilant maintenance and updates to survive, let alone thrive. On the last day of the Constitutional Convention, September 18, 1787, a prominent woman in Philadelphia's social and political circles, Elizabeth Willing Powel, asked Benjamin Franklin, "Well, Doctor, what have we got—a republic or a monarchy?" to which Franklin replied, "A republic, if we can keep it."[1]

We have kept it, more or less, for over two hundred years, but it seems acutely up for grabs (an unfortunately apt term) these days. In his January 6, 2021, speech on the Ellipse in Washington, DC egging his supporters to storm the Capitol and "stop the steal" of the 2020 election, (lame duck) President Trump thundered, "We fight like hell. And if you don't fight like hell, you're not going to have a country anymore."[2] On the other side, concerned citizens feared that four more years of Trump, especially after his clear electoral defeat, would signal the hellish demise of our country. Republic lost, tyranny triumphs.

Fortunately, we dodged that bullet (another lamentably apt idiom). But here we are again (I'm writing this in December 2023) heading into the 2024 election with Trump as the presumptive nominee, with Biden's poll numbers sagging, with rumblings of third-party candidates (these usually hurt the incumbent)—and with evangelical Christians still overwhelmingly in favor of Trump and Trumpian authoritarian government,

1. Miller, "'A republic.'"
2. Naylor, "Read Trump's Jan. 6 Speech."

which is to say, government stripped to the bone to clear the way for strongman rule. Many evangelicals would readily sign on to the Heritage Foundation's Project 2025 conservative agenda, dedicated, according to Heritage president Kevin Roberts, to making the next US president "ready to govern in the most aggressive, ambitious, audacious way to destroy the Deep State and devolve power back to the individual Americans."[3] So "individual Americans" supposedly regain their power by ceding all power to one Big-I Individual autocrat? (My head hurts.)

And evangelical Jesus-followers are happy with that plan? Even granting that Jesus himself might not be suitable for the rough-and-tumble world of politics (he fits better in Sunday school classrooms and soup kitchens), they believe he would certainly, as a good gospeler (evangelical), endorse Trump or someone like him over all weak and "woke" alternatives. I might hasten to add that evangelicals normally believe that Jesus doesn't simply preach the gospel. He *is* the gospel; without Jesus there is no gospel.

I have argued in this book, however, via the time-honored medium of political riff and satire, that the portrait of Jesus Christ sketched by one writer with impeccable Gospel credentials, Luke the evangelist, ill suits a figure who embodies or endorses authoritarian ideology or politics. Luke's Jesus resists cooptation by any partisan platform but especially that which promotes muscular and monarchic mega-power (and MA-GA-power). If nothing else, the cross crosses out power politics through and through. And don't be fooled by the classic strongman trick that he is the (only) one who can save you from authoritarianism (I'm not the authoritarian—you are!).[4] Believe what he shows and tells you in plain sight who he really is and what he stands for. Don't believe it has anything to do with Jesus.

So where does all this leave us? I have no idea how the year 2024 will play out, including the November presidential election, arguably one of the most critical elections in our nation's history. And we can be certain that the polls will vacillate and never tell the full story. But perhaps we can make a couple of New Year's resolutions—and keep them for a change throughout the year and beyond. Consider the sage counsel of the eminent Old Testament scholar Walter Brueggemann concerning

---

3. Twitter message reported in Vandehei and Allen, "Behind the Curtain"; cf. Hirsch, "Inside the Next Republican Revolution."

4. See N. Klein, *Doppelganger*, 71–72; 145–46, 150–57.

America's current political crisis, counsel which I transpose below into two resolutions.

> I have no doubt that the Bible provides guidance and resources for our current political situation, and standing ground from which to resist current right-wing ideology, and to host alternative visions of social well-being. . . . The Bible, ancient as it is, continues to emit echoes that take the form of both assurance and summons. The assurance from biblical faith, variously expressed, is that there is a coherent governance of creation that is bent toward well-being, shaped as restorative justice, and enacted with generous compassion. The summons that echoes from the Bible, also variously voiced, is that we human agents are recruited into that work.[5]

Assurance and summons. Hope and action. Two vital resolutions which Luke supports (with a boost from Romans 8).

First, BE IT RESOLVED THAT the Bible overall—not least the Gospel of Luke that we've explored in this book—and Jesus Christ the Living Creative Word to whom the Bible witnesses, sustains a holistic vision of grace-suffused redemption, restoration, and reconciliation for all creation. In our present "groanings" with all creation, we persevere in aspirational saving hope, not abject cynical despair (Rom 8:18–30).[6] Luke shares that core message with the apostle Paul and the other biblical writers.[7] It's high time for evangelicals and other concerned Christians to "grab" hold again of this biblical good news for dear life,[8] to treat the Bible seriously again as a deep reservoir of rich multilayered truth, not as a cheap prop[9] or prooftext.

Second, BE IT RESOLVED THAT God recruits all of us, not just a special "chosen" one or few, as active coagents with God, Jesus Christ, and the Holy Spirit in the hard work of re-creating and renewing the world according to God's good purposes for the common good—of, by, and for common people—in solidarity with all creation. Hence, we must resolve

---

5. Brueggemann, *Ancient Echoes*, ix–x.

6. Wright, *Into the Heart*.

7. See the section on "Creational Theology" in Spencer, *Luke*, 674–90.

8. Cf. Friesen, "Grab 'Em by the Bible?"; M. Bird, "Someone Needs to Grab America by the Bible."

9. As when Trump posed with a Bible for a photo op in front of the St. John's Church Parish House sign in Washington, DC (June 1, 2020) amid protest in the city over police violence against George Floyd; cf. Schiess, *Bible and the Ballot*, 1–2; Montague, "Holding It Aloft."

to give active life service, not empty lip service, to the gospel, to "walk the same way [Jesus] walked" (1 John 2:6) as much as possible in our daily lives—our public and political lives as much as our private and personal ones. We must all do what we can, giving in neither to crippling cynicism nor to Pollyannaish optimism that somehow things will just magically work out as they're supposed to.

Forget the mistranslated and misapplied panacea-verse in Romans 8:28: "And we know that all things work together for good to them that love God, to them that are called according to his purpose" (KJV). The NRSV makes a few slight grammatical tweaks, such as "for those who love God."[10] The NRSVue makes no further changes. It would have been better, however, truer to the Greek and Paul's overall message in Romans 8, to follow the original RSV: "We know that in everything *God works* for good *with those* who love him, who are called according to his purpose." The Greek word order actually runs, "with those who love God, everything [God] works for good" (*tois agapōsin ton theon panta synergei eis agathon*), stressing up front God-lovers' active roles as God's working partners.[11] The verb (*synergei*) reinforces God's dynamic working *together* (synergy) *with* God's people in a common calling (vocation) for the common good—not "all things" perchance or even providentially working *themselves* out.

The holy "purpose" which we've been called to work out with God is not Democrat or Republican, conservative or liberal. It doesn't fit any partisan label. It's as big as all creation and as deep as incarnation. Its image is not a logo or photo but a living person: Jesus Christ, God's Son, in whose image God calls us "to be conformed" (8:29; cf. 12:1–2). "Do you want to know God's purpose for your life? Then be like Jesus! That is God's purpose. That is how we are restored to what we were always called to be, the image of God."[12]

Jesus is not on the ballot and endorses no candidate. But if we call ourselves Christian, the Jesus way—as spelled out in the canonical Gospels like Luke (how else do we know Jesus's way?)—must honestly and

---

10. See Keesmaat and Walsh, *Romans Disarmed*, 375–79; Wright, *Into the Heart*, 155–63.

11. The NRSV and NRSVue acknowledge in a footnote that some ancient authorities add the nominative *theos* to make God's role as the subject of *synergei* more explicit. The Creator and Redeemer God is the prime subject throughout Romans 8; see Wright, *Into the Heart*, 159–61.

12. Keesmaat and Walsh, *Romans Disarmed*, 378.

actively inform our political lives. Whatever else we might do, we must at least register our voices by voting. As Barack Obama never tires of responding during speeches when audiences bemoan the current state of political affairs, "Don't boo. Vote!" Amen.

Bibliography

Adams, John. *The Letters of John and Abigail Adams*. Edited by Abigail Adams. New York: Penguin Classics, 2003.
Alberta, Tim. *The Kingdom, the Power, and the Glory: American Evangelicals in an Age of Extremism*. New York: HarperCollins, 2023.
Allison, Dale C., Jr. *The New Moses: A Matthean Typology*. Eugene, OR: Wipf & Stock, 2013 (orig. 1993).
Alter, Alexandra, and Nicholas Confessore. "Republican Party spent nearly $100,000 on Donald Trump Jr's new book." *Atlanta Journal-Constitution*, November 22, 2019. https://www.ajc.com/news/republican-party-spent-nearly-100-100-donald-trump-new-book/Y4hNu8d1UjKr3Mxx7ouCyK/.
Alter, Jonathan. *His Very Best: Jimmy Carter, A Life*. New York: Simon & Schuster, 2020.
Anderson, Gary A. *Sin: A History*. New Haven: Yale University Press, 2009.
Anderson, Robert T. *The Samaritan Pentateuch: An Introduction to Its Origin, History, and Significance for Biblical Studies*. Atlanta: SBL, 2012.
Applebaum, Anne. *The Twilight of Democracy: The Seductive Lure of Authoritarianism*. New York: Doubleday, 2020.
Arendt, Hannah. *The Human Condition*. 2nd ed. Chicago: University of Chicago Press, 1998 (orig. 1958).
———. *Love and Saint Augustine*. Edited by Joanna Vecchiarelli Scott and Judith Chelius Stark. Chicago: University of Chicago Press, 1996.
———. *The Origins of Totalitarianism*. New ed. Boston: Mariner, 1968.
Aristotle. *Aristotle's Art of Rhetoric*. Translated by Robert C. Bartlett. Chicago: University of Chicago Press, 2019.
Ashdown, Nick. "'Radical Love Book' hailed as key to Turkish Opposition Election Success." *Middle East Eye*, April 11, 2019. https://www.middleeasteye.net/news/radical-love-book-hailed-key-turkish-opposition-election-success.
Austin, Emily A. *Living for Pleasure: An Epicurean Guide to Life*. New York: Oxford University Press, 2022.
Babota, Vasile. "In Search of the Origins of the Pharisees." In *The Pharisees*, edited by Joseph Sievers and Amy-Jill Levine, 23–40. Grand Rapids: Eerdmans, 2021.
Bailey, Kenneth E. *Jesus through Middle Eastern Eyes: Cultural Studies in the Gospels*. Downers Grove, IL: IVP Academic, 2008.
Balmer, Randall. *Bad Faith: Race and the Rise of the Religious Right*. Grand Rapids: Eerdmans, 2021.

———. *Redeemer: The Life of Jimmy Carter*. New York: Basic Books, 2014.
Barton, Bruce. *The Man Nobody Knows: A Rediscovery of the Real Jesus*. Indianapolis: Bobbs-Merrill, 1924.
Bauckham, Richard. "Son of Man." Vol. 1: *Early Jewish Literature*. Grand Rapids: Eerdmans, 2023.
Bean, Alan. "Jesus and John Wayne: Must we choose?" *Baptist News Global*, October 31, 2016. https://baptistnews.com/article/jesus-and-john-wayne-must-we-choose/.
Beard, Mary. *Emperor of Rome: Ruling the Ancient Roman World*. New York: Liveright, 2023.
Beaty, Katelyn. *Celebrities for Jesus: How Personas, Platforms, and Profits are Hurting the Church*. Grand Rapids: Brazos, 2022.
Begley, Sarah. "How 'In God We Trust' Got on the Currency in the First Place." *Time*, January 13, 2016. https://time.com/4179685/in-god-we-trust-currency-history/.
Ben-Ghiat, Ruth. *Strongmen: Mussolini to the Present*. New York: Norton, 2020.
Berkowitz, Roger. "The Double Weaponization of Loneliness." *Amor Mundi*, August 13, 2023. https://hac.bard.edu/amor-mundi/the-double-weaponization-of-loneliness-2023-28-13.
Bird, Kai. *The Outlier: The Unfinished Presidency of Jimmy Carter*. New York: Crown, 2022.
Bird, Michael F. *A Bird's-Eye View of Luke-Acts: Context, Story, and Themes*. Downers Grove, IL: IVP Academic, 2023.
———. *Evangelical Theology: A Biblical and Systematic Introduction*. Grand Rapids: Zondervan, 2013.
———. "Someone Needs to Grab America by the Bible." *Substack*, September 29, 2023. https://michaelfbird.substack.com/p/someone-needs-to-grab-america-by?utm_source=%2Fsearch%2Fsomeone%2520needs%2520to%2520grab&utm_medium=reader2.
Boller, Paul F., Jr. *Presidential Campaigns from George Washington to George W. Bush*. New York: Oxford University Press, 1984.
Boring, M. Eugene. *Deuteronomy for the Church: Who We Are, What God Requires*. Minneapolis: Fortress, 2022.
Brodie, Thomas L. "Towards Unravelling Luke's Use of the Old Testament: Luke 7:11–17 as an Imitatio of 1 Kings 17:17–24." *NTS* 32 (1986) 247–67.
Brown, Raymond E. *The Death of the Messiah from Gethsemane to the Grave: A Commentary on the Passion Narratives in the Four Gospels*. Vol. 2. ABRL. New York: Doubleday, 1994.
Brueggemann, Walter. *Ancient Echoes: Refusing the Fear-Filled, Greed-Driven Toxicity of the Far Right*. Minneapolis: Fortress, 2023.
Bush, George W. "2000 Presidential Victory Speech." *American Rhetoric*, December 13, 2000. https://www.americanrhetoric.com/speeches/gwbush2000victoryspeech.htm.
Canin, Ethan. *America America: A Novel*. New York: Random House, 2008.
Capa, Cornell (photographer). "Politics: A Great Game and a Sight to Behold." Photo essay in *Life*, July 4, 1960, 12–21.
Caponegro, Ramon Anne. "Sister Helen Prejean: American Nun." *Britannica*. https://www.britannica.com/biography/Sister-Helen-Prejean.
Caputo, John D. *The Weakness of God: A Theology of the Event*. Bloomington: Indiana University Press, 2006.
———. *What To Believe: Twelve Brief Lessons in Radical Theology*. New York: Columbia University Press, 2023.

Carlson, Stephen C. "The Accommodations of Joseph and Mary in Bethlehem: Κατάλυμα in Luke 2.7." *NTS* 56 (2010) 326–42.

Carroll, John T. *Luke: A Commentary*. NTL. Louisville: Westminster John Knox, 2012.

Carter Center. "Guinea Worm Case Totals." https://www.cartercenter.org/health/guinea_worm/case-totals.html.

———. "Jimmy Carter." https://www.cartercenter.org/about/experts/jimmy_carter.html.

Carter, Jimmy. *A Call to Action: Women, Religion, Violence, and Power*. New York: Simon & Schuster, 2014.

———. "Inaugural Address," January 20, 1977. https://www.presidency.ucsb.edu/documents/inaugural-address-0.

Carter, Warren. *Matthew and the Margins: A Sociopolitical and Religious Reading*. Maryknoll, NY: Orbis, 2000.

Charlesworth, James H. "Paradise." In *The Anchor Bible Dictionary*, edited by David Noel Freedman et al., 5:154–55. New York: Doubleday, 1992.

Cicero, Marcus Tullius. *De Amicitia*. Translated by William Armistead Falconer. Cambridge: Harvard University Press, 1923. https://www.perseus.tufts.edu/hopper/text?doc=Perseus%3Atext%3A2007.01.0041%3Asection%3D98.

———. *For Aulus Cluentius*. In *The Orations of Marcus Tullius Cicero*. Translated by C. D. Yonge, B. A. London, and Henry G. Bohn (1856). https://www.perseus.tufts.edu/hopper/text?doc=Perseus%3Atext%3A1999.02.0019%3Atext%3DClu.%3Asection%3D51.

———. *How to Win an Argument: An Ancient Guide to the Art of Persuasion*. Translated by James M. May. Princeton: Princeton University Press, 2016.

Cicero, Quintus Tullius. *How to Win an Election: An Ancient Guide for Modern Politicians*. Translated by Philip Freeman. Princeton: Princeton University Press, 2012.

Clapp, Rodney. *Naming Neoliberalism: Exposing the Spirit of Our Age*. Minneapolis: Fortress, 2021.

Clinton, Hillary Rodham. *It Takes a Village and Other Lessons Children Teach Us*. New York: Simon & Schuster, 1996.

———. "The Weaponization of Loneliness." *Atlantic*, August 7, 2023. https://www.theatlantic.com/ideas/archive/2023/08/hillary-clinton-essay-loneliness-epidemic/674921/.

Collins, Adela Yarbro, and John J. Collins. *King and Messiah as Son of God: Divine, Human, and Angelic Figures in Biblical and Related Literature*. Grand Rapids: Eerdmans, 2008.

Crossan, John Dominic. *Jesus: A Revolutionary Biography*. New York: HarperCollins, 1994.

Croston, Glenn. "The Thing We Fear More than Death." *Psychology Today*, November 29, 2012. https://www.psychologytoday.com/us/blog/the-real-story-risk/201211/the-thing-we-fear-more-death#:~:text=Surveys%20about%20our%20fears%20commonly,least%20according%20to%20some%20surveys.

Culy, Martin M., Mikeal C. Parsons, and Joshua J. Stigall. *Luke: A Handbook on the Greek Text*. Waco, TX: Baylor University Press, 2010.

Danby, Herbert. *The Mishnah*. London: Oxford University Press, 1933.

Danker, Frederick W. *Jesus and the New Age: A Commentary on St. Luke's Gospel*. 2nd ed. Philadelphia: Fortress, 1988.

D'Angelo, Mary Rose. "Reconstructing 'Real' Women from Gospel Literature: The Case of Mary Magdalene." In *Women and Christian Origins*, edited by Ross Kraemer Shepard and Mary Rose D'Angelo, 105–28. New York: Oxford University Press, 1999.

DeSteno, David. *Emotional Success: The Power of Gratitude, Compassion, and Pride*. Boston: Houghton Mifflin Harcourt, 2018.

Detrow, Scott. "Russell Moore on an 'altar call' for Evangelical America." NPR interview, August 5, 2023. https://www.npr.org/2023/08/05/1192374014/russell-moore-on-altar-call-for-evangelical-america.

Dostoevsky, Fyodor. *The Brothers Karamazov*. Translated by Richard Pevear and Larissa Volokhonshy. Princeton: Princeton University Press, 1990.

Du Mez, Kristin Kobes. *Jesus and John Wayne: How White Evangelicals Corrupted a Faith and Fractured a Nation*. New York: Liveright, 2020.

Dwyer, Colin. "Donald Trump: 'I Could Shoot Somebody . . . and I Wouldn't Lose Any Voters.'" *The Two-Way*, NPR, January 23, 2016. https://www.npr.org/sections/thetwo-way/2016/01/23/464129029/donald-trump-i-could-shoot-somebody-and-i-wouldnt-lose-any-voters.

Dwyer, Karen Kangas, and Marlin M. Davidson. "Is Public Speaking Really More Feared than Death?" *Communication Research Reports* 29 (2012) 99–107.

Ebrahimi, Omid V, Ståle Pallesen Robin M. F. Kenter, and Tine Nordgreen. "Psychological Interventions for the Fear of Public Speaking: A Meta-Analysis." *Frontiers in Psychology* 10 (2019) 1–27. doi: 10.3389/fpsyg.2019.00488.

Eizenstat, Stuart E. *President Carter: The White House Years*. New York: Thomas Dunne, 2018.

Ekblad, Bob. *Reading the Bible with the Damned*. Louisville: Westminster John Knox, 2005.

Epictetus. *The Complete Works: Handbook, Discourses, and Fragments*. Edited and translated by Robin Waterfield. Chicago: University of Chicago Press, 2022.

Evans, Craig A., and James A. Sanders. *Luke and Scripture: The Function of Sacred Tradition in Luke-Acts*. Eugene, OR: Wipf and Stock, 2001.

Farmer, William R., ed. *Anti-Judaism and the Gospels*. Harrisburg, PA: Trinity Press International, 1999.

Fea, John. *Believe Me: The Evangelical World of Donald Trump*. Grand Rapids: Eerdmans, 2018.

Fredriksen, Paula, and Adele Reinhartz, eds. *Jesus, Judaism, and Christian Anti-Judaism*. Louisville: Westminster John Knox, 2002.

Friedersdorf, Conor. "Why Do Parents Hand Their Babies to Politicians?" *Atlantic*, August 19, 2011. https://www.theatlantic.com/politics/archive/2011/08/why-do-parents-hand-their-babies-to-politicians/243848/.

Friesen, Courtney. "Grab 'Em by the Bible? Wayne Grudem and Trumpian Biblical Ethics." *Sojourners*, August 29, 2018. https://sojo.net/articles/grab-em-bible.

Garber, Megan. "Who Cares If a Politician Is Likeable?" *Atlantic*, October 6, 2016. https://www.theatlantic.com/culture/archive/2016/10/who-cares-if-a-politician-is-likable/623074/.

Garnsey, Peter, and Richard Saller, with Jaś Elsner, Martin Goodman, Richard Gordon, and Greg Woolf (and Marguerite Hirt). *The Roman Empire: Economy, Society and Culture*. 2nd ed. Oakland: University of California Press, 2015.

Gessen, Masha. *Surviving Autocracy*. New York: Riverhead, 2021.

Gibbs, Nancy, David Aikman, and Richard N. Ostling. "America's Holy War." *Time*, December 9, 1991. https://content.time.com/time/subscriber/article/0,33009, 974430-4,00.html.

Glancy, Jennifer A. *Slavery as Moral Problem in the Early Church and Today*. Minneapolis: Fortress, 2011.

———. *Slavery in Early Christianity*. Minneapolis: Fortress, 2006.

Goodwin, Doris Kearns. *Leadership in Turbulent Times*. New York: Simon & Schuster, 2018.

———. *Team of Rivals: The Political Genius of Abraham Lincoln*. New York: Simon & Schuster, 2005.

Gore, Al. "2000 Presidential Concession Speech." *American Rhetoric*, December 13, 2000. https://www.americanrhetoric.com/speeches/algore2000concessionspeech.html.

Gray, Rebecca. *Prophetic Figures in Late Second Temple Jewish Palestine*. New York: Oxford University Press.

Gushee, David P. *Defending Democracy from Its Christian Enemies*. Grand Rapids: Eerdmans, 2023.

Haidt, Jonathan. "The Emotional Dog and Its Rational Tail: A Social Intuitionist Approach to Moral Judgment." *Psychological Review* 108 (2001) 814–34.

———. *The Righteous Mind: Why Good People Are Divided by Politics and Religion*. New York: Pantheon, 2012.

Hanson, K. C. "The Galilean Fishing Economy and the Jesus Tradition." *BTB* 27 (1997) 99–111.

Hanson, K. C., and Douglas E. Oakman. *Palestine in the Time of Jesus: Social Structures and Social Conflicts*. Minneapolis: Fortress, 1998.

Hart, Bradley W. *Hitler's American Friends: The Third Reich's Supporters in the United States*. New York: Thomas Dunne, 2018.

Hawn, C. Michael. "History of Hymns: 'There Is a Balm in Gilead.'" *Discipleship Ministries*, March 18, 2019. https://www.umcdiscipleship.org/resources/history-of-hymns-there-is-a-balm-in-gilead.

Hendricks, Obery, Jr. *Christians Against Christianity: How Right-Wing Evangelicals Are Destroying Our Nation and Our Faith*. Boston: Beacon, 2021.

———. *The Politics of Jesus: Rediscovering the True Revolutionary Nature of Jesus' Teachings and How They Have Been Corrupted*. New York: Doubleday, 2006.

Herzog, William R., II. "Dissembling, a Weapon of the Weak: The Case of Christ and Caesar in Mark 12:13–17 and Romans 13:1–7." *PRSt* 21 (1994) 339–60.

———. "Sowing Discord: The Parable of the Sower." *RevExp* 109 (2012) 187–98.

Hill, Samantha Rose. "When Hope Is a Hindrance." *Aeon*, October 4, 2021. https://aeon.co/essays/for-arendt-hope-in-dark-times-is-no-match-for-action.

Hirsch, Michael. "Inside the Next Republican Revolution." *Politico*, September 19, 2023. https://www.axios.com/2023/12/01/trump-government-job-applications-2025?utm_source=newsletter&utm_medium=email&utm_campaign=newsletter_axiosam&stream=top.

Hoffer, Eric. *The True Believer: Thoughts on the Nature of Mass Movements*. New York: Harper & Row, 1951.

Hoover, Herbert. "October 22, 1928: Principles and Ideals of the United States Government." Transcript of presidential campaign speech on website of the Miller Center, University of Virginia. https://millercenter.org/the-presidency/presidential-speeches/october-22-1928-principles-and-ideals-united-states-government.

Horsley, Richard A. *Jesus and the Spiral of Violence: Popular Jewish Resistance in Roman Palestine.* New York: Harper & Row, 1987.

Horsley, Richard A., and John S. Hanson. *Bandits, Prophets, and Messiahs: Popular Movements at the Time of Jesus.* Minneapolis: Winston, 1985.

Imamoğlu, Ekrem. "How I won the race for mayor of Istanbul—and how I'll win again." *Washington Post*, June 4, 2019. https://www.washingtonpost.com/opinions/2019/06/04/how-i-won-race-mayor-istanbul-how-ill-win-again/.

Immerwahr, Daniel. *How to Hide an Empire: A History of the Greater United States.* New York: Farrar, Straus and Giroux, 2019.

Ingleby, Melvyn. "A Turkish Opposition Leader Is Fighting Erdoğan with 'Radical Love.'" *Atlantic*, June 14, 2019. https://www.theatlantic.com/international/archive/2019/06/ex-istanbul-mayor-imamoglu-fights-erdogan-radical-love/591541/.

Jenkins, Jack. "In 'God made a fighter' ad." *Religion News*. https://religionnews.com/2022/11/07/new-desantis-ad-signals-potential-vie-for-trumps-religious-base/.

Johnson, Luke Timothy. *Prophetic Jesus, Prophetic Church: The Challenge of Luke-Acts to Contemporary Christians.* Grand Rapids: Eerdmans, 2011.

Josephus, Flavius. *The New Complete Works of Josephus.* Translated by William Whiston with commentary by Paul L. Maier. Rev. and expanded ed. Grand Rapids: Kregel, 1999.

Joshel, Sandra R. *Slavery in the Roman World.* Cambridge: Cambridge University Press, 2010.

Juvenal. *Satires.* Translated by A. S. Kline. Online, 2011. https://www.poetryintranslation.com/klineasjuvenal.php.

Keddie, Tony. *Republican Jesus: How the Right Has Rewritten the Gospels.* Oakland: University of California Press, 2020.

Kee, Howard C. *Miracle in the Early Christian World: A Study in Sociohistorical Method.* New Haven: Yale University Press, 1983.

Keesmaat, Sylvia C., and Brian J. Walsh. *Romans Disarmed: Resisting Empire, Demanding Justice.* Grand Rapids: Brazos, 2019.

Kendall, Joshua. *American Obsessives: The Compulsive Energy that Built a Nation.* New York: Grand Central, 2013.

Kennedy, George A. *Progymnasmata: Greek Textbooks of Prose Composition and Rhetoric.* Atlanta: SBL, 2003.

King, Martin Luther, Jr. "Facing the Challenge of a New Age." Address delivered at the First Annual Institute on Nonviolence and Social Change, Montgomery, AL, December 3, 1956. https://okra.stanford.edu/transcription/document_images/Vol03Scans/451_3-Dec-1956_Facing%20the%20Challenge%20of%20a%20New%20Age.pdf.

Klein, Christopher. "Election 101: How did the tradition of kissing babies begin?" *History*, September 1, 2018. https://www.history.com/news/election-101-how-did-the-tradition-of-kissing-babies-begin .

Klein, Naomi. *Doppelganger: A Trip into the Mirror World.* New York: Farrar, Straus and Giroux, 2023.

———. *No Is Not Enough: Resisting Trump's Shock Politics and Winning the World We Need.* Chicago: Haymarket, 2017.

Klutz, Todd E. *The Exorcism Stories in Luke-Acts: A Sociostylistic Reading.* SNTMS 129. Cambridge: Cambridge University Press, 2004.

Klepper, David. "Trump arrest prompts Jesus comparisons: 'Spiritual warfare.'" *AP*, April 5, 2023. https://apnews.com/article/donald-trump-arraignment-jesus-christ-conspiracy-theory-670c45bd71b3466dcd6e8e188badcd1d.

Kolbert, Elizabeth. "You Can't Make It Up: What P. T. Barnum Understood about America." *The New Yorker*, August 5, 2019. https://www.newyorker.com/magazine/2019/08/05/what-p-t-barnum-understood-about-america.

Kurlander, Eric. *Hitler's Monsters: A Supernatural History of the Third Reich*. New Haven: Yale University Press, 2017.

Lane, Melissa. *The Birth of Politics: Eight Greek and Roman Political Ideas and Why They Matter*. Princeton: Princeton University Press, 2014.

———. "The Origins of the Statesman: Demagogue Distinctions in and after Athens." *Journal of the History of Ideas* 73 (2012) 179–200.

Lee, Bandy X., ed. *The Dangerous Case of Donald Trump: 37 Psychiatrists and Mental Health Experts Assess a President*. New York: Thomas Dunne, 2019.

Lepore, Jill. *These Truths: A History of the United States*. New York: Norton, 2018.

Levitsky, Steven, and Daniel Ziblatt. *How Democracies Die*. New York: Broadway, 2018.

Lincoln, Abraham. "House Divided." June 16, 1858. Illinois Republican State Convention, Springfield, IL. Abraham Lincoln Online: Speeches and Writings. https://www.abrahamlincolnonline.org/lincoln/speeches/house.htm.

———. "Second Inaugural Address." March 4, 1865. Website of the Lincoln Memorial, National Park Service, US Department of the Interior. https://www.nps.gov/linc/learn/historyculture/lincoln-second-inaugural.htm.

Long, D. Stephen. "Debt." In *Dictionary of Scripture and Ethics*, edited by Joel B. Green et al., 209–10. Grand Rapids: Baker Academic, 2011.

Louw, Johannes P., and Eugene A. Nida, eds. *Greek-English Lexicon of the New Testament Based on Semantic Domains*. Vol. 1. 2nd ed. New York: United Bible Societies, 1988.

Lovelace, Berkely, Jr. "Donald Trump used campaign funds to buy his own book: Report." CNBC, August 24, 2016. https://www.cnbc.com/2016/08/24/donald-trump-used-campaign-funds-to-buy-his-own-book-report.html.

Machiavelli, Niccolò. *The Art of War*. Translated by Christopher Lynch. Chicago: University of Chicago Press, 2003.

Maiz, Ramón. "The Political Mind and Its Other: Rethinking the Non-Place of Passions in Political Theory." In *Politics and Emotions*, edited by Marcos Engelken-Jorge, Pedro Ibarro Güell, and Carmelo Moreno del Río, 29–70. Wiesbaden: Springer Fachmedien, 2011.

Mark, David, and Adelle M. Banks. "Repentant 'Hatchet Man,' Colson was Evangelical Icon." *Christian Century*, May 16, 2012. http://www.christiancentury.org/article/2012-14/nixon-felon-and-evangelical-icon-charles-colson-dies-80.

Martin, Jonathan, and Mike Allen. "McCain unsure how many houses he owns." *Politico*, August 21, 2008. https://www.politico.com/story/2008/08/mccain-unsure-how-many-houses-he-owns-012685.

May, Rollo. *Freedom and Destiny*. New York: Norton, 1981.

Mayo, Maria. *The Limits of Forgiveness: Case Studies in the Distortion of a Biblical Ideal*. Minneapolis: Fortress, 2015.

McKnight, Scot. *The Bible Is Not Enough: Imagination and Making Peace in the Modern World*. Minneapolis: Fortress, 2023.

McLuhan, Marshall. *Understanding Media*. Cambridge: MIT Press, 1994 (original ed. 1964).

Meacham, Jon. *And There Was Light: Abraham Lincoln and the American Struggle.* New York: Random House, 2022.

Meier, John P. *A Marginal Jew: Rethinking the Historical Jesus.* 5 vols. AYBRL. New Haven: Yale University Press, 1991–2016.

Miller, Julie. "'A republic if you can keep it': Elizabeth Willing Powel, Benjamin Franklin, and the James McHenry Journal." *Library of Congress Blogs,* January 6, 2022. https://blogs.loc.gov/manuscripts/2022/01/a-republic-if-you-can-keep-it-elizabeth-willing-powel-benjamin-franklin-and-the-james-mchenry-journal/.

Montague, Zach. "Holding It Aloft, He Incited a Backlash. What Does the Bible Mean to Trump?" *New York Times,* June 1, 2020. https://www.nytimes.com/2020/06/02/us/politics/trump-bible-st-johns.html.

Moore, Christopher. *Lamb: The Gospel according to Biff, Christ's Childhood Pal.* New York: William Morrow, 2002.

Moore, Russell D. *Losing Our Religion: An Altar Call for Evangelical America.* New York: Sentinel, 2023.

Morabito, Stella. *The Weaponization of Loneliness: How Tyrants Stoke Our Fear of Isolation to Silence, Divide, and Conquer.* New York: Bombardier, 2021.

Morgan, Teresa. *The New Testament and the Theology of Trust: "The Rich Trust."* Oxford: Oxford University Press, 2022.

———. *Roman Faith and Christian Faith:* Pistis *and* Fides *in the Early Roman Empire and Early Churches.* Oxford: Oxford University Press, 2015.

Naím, Moisés. *Revenge of Power: How Autocrats are Reinventing Power for the 21st Century.* New York: St. Martin's, 2022.

Naylor, Brian. "Read Trump's Jan. 6 Speech, A Key Part of Impeachment Trial." *NPR,* February 10, 2021. https://www.npr.org/2021/02/10/966396848/read-trumps-jan-6-speech-a-key-part-of-impeachment-trial.

Neuman, Scott. "Trump Doubles Down on McCain Criticism, Refusing to Apologize." NPR *Two Way,* July 19, 2015. https://www.npr.org/sections/thetwo-way/2015/07/19/424382469/trump-doubles-down-on-mccain-criticism-refusing-to-apologize.

Neveu, Cameron. "Evel Empire: Knievel's Stranglehold on the Seventies." *Hagerty Media,* March 26, 2021. https://www.hagerty.com/media/people/evel-empire-knievel-stranglehold-seventies/.

Novakovic, Lidija. "Jews and Samaritans." In *The World of the New Testament: Cultural, Social, and Historical Contexts,* edited by Joel B. Green and Lee Martin McDonald, 207–15. Grand Rapids: Baker Academic, 2013.

Novenson, Matthew V. *The Grammar of Messianism: An Ancient Jewish Political Idiom and Its Users.* Oxford: Oxford University Press, 2017.

Nussbaum, Martha C. *Anger and Forgiveness: Resentment, Generosity, Justice.* New York: Oxford University Press, 2016.

Oakman, Douglas E. *Jesus, Debt, and the Lord's Prayer: First-Century Debt and Jesus' Intentions.* Eugene, OR: Cascade, 2014.

Oh, Inae. "Trump Brags About Eating 'the Most Beautiful' Chocolate Cake During Syrian Missile Strike Decision." *Mother Jones,* April 12, 2017. https://www.motherjones.com/politics/2017/04/trump-syria-chocolate-cake-mar-a-lago/.

Omanson, Roger L. *A Textual Guide to the Greek New Testament.* Stuttgart: German Bible Society, 2006.

Bibliography

Oord, Thomas Jay. *Death of Omnipotence and Birth of Amipotence*. Grasmere, ID: SacraSage, 2023.

———. *God Can't: How to Believe in God after Tragedy, Abuse, and other Evils*. Grasmere, ID: SacraSage, 2019.

———. *The Uncontrolling Love of God: An Open and Relational Account of Providence*. Downers Grove, IL: IVP Academic, 2015.

Oster, Richard E. "'Show Me a Denarius': Symbolism of Roman Coinage and Christian Beliefs." *RestQ* 28 (1985/86) 107–15.

Parsons, Mikeal C. *Luke: Storyteller, Interpreter, Evangelist*. Peabody, MA: Hendrickson, 2007.

Peppard, Michael. *The Son of God in the Roman World: Divine Sonship in Its Social and Political Context*. New York: Oxford University Press, 2012.

Perry, Patrick. "Something Serious: Deviating from lighthearted fare for a change, Norman Rockwell interprets the Golden Rule." *Saturday Evening Post*, February 2, 2015. https://www.saturdayeveningpost.com/2015/02/something-serious/.

Peterson, Eugene H. *Tell It Slant: A Conversation on the Language of Jesus in His Stories and Prayers*. Grand Rapids: Eerdmans, 2008.

Philodemus. *On Frank Criticism*. Introduction, Translation, and Notes by David Konstan, Diskin Clay, Clarence E. Glad, Johan C. Thom, and James Ware. SBLTT 43. Atlanta: Scholars, 1998.

Plutarch. *Comparitio Thesei et Romuli*. In *Plutarch's Lives*, translated by Bernadotte Perrin. Cambridge: Harvard University Press, 1914.

Poirier, John C. "The Endtime Return of Elijah and Moses at Qumran." *DSD* 10 (2003) 221–42.

Porter, Stanley E. "The Parable of the Unjust Steward (Luke 16:1-13): Irony Is the Key." In *The Bible in Three Dimensions: Essays in Celebration of Forty Years of Biblical Study at the University of Sheffield*, edited by David J. A. Clines, Stephen E. Fowl, and Stanley E. Porter, 127–53. JSOTSup 87. Sheffield: JSOT, 1990.

Posner, Eric A., Kathryn E. Spier, and Adrian Vermeule. "Divide and Conquer." *Journal of Legal Analysis* 2 (2010) 417–71.

Prejean, Helen. *Dead Man Walking: An Eyewitness Account of the Death Penalty in the United States*. New York: Random House, 1993.

Pummer, Reinhard. *The Samaritans: A Profile*. Grand Rapids: Eerdmans, 2016.

Reich, Robert. *The Common Good*. New York: Vintage, 2019.

———. "Why I'm so short. Thoughts about heightism." *Substack*, July 11, 2023. https://robertreich.substack.com/p/why-im-so-short.

Reid, Barbara E. "Beyond Petty Pursuits and Wearisome Widows: Three Lukan Parables." *Int* 53 (2002) 284–94.

Rhee, Helen. *Illness, Pain, and Health Care in Early Christianity*. Grand Rapids: Eerdmans, 2022.

Richardson, Heather Cox. *Democracy Awakening: Notes on the State of America*. New York: Viking, 2023.

Riesner, Rainer. "Praetorium." In vol. 4 of *The New Interpreter's Dictionary of the Bible*, edited by Katherine Doob Sakenfeld et al., 577–78. Nashville: Abingdon, 2009.

Robin, Corey. *The Reactionary Mind: Conservatism from Edmund Burke to Donald Trump*. 2nd ed. New York: Oxford University Press, 2018.

Roth, Philip. *The Plot Against America*. New York: Houghton Mifflin, 2004.

Rothman, Lily. "The Long History Behind Donald Trump's 'America First' Foreign Policy." *Time*, March 28, 2016. https://time.com/4273812/america-first-donald-trump-history/.

Rousseau, Jean-Jacque. *Confessions*. Anonymous translator, 1903. https://www.gutenberg.org/files/3913/3913-h/3913-h.htm.

Rousseau, John J., and Rami Arav. *Jesus and His World: An Archaeological and Cultural Dictionary*. Minneapolis: Fortress, 1995.

Saldarini, Anthony J. *Pharisees, Scribes and Sadducees in Palestinian Society: A Sociological Approach*. Grand Rapids: Eerdmans, 2001.

Sample, Ian. "If they could turn back time: how tech billionaires are trying to reverse the ageing process." *Guardian*, February 17, 2022. https://www.theguardian.com/science/2022/feb/17/if-they-could-turn-back-time-how-tech-billionaires-are-trying-to-reverse-the-ageing-process.

Sawicki, Marianne. *Crossing Galilee: Architectures of Contact in the Occupied Land of Galilee*. Harrisburg, PA: Trinity Press International, 2000.

———. "Magdalenes and Tiberiennes: City Women in the Entourage of Jesus." In *Transformative Encounters: Jesus and Women Re-viewed*, edited by Ingrid R. Kitzberger, 181–202. Biblical Interpretation 43. Boston: Brill, 1999.

Schiess, Kaitlyn. *The Bible and the Ballot: How Scripture Has Been Used and Abused in American Politics and Where We Go from Here*. Grand Rapids: Brazos, 2023.

Schneemelcher, William, ed. *New Testament Apocrypha*, vol. 2. Rev. ed. Translated by R. McL. Wilson. Cambridge: James Clarke/Louisville: Westminster John Knox, 1992.

Sharlet, Jeff. *The Family: The Secret Fundamentalism at the Heart of American Power*. New York: Harper Perennial, 2008.

———. *The Undertow: Scenes from a Slow Civil War*. New York: Norton, 2023.

Schreiber, Melody. "George W. Bush's anti-HIV program is hailed as 'amazing'—and still crucial at 20." NPR *Goats and Soda*, February 28, 2023. https://www.npr.org/sections/goatsandsoda/2023/02/28/1159415936/george-w-bushs-anti-hiv-program-is-hailed-as-amazing-and-still-crucial-at-20#:~:text=Bush's%20anti%2DHIV%20program%20is,and%20still%20crucial%20at%2020&text=via%20Getty%20Images-,In%202003%2C%20President%20George%20W.,over%20the%20next%205%20years.

Scott, Eugene. "Trump believes in God, but hasn't sought forgiveness." *CNN*, July 18, 2015. https://www.cnn.com/2015/07/18/politics/trump-has-never-sought-forgiveness/index.html.

Scott, Joanna Vechiarelli, and Judith Chelius Start. "Thought Trains." In Hannah Arendt, *Love and Saint Augustine*, edited by J. Scott and Start, 142–72. Chicago: University of Chicago Press, 1996.

Skinner, Matthew L. *The Trial Narratives: Conflict, Power, and Identity in the New Testament*. Louisville: Westminster John Knox, 2010.

Snodgrass, Klyne R. *Stories with Intent: A Comprehensive Guide to the Parables of Jesus*. Grand Rapids: Eerdmans, 2008.

Snyder, Timothy. *On Tyranny: Twenty Lessons from the Twentieth Century*. New York: Crown, 2017.

Specter, Michael. "1992 Campaign: Treading a Mosaic of Nerve Endings." With verbatim under the heading, "Heckler Stirs Clinton Anger: Excerpts from the Exchange." *New York Times*, March 28, 1992. https://www.nytimes.com/1992/03/28/us/1992-campaign-verbatim-heckler-stirs-clinton-anger-excerpts-exchange.html.

Spencer, F. Scott. "And the Word 'Felt' Among us." Guest blog series posted by Nijay K. Gupta, *Crux Sola*, May 26, 2021. https://www.patheos.com/blogs/cruxsola/2021/05/part-3-and-the-word-felt-among-us-are-jesus-emotions-readable-spencer/.

———. "Faith on Edge: The Difficult Case of the Spirit-Seized Boy in Mark 9:14–29." *RevExp* 107 (2010) 419–24.

———. "'Follow Me': The Imperious Call of Jesus in the Synoptic Gospels." *Int* 59 (2005) 142–53.

———. *The Gospel of Luke and Acts of the Apostles*. Nashville: Abingdon, 2008.

———. "Jubilee." In *Dictionary of Scripture and Ethics*, edited by Joel B. Green et al., 428–29. Grand Rapids: Baker Academic, 2011.

———. *Luke*. Two Horizons New Testament Commentary. Grand Rapids: Eerdmans, 2019.

———. *Passions of the Christ: The Emotional Life of Jesus in the Gospels*. Grand Rapids: Baker Academic, 2021.

———. *The Portrait of Philip in Acts: A Study of Roles and Relations*. JSNTSupp 66. Sheffield: Sheffield Academic, 1992.

———. *Salty Wives, Spirited Mothers, and Savvy Widows: Capable Women of Persistence and Purpose in Luke's Gospel*. Grand Rapids: Eerdmans, 2012.

———. *Seven Challenges That Shaped the New Testament Writings: Understanding the Inherent Tensions of Early Christian Faith*. Grand Rapids: Baker Academic, 2024.

———. "To Fear and Not to Fear God: A Theological and Therapeutic Interpretation of Luke 12:1–34." *JTI* 8 (2014) 75–96.

———. *What Did Jesus Do? Gospel Profiles of Jesus' Personal Conduct*. Harrisburg, PA: Trinity Press International, 2003.

———. "A Woman's Touch: Manual and Emotional Dynamics of Female Characters in Luke's Gospel." In *Characters and Characterization in Luke-Acts*, edited by Frank E. Dicken and Julia A. Snyder, 73–94. LNTS 548. London: Bloomsbury T. & T. Clark, 2016.

Stassen, Glen Harold. *A Thicker Jesus: Incarnational Discipleship in a Secular Age*. Louisville: Westminster John Knox, 2012.

Stossel, Scott. *My Age of Anxiety: Fear, Hope, Dread, and the Search for Peace of Mind*. New York: Viking, 2015.

Strahan, Joshua Marshall. *The Limits of a Text: Luke 23:34a as a Test case in Theological Interpretation*. JTISup 8. Winona Lake, IN: Eisenbrauns, 2013.

Streett, R. Alan. *Songs of Resistance: Challenging Caesar and Empire*. Eugene, OR: Cascade, 2020.

Stulp, Gert, Abraham P. Buunk, Simon Verhulst, and Thomas V. Pollet. "Tall claims? Sense and nonsense about the importance of height of US presidents." *Leadership Quarterly* 24 (2013) 159–71.

Tannehill, Robert C. *Luke*. ANTC. Nashville: Abingdon, 1996.

———. *The Shape of Luke's Story: Essays on Luke-Acts*. Eugene, OR: Cascade, 2005.

Taylor, Joan E. *The Immerser: John the Baptist within Second Temple Judaism*. Grand Rapids: Eerdmans, 1997.

Taylor, Shelley E. *The Tending Instinct: How Nurture Is Essential to Who We Are and How We Live*. New York: Times Books, 2002.

Theissen, Gerd. *The Shadow of the Galilean: The Quest of the Historical Jesus in Narrative Form*. Translated by John Bowman. Philadelphia: Fortress, 1987.

Tiede, David L. *Prophecy and History in Luke-Acts*. Philadelphia: Fortress, 1980.

Trudinger, Paul. "Ire or Irony? The Enigmatic Character of the Parable of the Dishonest Steward (Luke 16:1-13)." *DRev* 116 (1998) 85–102.

Udoh, Fabian E. *To Caesar What Is Caesar's: Tribute, Taxes, and Imperial Administration in Early Roman Palestine (63 B.C.E.–70 C.E.)*. BJS. Providence, RI: Brown University, 2020.

Vandehei, Jim, and Mike Allen. "Behind the Curtain—Scoop: the Trump job applications revealed." *Axios*, December 1, 2023. https://www.axios.com/2023/12/01/trump-government-job-applications-2025?utm_source=newsletter&utm_medium=email&utm_campaign=newsletter_axiosam&stream=top.

VanderKam, James C. *The Dead Sea Scrolls Today*. Grand Rapids: Eerdmans, 1994.

Vermes, Geza. *The Complete Dead Sea Scrolls in English*. 7th ed. London: Penguin, 2007.

———. *An Introduction to the Complete Dead Sea Scrolls*. Minneapolis: Fortress, 1999.

Vishnia, Rachel Feig. *Roman Elections in the Age of Cicero: Society, Government, and Voting*. New York: Routledge, 2012.

Von Drehle, David, Jay Newton-Small, and Maya Rhodan. "How Do You Forgive a Murder?" *Time*, November 23, 2015. https://time.com/time-magazine-charleston-shooting-cover-story/.

Wainwright, Loudon. "One More Try for the Heights." *Life*, March 1, 1968, 60–68.

Wall, Robert W. "'The Finger of God': Deuteronomy 9.10 and Luke 11.20." *NTS* 33 (1987) 144–50.

Wallace, David Foster. *McCain's Promise: Aboard the Straight Talk Express with John McCain and a Whole Bunch of Actual Reporters, Thinking About Hope*. Foreword by Jacob Weisberg. New York: Back Bay, 2008.

Webber, Andrew Lloyd, and Tim Rice. "Don't Cry for Me, Argentina." MCA, 1976.

Westen, Drew. *The Political Brain: The Role of Emotion in Deciding the Fate of the Nation*. New York: PublicAffairs, 2008.

Whitaker, Robyn J. *Even the Devil Quotes Scripture: Reading the Bible on Its Own Terms*. Grand Rapids: Eerdmans, 2023.

Wiggins, Marianne. *Evidence of Things Unseen: A Novel*. New York: Simon & Schuster, 2004.

Wilson, Brittany E. *Unmanly Men: Refigurations of Masculinity in Luke-Acts*. Oxford: Oxford University Press, 2015.

Wink, Walter. *The Human Being: Jesus and the Enigma of the Son of Man*. Minneapolis: Fortress, 2002.

Wright, N. T. *Into the Heart of Romans: A Deep Dive into Paul's Greatest Letter*. Grand Rapids: Zondervan Academic, 2023.

Wright, R. B. "Psalms of Solomon." In *The Old Testament Pseudepigrapha*, vol. 2, edited by James H. Charlesworth, 639–70. London: Darton, Longman & Todd, 1985.

Xeravits, Géza G. *King, Priests, Prophet: Positive Eschatological Protagonists of the Qumran Library*. STDJ 47. Leiden: Brill, 2003.

www.ingramcontent.com/pod-product-compliance
Lightning Source LLC
Chambersburg PA
CBHW031809220426
43662CB00007B/579